North East England:

places, history, people and legends

David Simpson

© David Simpson

ISBN 1 901888 37 1

First published 2003

Cover Design Dominic Edmunds

Published in Great Britain by
Business Education Publishers Limited
The Teleport
Doxford International
Sunderland
SR3 3XD

Tel: 0191 5252410
Fax: 0191 5201815

Including illustrations from the Monthly Chronicle of North Country Lore and Legend 1887-1891.
All photographs by David Simpson.
Sections of this book first appeared in a series of booklets written and published by David Simpson
1991-1992.

British Cataloguing-in-Publications Data
A catalogue record for this book is available from the British Library

Printed in Great Britain by Athenaeum Press, Gateshead.

Biography

David Simpson was born in 1967. He is the author of ten books on Northern English history including *The Millennium History of North East England* hailed by the Prime Minister, Tony Blair in his 'Millennium Address to the Nation' 1999. David lives in Durham with his wife, Abi and two cats. He is well known as a public speaker and has made numerous appearances on television and radio.

Preface

Stretching from the River Tees to the River Tweed, the North East of England was the ancient heartland of the Kingdom of Northumbria.

It was the birthplace of the railways, the 'borderland zone' of the Scottish raids and the quiet retreat of the ancient Celtic saints.

It is a region steeped in history and a home to wonderful sites like Durham Cathedral, Hadrian's Wall and the bustling Quayside of Newcastle upon Tyne.

Travelling across the region from Durham and Teesside to England's northernmost county of Northumberland, this book explores the places, history, people and legends of this remarkable northern region.

For Mum and Dad

North East England

Contents

Introduction
Setting the Scene

North East England is a distinct region, with a unique culture and history. It is England's most northerly region stretching from the Tees Valley and Cleveland Hills on the fringe of Yorkshire, one hundred miles north, to Berwick and the border with Scotland.

On its western flank, the Pennines and Cheviots form the backbone of England and separate the region from the Cumbrian Lake District. The North Sea, provides the eastern border of the region, with Norway and Denmark being its nearest neighbours, hundreds of miles to the east.

The North East was historically divided into two parts, namely County Durham and Northumberland, separated from each other by the course of the Rivers Tyne and Derwent.

Small pockets of old Yorkshire on the south bank of the Tees are also often included in the North East. Most notable is the ancient Cleveland region which is separated from the rest of Yorkshire by the Cleveland Hills. In industrial terms Cleveland's history is more closely tied to Durham and its coalfield than it is to rural North Yorkshire.

It is the three great rivers of the Tyne, the Wear and the Tees that dominate the most industrial parts of the North East. The ports of Newcastle, Sunderland and Middlesbrough lie close to the three river estuaries and are the major centres of population. But the North East is not just about ports and industry. In fact the region is one of the most rural in England and its landscape and scenery are as varied as anywhere in the country.

From the sleepy vale of the middle Tees, to the rugged mountains and trickling streams of the Cheviots and the unspoilt beaches of the Northumberland coast, the region is dominated by a rural rather than an industrial landscape.

Of course there are exceptions to this rule, but in the past it was often mistakenly thought that the North East was not a place for the tourist to visit. It was often perceived as a region dominated by the industrial scars of mining.

This was indeed partly true in the heyday of the Northumberland and Durham coalfield, but even in those distant days, when mining dominated the region, the North East kept many secrets hidden in its history and landscape.

Industrial scars are no longer so apparent today and the old pit heaps have long since gone. Former mining villages are still easy to recognise but there is no doubting the beauty of the region.

Northumberland is one of England's largest counties and is the least densely populated county in England. It has vast open skies and varied scenery that includes hills, dales, countless castles and beaches that run for miles. County Durham is slightly more populous but even this county is mostly rural and the western part of the region is home to the unspoilt beauty of the northern Pennines.

A Rich History

The landscape of North East England may be wonderful, rugged and dramatic but for me it is not the scenery that makes the region so special. There is something more to it than that.

This book is essentially about places and the part such places have played in the region's history. It will focus on the people, legends and history associated with each locality. There are a great variety of stories, legends and historical facts to discover in this book, but there are three major historical themes that occur again and again. They are themes that can be found wherever we travel in the region and each has played its part in shaping, not just the history of the region, but also the history of Britain and the world. The three themes can be described as 'Border History', 'Industrial History' and the 'Christian Heritage' associated with the ancient kingdom of Northumbria.

Border History

The region's historical role as a border zone between England and Scotland has its roots in Roman times when the Emperor Hadrian built his famous wall, but the border history was most prominent in the centuries that followed the Norman Conquest.

Northumberland in particular was ravaged by the Border raids and the Border Reivers who inhabited its dales. It was during this period that the region played host to major battles like Flodden Field, Otterburn and Nevilles Cross.

The numerous castles and fortifications of Northumberland and Durham are testament to the North East's role as a Border zone and Northumberland has more castles than any other part of England. Indeed, Northumberland has been described by the architectural historian Sir Nicholas Pevsner as the 'English Castle County Par Excellence'.

County Durham's role in the border history was not quite so important, but Scottish raids penetrated deep into its territory and even the northern reaches of Yorkshire fell well within the zone of Scottish raids.

In the medieval period the Prince Bishops of Durham held certain political powers within their diocese and were partly responsible for defending the north from the Scots. Such were the bishops' powers that one medieval observer remarked:

> *"There are two kings in England - the Lord King of England, wearing a crown in sign of his regality and the Lord Bishop of Durham wearing a mitre in place of a crown in sign of his regality in the diocese of Durham"*

Northumbria's Christian Heritage

The Christian heritage of the North East has its origins in the ancient Kingdom of Northumbria, one of the most powerful kingdoms of the Anglo-Saxon period.

In the fifth and sixth centuries AD, a Pagan race called the Angles, from what is now Germany and Denmark began their invasion of Britain and settled on the North East coast of England. These settlements developed into the Kingdom of Northumbria, stretching from the Humber to the Firth of Forth, with the North East located at its very heart.

It was Oswald, King of Northumbria (634-641 A.D), who brought Christianity to the north. He employed St. Aidan, a Celtic monk to convert the Northumbrians and Aidan chose the island of Lindisfarne as his base. Other great religious houses like Hexham, Hartlepool, Jarrow and Wearmouth would follow, each associated with Northumbrian saints like Wilfrid, Cuthbert, Hild and the Venerable Bede.

Many legends and stories surround the lives of these saints, but none more so than St. Cuthbert of Lindisfarne who is best described as the 'Patron Saint' of Northumbria.

It was to the life of Cuthbert that the 7th Century Lindisfarne Gospels were dedicated. These are as beautiful and as important a symbol of the region's history as the Book of Kells are to Irish history, but sadly they lie exiled in the British Museum in London. They were 'stolen' from Durham Cathedral on the orders of King Henry VIII and have remained in London ever since.

The Christian heritage of Northumbria suffered a great setback at the time of the Viking raids that ravaged the coast of Northumbria in the ninth century, but their settlement fell largely upon neighbouring Yorkshire and Cumbria

and was only noticeable in the North East along the valley of the Tees.

After 1066, the Normans were keen to preserve the Christianity of the North and monasteries like Lindisfarne were rebuilt in the Norman style. At Durham an Anglo-Saxon minster, that had been the resting place of St. Cuthbert since 995 AD was replaced by a magnificent Norman Cathedral.

The Industrial Past

It was the Normans who established the 'New Castle' on the banks of the River Tyne close to the site of an old Roman fort in 1080. This castle became the focus for a town that has been without a doubt the busiest, most populous and most commercially powerful place in the whole region for the last thousand years.

In 1286, the town of Newcastle was the leading English town for the export of leather, but it was already noted for the shipping of coal, a resource for which there was a plentiful, accessible supply in and around the Tyne. Coal became Newcastle's lifeblood, and it was continuously shipping coal to London in ever increasing amounts. Keelmen, a distinct community of boatmen helped to load the ships with coal and powerful Newcastle merchants called the hostmen were the leading figures in the trade.

By the 1600s coal mines were opening further away from the Tyne and spread deeper into the Counties of Durham and Northumberland. Unique railroads were built. These were the first railways in the world, where horse-drawn wagons transported coal from the mines to the banks of the Tyne.

Innovation was a major feature of the industrial developments of the region in the nineteenth century. Steam locomotives were developed by local engineers like George Stephenson, Timothy Hackworth and William Hedley and the opening of the Stockton and Darlington Railway to passengers in 1825 was a major event in the history of the world.

At Newcastle, industrial pioneers like the Stephensons, Joseph Swan, William Armstrong and later Charles Parsons, literally changed the world forever with their inventions and developments.

Shipbuilding, engineering, coal mining, lead mining and steel making brought employment and pride to the North and North East steel was used in the building of bridges across the world. The industries would shape the character, pride and history of the region in a way that would have a lasting effect.

In the twentieth century there were periods of industrial decline and today only one coal mine remains in Northumberland. There are none in County Durham.

New industries have sprung up here and there but some parts of the region are still suffering from the effects of economic decline. However, there is a greater recognition of the region's natural assets, namely its people, history and scenery than ever there was before. With this recognition new developments and an ever increasing confidence have brought new hope for the future.

A walk along the quayside at Newcastle with the view of the magnificent bridges and buildings, both new and old cannot fail to inspire and impress and leave the visitor or resident believing that they are in indeed in a special place.

In fact, the phrase 'special place' can be applied to the North East as a whole and one of the aims of this book is to give a sense of place and an insight into the North East that will inspire us to explore further and appreciate this unique part of England.

Part One
Teesdale and Darlington

Darlington in 1760

Part One
Teesdale and Darlington

Where Tees is Born

The River Tees begins its journey in the bleak North Pennine moorlands of east Cumbria on the southern slopes of Cross Fell, where it rises less than a mile from the source of the South Tyne. Cross Fell is the highest point in the Pennines and at 2,930 feet is a familiar sight to walkers on the Pennine Way. From these boggy origins the Tees flows five miles east before entering County Durham near Viewing Hill, (2,099 feet). It is soon engulfed by the two mile long Cow Green Reservoir, built between 1967 and 1971 to supply the industries of Teesside.

Environmentally speaking this part of upper Teesdale is of great importance and the reservoir was opposed by conservationists primarily concerned with protecting rare alpine plants like the unique Teesdale violet. Around a tenth of this plant's habitat was destroyed by the construction of the reservoir but the remaining area was designated a National Nature Reserve in 1969.

Peg Powler the Mermaid

According to legend, the creation of the Cow Green Reservoir may have destroyed the habitat of a certain Peg Powler, the grotesque green-haired mermaid of the Tees who used to inhabit the valley now occupied by the reservoir. Her presence could be indicated by frothy substances on the river known as Peg Powler's Suds and children were always warned to stay clear as she had an insatiable appetite for youngsters. Beware she may still be there!

The Teesdale Waterfalls

At the eastern end of the Cow Green Reservoir beyond the dam, the Tees rushes in a series of cataracts over a 200 yard long rocky stairway called Cauldron Snout. The vertical distance from the first cataract to the last is 200 feet, making this waterfall the highest in England.

Ghost of the Waterfall

Cauldron Snout is said to be haunted by a ghost called the 'Singing Lady' who was apparently a Victorian farm girl who drowned herself in the waterfall when her love affair with a lead miner came to an end. On cold moonlit nights it is said that she sits on a rock near the falls lamenting the loss of her loved one.

From Cauldron Snout, the Tees meanders around the huge whin sill cliffs of Cronkley Scar and Falcon Clints and is joined by the Maizebeck, Merrygill, Harwood and Blea Becks as it makes its way towards High Force, undoubtedly England's 'biggest' waterfall. It is best seen, with some care after a heavy downpour when the sound of the Tees roaring over a vertical drop of seventy feet almost deafens the observer.

High Force.

Tees is crossed by an iron suspension footbridge of 1830 which replaced the earliest suspension bridge in Europe.

Not far from Low Force the Tees is joined by the Bowlees Beck. At Summerhill Force, the stream flows over a band of limestone where the fall has undercut the limestone to form a cavern known as Gibson's Cave.

Middleton in Teesdale

Four miles downstream from High Force the little town of Middleton in Teesdale is located on the north bank of the river where the Tees is joined by the Hudeshope Beck. It is an ancient village but grew significantly in the nineteenth century when it was an important lead mining centre.

In 1880 Middleton was the headquarters of the benevolent Quaker owned, London Lead Company which built houses, schools and libraries for its workers and became the first British company to introduce the five day week.

High Force is in fact two falls, each situated on either side of a massive central rock, but the smaller northern fall is only occasionally seen in action. One such occasion was the 24th of June, 1880 when two men were trapped on the central rock after a sudden surge of the Tees known locally as the 'roll' occurred. The first man was pulled free by means of a rope, but the second was not so lucky, his rope snapped and he drowned. Tragically both men may have survived had they stayed where they were as there are no recorded instances of the two falls ever merging over the central rock.

A number of other waterfalls can be found in Teesdale, including White Force, Bleabeck Force, Maizebeck Force and Low Force. Low Force is only a short distance downstream from its more famous brother. Unlike High Force it is formed by a series of cascades. Here the

---

The Teesdale Poet

One of the London Lead Company's employees at Middleton was a certain Richard Watson known as 'the Teesdale Poet' (1833-1891). He once wrote;

"I've wandered many a weary mile,
And in strange countries been;
I've dwelt in towns and on wild moors,
And curious sights I've seen;
But still my heart clings to the dale
Where Tees rolls to the sea,
Compared with what I've seen I'll say
The Teesdale hills for me."

Romaldkirk and Cotherstone

East of Middleton, the Tees is joined by the Rivers Lune and Balder, which in their upper valleys form a miniature lake district of reservoirs called Selset, Grassholme, Balderhead, Blackton and Hury. Baldersdale is divided from Lunedale by the moors of Hunderthwaite and Romaldkirk and both are named from nearby villages.

Hunderthwaite is a Viking place-name which may mean 'Hunrothr's' or 'Hundor's meadow' and was the scene of a devastating Scottish raid in 1070. Romaldkirk is a picturesque little village on the south bank of the Tees between the Lune and Balder and is named from a Northumbrian saint called Romald.

Romaldkirk.

Romaldkirk's church is dedicated to St. Romald about whom we know very little, as he died whilst a baby. The village pubs have a tradition for good beer dating back to the days when the village had its own brewery but those with an unquenchable thirst might like to sample the qualities of the village stream - it is called the Beer Beck.

Two miles downstream from Romaldkirk we find the equally picturesque village of Cotherstone, famous as the home of Cotherstone cheese, a delicatessen unique to the North. Cotherstone is situated at the confluence of the Tees and Balder. It is Cotherstone and the Balder that are closely associated with the famous TV personality and daleswoman Hannah Hauxwell.

Barnard Castle

Barnard Castle on the north side of the Tees is the 'capital' of Teesdale and is one of the North's most historic towns. Known locally as 'Barney', the town owes its origins to Bernard Baliol, who built a castle here in the twelfth century. Bernard's family were of Norman origin and of high influence. His descendants included two kings of Scotland and the founder of Balliol College in Oxford.

Bernard's Castle is now a picturesque ruin on a high bank overlooking the Tees. The castle has seen plenty of history and is connected with historic figures like Richard III, Henry VII, Warwick the Kingmaker, and the Prince Bishops of Durham.

Barnard Castle.

The Market Cross

Horsemarket, Galgate, Bridgegate, Newgate and Thorngate are the main streets in Barnard Castle and are lined by beautiful stone built houses. At the centre of the town is the market place dominated by an intriguing octagonal building called the 'Market Cross' built by a local resident called Thomas Breaks in 1747. At various times in history this building has served as a court, a gaol, a town hall and a butter market. A weather vane on top of the building is damaged by two bullet holes reputedly made by a soldier and a gamekeeper in a competition to test their shooting abilities.

Market Cross.

At the northern end of the market place, Galgate runs north-east following the ancient course of a Roman road that ran from Stainmore to join Dere Street near West Auckland. The name Galgate originates from post Roman times and once led to gallows where public hangings took place.

The Bowes Museum

The market cross forms the centrepiece of a small roundabout at Barnard Castle from where a road called Newgate leads us into what is arguably Barnard Castle's biggest attraction - the Bowes Museum.

The Bowes Museum.

Visitors are surprised to find this huge and magnificent building in such a small north country town. Built in the style of a French chateau it has one of the most impressive collections of pictures, ceramics, textiles, tapestries, clocks and costumes in the north of England.

Its exhibits include a famous life size, silver swan, which can delicately lift a silver fish from a salver to swallow it. The Bowes Museum developed from the collection of John Bowes, Earl of Strathmore, who with his French actress wife, Josephine purchased most of the wonderful items displayed in the museum. Sadly both died before the completion of their museum in 1892.

Bowes and Stainmore

Bowes village, on the River Greta three miles south west of Barnard Castle is the home of a ruined twelfth century castle and the site of a once important Roman fort called Lavatrae. The village stands at the entrance to the bleak and lonely Stainmore Pass which has been one of the main Pennine crossing places for thousands of years. In 954 AD Stainmore was the site of an ambush in which the northern Viking king Eric Bloodaxe was murdered along with many of his followers. A tenth century chronicler recalled the incident:

"King Eric was treacherously killed in a certain lonely place which is called Stainmore with his son Haeric and his brother Ragnald, betrayed by Earl Oswulf."

The death of Bloodaxe brought about the downfall of the Viking Kingdom of York and Viking power did not rise again until the time of King Canute. The point where Bloodaxe met his death is marked by the ancient Rey Cross, situated alongside the busy A66 five miles west of Bowes.

Rey Cross once marked a boundary between ancient kingdoms on either side of the Pennines. 'Rey' is a Viking word simply meaning boundary.

Rokeby and the Greta

The River Greta, a tributary of the Tees which flows through the Stainmore Pass and rises to the west of the Rey Cross derives its name from the Viking word 'Griota' meaning a stony stream.

From Stainmore, the Greta makes a fourteen mile journey east before joining the Tees at Rokeby near Barnard Castle.

Rokeby was the site of a village that was probably deserted following Scottish attacks upon Teesdale. Its name lives on at Rokeby Park and Rokeby Hall, the latter an 18th century building belonging to the Morritt family.

The artists, J. M. W. Turner and J. S. Cotman had a particular affection for this part of Teesdale and Turner's famous picture 'The Meeting of the Waters' depicts the confluence of the Tees and Greta at Rokeby.

Another artist, Velazquez, is associated with the hall. His famous painting, 'The Rokeby Venus' was housed at Rokeby Hall between 1805 and 1905. Today it can be seen at the National Gallery in London. Across the River Greta from Rokeby Park are the remains of a fourteenth century fortified Pele Tower. It is a reminder that Teesdale often suffered from Border raids.

Sir Walter Scott in Teesdale

In the early nineteenth century Sir Walter Scott was a frequent visitor to Rokeby Hall and named his lengthy poem, Rokeby after the area. The poem includes verses with strong references to Teesdale and particularly its Viking past,

> *"When Denmark's raven soared on high,*
> *Triumphant through Northumbrian sky,*
> *Till, hovering near, her fatal croak*
> *Bade Reged's Britons dread the yoke.*

> *And the broad shadow of her wing*
> *Blackened each cataract and spring,*
> *Where Tees in tumult leaves his source,*
> *Thundering o'er Caldron and High Force.*

> *Balder named from Odin's son;*
> *And Greta, to whose banks ere long*
> *We lead the lovers of the song;*
> *And silver Lune from Stainmore wild*
> *And fairy Thorsgill's murmuring child."*

These verses from 'Rokeby' refer to the Viking sounding Thorsgill Beck, a stream that joins the River Tees to the west of Rokeby near Barnard Castle.

Raby Castle and Staindrop

From Rokeby the River Tees passes through Whorlton, Wycliffe and Ovington to Winston on Tees, where a road leads two miles north to Raby Castle and the adjacent village of Staindrop. Canute the Dane (c 994 - 1035), King of England, Denmark and Norway owned a mansion and estate in the vicinity of Staindrop in the tenth century.

It has been suggested that the mansion owned by Canute was on the site of the nearby Raby Castle and some argue that it was from here that he ruled his kingdom and Empire. Raby Castle's historic 'Bulmer Tower' is believed to incorporate Canute's mansion.

The name of Raby is Viking-Danish in origin and could mean either 'settlement on the boundary mark' - or 'settlement with roe deer'. Raby lies on the course of an old Roman road that leads to Stainmore and Rey Cross. Staindrop is historically the estate village for Raby Castle.

Raby Castle.

The Rising of the North

Raby is one of the best medieval castles in northern England, and for many years belonged to the influential Norman family called the Nevilles who were the most important barons in the Bishopric of Durham from the twelfth century onwards. The famous Rising of the North was plotted by the Nevilles at Raby in 1569, with the help of the equally powerful Percy family of Northumberland. Support for this rising came from all parts of the North East;

> *"Now was the North in arms: they shine*
> *In warlike trim from Tweed to Tyne,*
> *At Percy's voice : and Neville Sees*
> *His followers gathering in from Tees,*
> *From Wear and all the little rills*
> *Concealed among the forked hills-*
> *Seven hundred knights Retainers all*
> *Of Neville at their master's call*
> *Had sate together at Raby Hall."*

William Wordsworth.

'The Rising' was an attempt to replace Elizabeth I with her cousin, the Catholic Mary Queen of Scots, at a time when the people of northern England were mostly of the Catholic faith. Unfortunately for the Nevilles the Rising failed and Raby was confiscated from the family by the Crown along with their other great properties at Barnard Castle and Brancepeth.

Whitewashed Houses

In 1626 Raby became the seat of the Vanes who were Earls of Darlington and Dukes of Cleveland. The present owner, Lord Barnard is a member of this family. He is the owner of the vast Raby Estate which extends over a large area of south Durham. Farmhouses and cottages belonging to this estate can be found throughout the northern side of Teesdale and are easily identified by their attractive whitewashed exteriors.

Whitewashing goes back to the days when a Duke of Cleveland became stranded in a storm while out hunting in Teesdale. He was refused shelter at a local farmhouse which he had mistaken for one of his own properties. The Duke was determined not to suffer such a humiliation ever again and ordered that from that day on all buildings belonging to his estate were to be painted white for identification.

Raby Castle is said to be haunted by three ghosts, they are the headless Henry Vane the Younger, Sir Charles Neville and the First Lady Barnard, who is known as 'Old Hell Cat'.

Gainford - A Spa Village

Gainford on Tees, near Winston to the south east of Raby was in Anglo-Saxon times the centre of an important estate belonging to the Northumbrian

Congregation of St. Cuthbert. In the later Dark Ages this area was taken by the Vikings, whose settlement in the area is indicated by the names of the nearby villages ending in 'by' like Selaby, Eppleby and Killerby.

Gainford is an attractive village and has long been a popular place of retirement for residents of nearby Darlington. The origins of its name are disputed, though there is a legend concerning a ford that once existed on the river. Its ownership was disputed by the residents on either side of the Tees.

In the end a battle was fought in which the residents of the Durham side of the river gained the ford - hence Gainford. On the Yorkshire side of the river we find the site of the deserted village of Barforth or Barford. The name is said to be a reminder of an attempt by its residents to barricade the ford during the battle with Gainford.

In the nineteenth century Gainford village had its own spa. Today its main features are a village green, a Jacobean hall and an attractive Georgian street called High Row.

The village church of St. Mary's, Gainford is also of interest. It is on the site of an Anglo-Saxon church built by Bishop Ecgred of Lindisfarne in the early 9th century and is said to be the resting place of a Northumbrian chieftain called Ida or Eda. In more recent times the church became famed in local folklore as the place where a vicar married a Pigg, christened a Lamb and buried a Hogg all in the same week. Of course, these were all the family names of local residents.

Piercebridge Roman Fort

Piercebridge is situated at the point where the old Roman road called Dere Street crossed the River Tees. This road ran north from the Roman military headquarters at York well up into Tweeddale in Scotland.

Piercebridge Roman Fort.

A large area of Piercebridge occupies the site of a Roman fort that stood on the road guarding the crossing of the Tees. This fort at Piercebridge will have been of strategic importance as the fierce ancient British tribe called the Brigantes, were closely associated with the area.

The Brigantes were the largest tribe in Roman Britain with territory extending over Yorkshire, Durham, Cumbria and southern Northumberland. South west of Piercebridge can be seen one of the most significant remains associated with the Brigantes at a place called Stanwick St. John. Here we find the ancient earthworks of a Brigantian camp from where the tribe fought the Romans at the Battle of Scotch Corner in 71 AD.

East of Piercebridge, the Tees meanders its way towards the outskirts of Darlington, where it is crossed by the A1(M) Motorway. There are a number of Viking place names in this area, examples of which are Cleasby, Jolby, Brettanby and Ulnaby.

The Piercebridge Clock

"My Grandfather's Clock
was too tall for the shelf
So it stood ninety years on the floor."

Piercebridge, on the north bank of the River Tees, two miles downstream from Gainford is in County Durham but its Hotel 'The George' is across the river in Yorkshire. The hotel is famed as the home of the clock which is said to have inspired a visiting American composer called Henry Clay Work to write his famous song 'My Grandfather's Clock ' (1878), from which all long case clocks now take their name. The clock is notable in that it stopped at the very moment of its owner's death and never worked again.

"It rang an alarm in the dead of the night,
an alarm that for years had been dumb
And we knew that his spirit
was pluming for flight,
that his hour of departure had come.

Still the clock kept the time with
a soft and muffled chime
as we silently stood by its side.
But it Stopped, Short, never to go again
When the old man died."

The George, Piercebridge.

Darlington

Darlington began as an Anglo-Saxon settlement on the River Skerne which is a northern tributary of the Tees. Since Norman times Darlington has been a borough and the site of an important market and today it is arguably the 'capital' of southern County Durham with its population of over eighty thousand greater than that of Durham City. However, Darlington is no longer officially part of the County of Durham although it remains so in historic and cultural terms.

Darlington's name derives from the Anglo-Saxon Dearthington, which meant 'the settlement of Deornoth's people' but by Norman times its name had changed to Derlinton.

15

Confusion does not end here however, because during the seventeenth and eighteenth centuries the town was generally known by the name of 'Darnton' or somewhat less politely as 'Darnton i' the Dirt'. This unfortunate name was probably due to the once unpaved streets of the town which are said to have inspired King James of Scotland to write the following uncomplimentary verses during a visit of 1603;

"Darnton has a bonny, bonny church
With a broach upon the steeple
But Darnton is a mucky, mucky town
And mair sham on the people."

'Mucky town' is certainly not a good description of Darlington today, as like many large towns in North East England it has a pleasant and attractive appearance. It is especially well endowed with town parks and leafy suburbs.

St. Cuthbert's, the "bonny church" referred to in the rhyme is still one of the most admirable features of Darlington. Built in the twelfth century by Hugh Pudsey, Prince-Bishop of Durham, it is sometimes referred to as the 'Lady of the North'. It is one of the largest churches in the region.

Darlington.

The Cradle of the Railways

In the seventeenth century Darlington became a popular place of residence for members of the Quaker faith, who formed an influential and wealthy community in the town by the 1800s. The best known member of this Darlington fraternity was Edward Pease, the man responsible for Darlington's fame as the 'Cradle of the Railways'.

George Stephenson.

It was Pease who rejected an early nineteenth century plan by local businessmen to build a canal for the shipment of coals from south Durham to the mouth of the Tees and made the innovative suggestion that steam locomotives be used instead. The suggestion was accepted.

George Stephenson, the famous engineer of Tyneside was employed by Pease to design the locomotives and develop the railway, though it was Pease who provided the financial support and he was very much in charge.

16

On one occasion Stephenson had suggested an alternative route for the railway which would have bypassed Darlington and altered the railway history books. Pease was clear with his reply;

"George thou must think of Darlington;
remember it was Darlington
that sent for thee."

The Stockton and Darlington Railway

The Stockton and Darlington Railway was opened in September 1825, and history was made, for as well as carrying coal, the train included six hundred passengers, most travelling in coal wagons, but some in a specially designed carriage called 'The Experiment'.

The Stockton and Darlington Railway was thus the world's first public railway. On the historic day, the coal wagons for the journey were linked up to the locomotive called 'Locomotion Number One' at Shildon and were brought there from Witton Park Colliery by inclines at Etherley and Brussleton.

From Shildon the Locomotion travelled for two hours with only minor hitches before arriving in Darlington, where coal was distributed to the poor. From Darlington the Locomotion and its train of passengers continued its journey to Stockton stopping only at Yarm Junction where more passengers, including a brass band climbed on board.

George Stephenson's original 'Locomotion Number One', the locomotive that hauled the train on the historic opening of the Stockton and Darlington Railway can still be seen in Darlington today on display in the town's fascinating North Road Station Museum. The museum occupies what was one of the oldest railway stations in the world.

A full size working replica of the 'Locomotion' can often be seen at the Beamish Open Air Museum near Stanley, in County Durham. The 'Locomotion Number One' is of course an older engine than Stephenson's more famous 'Rocket', which won the victory at Lancashire's Rainhill Trials in 1829.

Bridge Building and Journalism

Railways are not the only industry for which the town of Darlington is noted. Its engineering skills, particularly bridge building have long been important and famous bridges have been built at Darlington which span rivers as far away as the Amazon and the Nile.

Darlington also has an important publishing industry, as the headquarters for the Durham Advertiser, the Darlington and Stockton Times, and The Northern Echo, a newspaper with a readership area covering North Yorkshire and the North East. The paper was once edited by W. T Stead, an influential Northumbrian born social reformer who died on board the Titanic in 1912. Stead began his career as an editor with the 'Northern Echo' at the age of only 22.

Lewis Carroll at Croft

Croft on Tees, an attractive village just to the south of Darlington was the place where Charles Lutwidge Dodgson, better known to us as Lewis Carroll, grew up as a young boy. His father was the rector at Croft and the rectory gardens are thought to be one of the most likely settings for famous scenes in 'Alice in Wonderland'.

Hell's Kettles and the River Skerne

Although Darlington is undoubtedly located in the vale of the River Tees, it is a tributary of the Tees called the Skerne that flows through the centre of the town. The Skerne rises in eastern County Durham to the north of Sedgefield near the former colliery village of Trimdon and flows south before joining the River Tees at Croft near Darlington. Here it runs close to the famous 'Hell's Kettles' at Oxen-le-Field.

These three, supposedly bottomless pits also known as 'Devil's Kettles' or 'Kettles of Hell', have been the subject of numerous legends and superstitions. Said to have been created by a ferocious earthquake in 1179, locals may tell you that they are full of green, boiling sulphorous water. People and animals are allegedly drowned or eaten alive by the Pikes and Eels that infest their waters.

The pits once aroused the curiosity of people the length and breadth of Britain and were even visited by the writer and traveller Daniel Defoe, who dismissed them as 'old coal pits'. This they certainly are not, as coal has never been mined in the Darlington area.

Lewis Carroll always considered Croft his home and it was here in the company of his large family that his unequalled talent for composing nonsense verse developed on this pleasant spot by the Tees. His earliest pieces were written in a little home made magazine which he wrote for his family at Croft.

Pieces written at Croft by Lewis Carroll include the first verse of one his best known poems, the 'Jabberwocky', which was written in 1855 though not published until a number of years later. The rest of the poem was written further north during visits to relations at Whitburn near Sunderland, where he is also said to have composed 'The Walrus and the Carpenter'. The gravestone of Lewis Carroll's mother and father can be seen in the churchyard at Croft.

"Fair stands the ancient Rectory
The Rectory of Croft
The sun shines bright upon it,
The breezes whisper soft."

Lewis Carroll.

The Sockburn Worm

A mile to the east of Croft, the River Tees makes a large and unexpected meander which penetrates deep into North Yorkshire to form the most southerly portion of County Durham called the 'Sockburn Peninsula'. In local legend this area was once the domain of a notorious creature called the 'Sockburn Worm'.

This terrible beast, a kind of winged serpent or wyvern terrorised the local neighbourhood until it was eventually slain by a certain young man called John Conyers, a member of a wealthy local family.

From that day on each new Prince-Bishop of Durham was presented with the sword that killed the worm upon entering their new Bishopric for the first time at Croft on Tees. The ceremony includes the following presentation speech;

> "My Lord Bishop. I hereby present you with the falchion wherewith the champion Conyers slew the worm, dragon or fiery flying serpent which destroyed man, woman and child; in memory of which the king then reigning gave him the manor of Sockburn, to hold by this tenure, that upon the first entrance of every bishop into the county the falchion should be presented."

The Durham historian Hutchinson was of the opinion that the legend of the Sockburn worm is a reference to some long since forgotten Viking rover who sacked and plundered this part of the Tees valley.

The sword used in the presentation known as the 'Conyers Falchion' can still be seen today on display in Durham Cathedral. The Sockburn worm itself is almost certainly immortalised by Lewis Carroll in his brilliant piece of nonsense rhyme, 'Jabberwocky'

> "'Twas brillig, and the slithy toves
> Did gyre and gimble in the wabe:
> All mimsy were the borogroves
> And the mome raths outgrabe."

Today Sockburn is home to a private residence but in Anglo-Saxon times it was a place of importance as it was here that Higbald, Bishop of Lindisfarne and Eanbald, Archbishop of York were consecrated in the 8th century AD. In later years the Sockburn area was settled by the Vikings and like the Teesdale village of Gainford, Sockburn was an important centre of Viking age sculpture.

Surtees and Pons Tees

From the southern tip of the Sockburn peninsula, the Tees flows three miles north, before reaching the villages of Dinsdale and Middleton St. George. Dinsdale is the site of a manor owned in Norman times by a family called Siward.

When the Siwards settled at Dinsdale in the eleventh century they changed their name to Sur Tees which in Norman French meant 'on the Tees'. Descendants of this Dinsdale family later included Robert Smith Surtees, the author, Bessie Surtees, the famous eloping daughter of a Newcastle merchant and Robert Surtees the great historian of County Durham.

Under the entry for Dinsdale in 'the History of the County Palatine of Durham' Robert Surtees compares this sleepy place of his ancestors to the 'Border Country' of the north

> "The knights of the Tees might mingle in the border warfare; but the bugle horn of an assailant would seldom startle the inmates of their quiet halls. Their mansions stood without tower or peel."

An important Roman road once crossed the Tees near Dinsdale on its way to the Roman forts at Chester le Street and Newcastle. The road sometimes named Cade's Road after a Gainford historian, can be traced near the villages of Middleton St. George and Middleton One Row. Here the old road is known by the name of Pountey's Lane and is probably named after a Roman bridge which crossed the Tees here called Pons Tesie - 'Bridge of the Tees'.

The bridge has long since disappeared with some of its foundation stones used in the construction of buildings at Middleton St. George. The Roman road from Middleton St. George passes through the village of Sadberge a few miles to the north. This was a place of considerable importance in Viking times.

> **The Durham Ox**
>
> Brafferton on the northern outskirts of Darlington is where the famous Durham Ox was bred. It was developed by the brothers Charles and Robert Colling of nearby Ketton farm in 1796 and achieved such great fame that it was exhibited throughout England and Scotland in a specially designed carriage. Over a period of five years, the ox journeyed more than 3,000 miles before the unfortunate beast dislocated its hip while on show at Oxford in February 1807.
>
> It was slaughtered two months later and weighed in at 189 stones. During its lifetime, it reached an incredible maximum weight of 270 stones. The Collings achieved far reaching fame for their development and throughout the country there are many inns named after the Durham Ox of Ketton Farm.

Sadberge

The village of Sadberge half way between Stockton and Darlington was once the capital or wappentake of the Viking settled area north of the Tees known as the Earldom of Sadberge which stretched from Hartlepool to Teesdale. Wappentakes were found in those parts of England settled by the Danes and continued to be important administrative centres in medieval times.

There were neighbouring Wappentakes to Sadberge at Northallerton in Yorkshire and at Langbaurgh in Cleveland. The word wappentake literally means

'Weapon Taking' and refers to the way in which land was held in return for military service to a chief.

Sadberge is a name of Viking origin deriving from Setberg, meaning 'flat topped hill', - an accurate description of the location of the village from where good views of the surrounding countryside can be obtained. The place name Setberg from which Sadberge derives also occurs in Norway and in Viking settled Iceland. Closer to home in Norse settled Cumbria we may find the village of Sedbergh near Kendal which has the same meaning.

Sadberge.

Sadberge in Scotland

The history of Sadberge can be confusing because in early Norman times the Earldom of Sadberge, though north of the River Tees, was not part of Durham and was not initially under the rule of Durham's Prince Bishops. Instead, the district formed an outlying part of the county of Northumberland by virtue of the fact that it had been part of the old Earldom of Northumbria.

To further add to confusion Northumberland was given to Scotland by King Stephen of England in 1139 so that the Tees actually became the southern boundary of the kingdom of Scotland. This situation continued for eighteen years until Northumberland was repossessed for England by King Henry II in 1157.

Hugh Pudsey, Prince Bishop of Durham (1153-1195) was the man largely responsible for the decline in importance of the Sadberge district. He added the 'earldom' to Durham in 1189 and from then on Sadberge was ruled by Durham's Prince Bishops.

The Earldom of Sadberge included the old parishes of Hart, Hartlepool, Greatham, Stranton, Elwick, Stainton (near Sedgefield), Elton, Long Newton, Egglescliffe, Middleton St. George, Low Dinsdale, Coatham Mundeville, Coniscliffe and the Barony of Gainford in Teesdale. It never included Stockton or Darlington.

Despite its fall in status, Sadberge retained a degree of independence and continued to be administered as an almost separate county until 1576. Even as late as the nineteenth century there were still occasionally references to 'the Counties of Durham and Sadberge'. In 1836 the revenues of the Bishopric of Durham including Sadberge passed to the Crown. A plaque attached to a large ice age stone on the village green reminds us how important Sadberge once was:

> *"This stone was placed here*
> *to commemorate the Golden*
> *Jubilee of Victoria, Queen*
> *of the United Kingdom,*
> *Empress of India,*
> *and Countess of Sadberge 1867."*

Part Two
Cleveland and Teesside

Middlesbrough Town Hall

Part Two
Cleveland and Teesside

Worsall Piersport

Low Worsall, on the River Tees near Yarm lies to the east of Middleton St. George and was situated at the highest tidal point on the River Tees until the construction of the Tees Barrage at Stockton in 1995.

In the eighteenth century, a small agricultural port called Piersport was established here by Thomas and Richard Pierse. Piersport was used for agricultural products but was never a real threat to Yarm, the chief port on the river at the time. The main feature of Worsall today is Worsall Hall which was the residence of Thomas Pierse from 1730 to 1767 when he moved to Acklam Hall. Worsall Hall has a secret tunnel which is said to have been used by smugglers.

Not far from Worsall, on the north side of the Tees is the village of Aislaby, a Viking place name that means Aislac's village. It is one of only a small number of Viking 'by' names on the north side of the river.

Yarm - The First Great Teesside Port

The River Tees at Yarm forms a northward pointing horse-shoe meander which encloses this attractive little Georgian market town on three sides. For many centuries Yarm was called Yarum, a name deriving from the Anglo-Saxon word Gear.

Pronounced 'yair', this was a pool for catching fish and would have been formed by a weir with a specially constructed channel to trap the fish. The 'um' on the end of the original name Yarum was an Anglo-Saxon plural, so Yarm means 'fish pools' or 'fish weirs'. Yarm may have been a place of importance in Anglo-Saxon times and there are traces of what are believed to be Anglo-Saxon stones in Yarm's parish church of St. Mary Magdalene.

From medieval times Yarm was the most important town and port on the River Tees and was a home to rope makers, brewers, tanners, nail makers, clock makers and shipbuilders.

In 1207 King John granted Yarm a weekly market and two annual fairs and from then on Yarm's prosperity grew. The wealth of Yarm was so great that it was frequently a target for Scottish raiders who sacked the town five times in the fourteenth century under the leadership of Robert the Bruce.

As ships grew in size and became unable to navigate far up river, Yarm's importance declined and the role of the old town was taken over by Stockton and ultimately Middlesbrough, both of which are much further downstream.

Yarm Town Hall.

Yarm High Street Pubs

Yarm's town centre is dominated by a cobbled High Street which runs along the centre of the loop formed by the Tees. It has the appearance of a typical North Yorkshire market town.

At the centre of the High Street is the little Dutch style Town Hall built in 1710 by Viscount Fauconberg, who was Lord of the Manor of Yarm. The High Street once boasted sixteen inns as Yarm was one of the most important coaching stops on the north-south route.

A number of Yarm's old inns still survive including the old 'Ketton Ox', named after a famous ox bred near Darlington. This inn was at one time noted for cock fighting.

The 'George and Dragon' was the site of the 1820 meeting at which the decision was made to build the Stockton and Darlington Railway.

Yarm Bridge and Viaduct.

Yarm Floods

Yarm's location within a tight bend of the River Tees resembles the situation of the city of Durham or the town of Warkworth in Northumberland. Yarm differs from both in that it is built on flat ground which, over the centuries has exposed it to the constant threat of flooding.

Most notable were the floods of 1753, 1771 and 1783 all of which inundated the town. A marker on Yarm's Town Hall in the High Street marks the height of the flood of 1771. It is seven feet above ground. The flood of 1753 was witnessed and recorded in a letter by a man from the nearby village of Redmarshall. The letter is dated 9th March;

"About one o' clock in the morning it came into Yarm, throwing down all the garden and orchard walls, and forcing its way through the windows of the houses in the middle of the street. The people got into their uppermost rooms, where they had the melancholy prospect of a perfect sea in the street: horses, cows, sheep and hogs and all manner of household goods floating. . . . There was one thing rather comical than otherwise happened in the midst of this doleful spectacle. A sow, big with young, had swum till her strength was quite exhausted; a wheelbarrow was carried by the torrent out of somebody's yard, which the sow being pretty near, laid her nose and forefeet into, and suffered herself to be carried by the flood till she got safe to land."

Yarm Bridge

Yarm is connected to the village of Egglescliffe on the north bank of the Tees by a stone bridge built by Walter Skirlaw, Bishop of Durham in 1400. During the Civil War there was a battle for control of this important strategic crossing of the Tees.

On February 1st 1643 a Royalist force under the command of General King and General Goring were on their way south to assist troops at York when they were set upon by 400 Parliamentarian troops at Yarm as they attempted to cross the bridge. The Parliamentarians were defeated but the Royalists soon recognised the importance of this crossing point.

A drawbridge had been incorporated into the northern arch of the bridge to restrict movements and on February 14th 1643 the commander of the Royalist force at Stockton ordered the rector of Egglescliffe, Isaac Basire that the bridge should be drawn every night.

In 1803 it was decided that Yarm's stone bridge should be replaced by a new one built of iron. When the new bridge was complete a celebration was held, at which the mayor of Stockton declared;

> *"May the almighty protect this undertaking, and may this bridge stand the test of time."*

The unfortunate mayor had to eat his words as shortly before the bridge was to be used by the public on the 12th January 1806 it fell into the river with a "tremendous crash". Fortunately the old bridge had not been destroyed and here it still stands to this day.

Until the building of Stockton bridge in 1771 Bishop Skirlaw's bridge was the most easterly crossing point of the Tees.

Egglescliffe or Eaglescliffe?

Egglescliffe Church.

Egglescliffe on the opposite side of the bridge to Yarm is an old village with a name that could mean 'church on the hill' This would certainly be a good description of the location of Egglescliffe's old church, however evidence suggests that Egglescliffe may mean Ecgi's Cliffe, the hill belonging to an Anglo-Saxon called Ecgi.

Whatever the origin of the name may be, it should not be confused with its larger modern neighbour called Eaglescliffe.

The name of this place apparently arose after a misspelling on a local railway station sign, in which an 'a' accidentally substituted the 'g'. There is not as might be expected, any record of Eaglescliffe ever being the domain of the eagle.

Preston Hall and Park

North of Eaglescliffe in the well-wooded Tees valley near Stockton is Preston Park and Hall. Preston on Tees is mentioned in the Boldon Buke, County Durham's equivalent of the Domesday Book in 1183, when the land was farmed by Orm son of Cockett, William son of Utting and Adam son of Walter de Stockton. Later owners included the Setons, Sayers and the Withams.

In 1722 Preston became the property of Sir John Eden of Windlestone, County Durham and in 1812 the property of David Burton Fowler. It was David Burton Fowler who commenced the construction of Preston Hall in 1825.

This was also the year of the opening of the famous Stockton and Darlington Railway which ran close to the grounds of Preston.

On the opening day of the railway, a famous race between a stagecoach and the Locomotion Number One is thought to have taken place along this particular stretch of the line. The victor is unrecorded.

Preston Hall was sold to the local shipbuilder Robert Ropner in 1882 and in the following century passed into the hands of Stockton Borough Council who opened the hall as a museum in 1953.

The museum has an outstanding collection of weapons, furniture, toys, costumes and armour, but is best known for its Victorian period rooms and a period street which are surprisingly not as well known as those at York or Beamish.

The shops in the museum street include a Grocers, Tobacconist, Taxidermist, Confectioner, Draper, Pawnbroker, Ironmongers, a Chemist and a Bank.

The most outstanding exhibit is the beautiful atmospheric painting by the French artist Georges De La Tour (1593-1652) entitled The Dice Players. The Dice Players was purchased by the avid collector Edwin Clephan, the son of a baker in Silver Street, Stockton. Mr Clephan later moved to Leicester but in a deed of 1911 his art collection passed to his daughter Miss Annie Elizabeth Clephan.

In 1930 the entire collection of paintings was left to the people of Stockton by Miss Clephan in memory of her father. The paintings were stored at Preston Hall for many years and it was only during a routine inspection of the collection in 1972 that the importance of the painting came to light. This was a remarkable discovery and is one of only two examples of De La Tour's work in this country, the other is at Hampton Court.

Stockton on Tees

Stockton-on-Tees began as an Anglo-Saxon settlement on high ground close to the northern bank of the River Tees. In later times this area became the site of a Norman castle belonging to the Prince-Bishops of Durham. Dating from at least the 12th century this castle was originally a hall belonging to Hugh Pudsey a famous Bishop of Durham. At what date the hall was fortified we do not know although it is first referred to as a castle in 1376.

During the Civil War Stockton castle was a Royalist stronghold and in 1640 when a treaty was signed making the Tees a boundary between the forces of Scotland and the King, the castle stayed in Royalist hands.

The Scottish forces finally captured Stockton castle in 1644 and it was garrisoned by them until 1646. At the end of the Civil War the castle was destroyed on the orders of Oliver Cromwell and only the castle barn was left standing. Sadly this barn was demolished in the nineteenth century and today nothing remains of the old castle of Stockton on Tees;

> *"Old Noll in his day*
> *out of pious concern.*
> *The castle demolished*
> *sold all but the barn."*

The site of Stockton castle is now occupied by a prominent hotel. Its former presence indicated by Tower Street and the Castlegate Shopping centre. Some of the stonework from the old castle was incorporated into Stockton's Green Dragon Yard, just off the High Street.

The Old Heart of Teesside

By the seventeenth century Stockton was beginning to take over Yarm's role as the main port on the River Tees and was developing an important Baltic trade. It was still nevertheless a largely agricultural district, with farmland described in 1647 as "Champion country, very fruitful though of a stiff clay".

With the increasing size of ships Yarm became an impractical place for vessels to reach and Stockton soon became the main port for North Yorkshire, Westmorland and south Durham.

The main goods exported from Stockton were local agricultural produce and lead from the dales of Durham and Yorkshire. Even at Stockton adjustments had to be made to improve the efficiency of this expanding port and great cuts were made across the river meanders at Portrack and Mandale, shortening the journey of sea vessels to Stockton by three miles.

The result was a dramatic straightening in the course of the River Tees east of Stockton and a resulting confusion in the exact local boundary between Durham and Yorkshire.

Stockton Town Hall.

Stockton and the Railways

The opening of the Stockton and Darlington Railway in 1825 brought about further significant increases in the trade and population of Stockton as lead from the dales could now be quickly brought to the town along with coal from mines in the Bishop Auckland area.

The history of this famous railway to Stockton can be traced by those who

29

explore the town. Of particular interest is Bridge Road where two plaques can be found highlighting Stockton's railway history.

One plaque commemorates the place where the first section of Stockton and Darlington track was laid by Thomas Meynell of Yarm on 23rd May 1822.

The second plaque marks the building that was arguably the world's first railway ticket office. In Stockton the railway ran along the course of the quayside by the Tees and linked up with four sets of coal staithes which were jetties from which coal could be loaded into the ships.

The old Stockton ticket office.

The railway which brought about such a rapid increase in the development of Stockton was ultimately to bring about the downfall of this port, with the extension of the Stockton and Darlington line to Middlesbrough in 1830.

Middlesbrough was six miles nearer to the sea than Stockton and had many advantages over the old heart of Teesside.

A nineteenth century writer records the change in Stockton's fortunes;

"Vessels now anchor at Middleburgh snug and comfortable, which before strove to mount the river and reach Stockton after overcoming the sad surf tossed over the bar by the easterly gales; so that Stockton as a maritime place has become insignificant."

Friction Matches

Considering all the heavy industries for which Teesside is known, it is perhaps surprising that one of Stockton's most widely famed industrial enterprises can be attributed to a humble High Street chemist. His name was John Walker, the inventor of the Friction Match.

In 1826 while at his home on the Stockton Quayside experimenting with a mixture of combustible materials he happened to scrape his mixing stick against his hearth causing the stick to catch fire.

Walker realised this could have a number of potential applications. He put the substance on sale in April 1827 in the form of friction matches. They came supplied with a piece of folded sandpaper for scraping against.

Walker's first matches were made of paste board which was later replaced with three inch wood splints cut by elderly people in the neighbourhood. They were generously paid by the chemist for their efforts.

In 1830 Walker was visited by Michael Faraday who is thought to have encouraged Walker to patent his invention. Sadly Walker seemed to have no interest in developing a wider market for his development and in 1830 his idea was taken on board by a Londoner called Samuel Johnson who patented the friction lights as Friction Matches.

Johnson termed the matches Lucifers, which is perhaps appropriate because he was a bit of a devil for taking all the credit for the invention of a Stockton man.

Norton-on-Tees

For many centuries Stockton was the most important settlement in the north Teesside area, but in more ancient times Norton and Billingham were places of significance.

Both were places of importance in Anglo-Saxon times, and both still have Anglo-Saxon churches. In 1984 excavations at Mill Lane, Norton revealed a large Anglo-Saxon pagan cemetery. More than one hundred burials were discovered at the site.

Norton today is a large suburb of Stockton but at its centre stands the unexpected haven of old Norton village, which still retains a rural atmosphere with cottages, a duck pond and a village green.

For centuries, old Norton and its Saxon church were the centre of an important parish which included Stockton. Today the status of these towns has been reversed and Norton is now a part of the borough of Stockton-on-Tees.

Salt Making

Salt may have been made in the Billingham area since Roman times although it was not specifically mentioned until 1290 when Robert de Brus (grandfather of Robert the Bruce King of Scotland) granted a salt pan in Hart village to Sir John Rumundebi.

The district of Hart or Hartness is thought to have included Billingham and the port of Hartlepool. The salt pan granted by De Brus may have been located at Cowpen near Billingham as this is known to have been an important centre of the salt making industry in medieval times.

The process of making salt was quite simple, it was extracted by perpetual boiling and reboiling of sea water. The water was boiled in huge shallow salt pans made of lead. Often this necessitated eight boilings before the salt could be obtained.

The local salt making industry achieved great heights in the fifteenth and sixteenth centuries when Greatham between Hartlepool and Billingham became a salt making centre. By 1650 the centre of salt making in Britain had moved to South Shields where there was a plentiful supply of coal for heating the salt water.

Large scale exploitation of salt did not return to Greatham until the nineteenth century when the salt was extracted in the form of brine extracted from 1,000 feet below the earth.

Old Billingham

Billingham, across the Billingham Beck, to the north east of Norton is very much a modern town, best known as the site of the huge petro-chemical works of ICI but like Norton it also has ancient origins and its church has an Anglo-Saxon tower dating from about 1000 AD.

Billingham's Saxon church.

In the late Anglo-Saxon period Billingham belonged to the followers of St. Cuthbert until it was captured by the Viking King Ragnald in the tenth century AD. Ragnald gave Billingham to one of his men, a Viking called Scula.

Billingham Industry

In the fourteenth century Billingham was a little village noted for a small brewery and the making of fish oil. In 1834 an extension of the Stockton and Darlington Railway called the Clarence Railway was brought to the deep water dock on the north bank of the Tees. The railway passed close to Billingham and helped stimulate industrial growth.

Despite this industry, Billingham was still largely a village in 1857.

World War One and the need to produce nitrates for the manufacture of explosives provided the spark which brought about the incredible development of Billingham as a chemical centre. In 1917 Billingham was chosen as the site for the production of Synthetic Ammonia to be used in the manufacture of explosives.

Billingham Chemical Works.

The war was over before the Billingham Chemical plant was completed, but the works were taken over in 1920 by Brunner Mond who adapted the production of synthetic ammonia to the manufacture of fertilisers. In 1926 Brunner Mond became part of Imperial Chemical Industries Ltd (ICI).

Cargo Fleet - A Medieval Port

Although Middlesbrough was not born until 1829 the area known as Cargo Fleet was a place of some importance in medieval times and was the site of a fishing port called Caldecotes. Somehow the name Caldecotes was corrupted into Cawker, then into Caudgatefleet and finally Cargo Fleet. During the eighteenth century Cargo Fleet was also known as Cleveland Port and was the point where large ships off-loaded their cargoes onto fleets of smaller vessels. From here these smaller vessels were able to continue the journey along the River Tees to Stockton which was the main port in the area.

The Birth of Middlesbrough

Mydilsburgh is the earliest recorded form of Middlesbrough's name and dates to Saxon times. In Anglo-Saxon times Middlesbrough was certainly the site of a chapel or cell belonging to Whitby Abbey but despite this early activity, Middlesbrough was still only a small farm of twenty five people as late as 1801.

In 1829 a group of Quaker businessmen headed by Joseph Pease of Darlington purchased this Middlesbrough farmstead and its estate and set about the development of what they termed 'Port Darlington' on the banks of the Tees nearby. A town was planned on the site of the farm to supply labour to the new coal port - Middlesbrough was born.

Joseph Pease, 'the father of Middlesbrough' was the son of Edward Pease, the man behind the Stockton and Darlington Railway. By 1830 this famous line had been extended to Middlesbrough, making the rapid expansion of the town and port inevitable. In 1828 Joseph Pease had predicted there would be a day when;

> ".. the bare fields would be covered with a busy multitude with vessels crowding the banks of a busy seaport."

His prophecy was to prove true, the small farmstead became the site of North Street, South Street, West Street, East Street, Commercial Street, Stockton Street, Cleveland Street, Durham Street, Richmond Street, Gosford Street, Dacre Street, Feversham Street and Suffield Street, all laid out on a grid-iron pattern centred on a Market Square.

New businesses quickly bought up premises and plots of land in the new town and soon shippers, merchants, butchers, innkeepers, joiners, blacksmiths, tailors, builders and painters were moving in. Labour was employed, staithes and wharves were built, workshops were constructed and lifting engines installed.

Indeed such was the growth of this port that in 1846 one local writer observed;

> "To the stranger visiting his home after an abscence of fifteen years, this proud array of ships, docks, warehouses, churches, foundries and wharfs would seem like some enchanted spectacle, some Arabian Night's vision."

By 1851 Middlesbrough's population had grown from 40 people in 1829 to 7,600 and it was rapidly replacing Stockton as the main port on the Tees. A Teesside proverb was proven true;

> "Yarm was, Stockton is, Middlesbrough will be."

Iron and Steel

In 1850 iron ore was discovered in the Cleveland Hills near Eston to the south of Middlesbrough and iron gradually replaced coal as the lifeblood of the town. The ore was discovered by John Vaughan, the principal ironmaster of Middlesbrough who along with his German business partner Henry Bolckow had already established a small iron foundry and rolling mill at Middlesbrough using iron stone from Durham and the Yorkshire coast. The new discovery of iron ore on their doorstep prompted them to build Teesside's first blast furnace in 1851.

Iron was now in big demand in Britain, particularly for the rapid expansion of the railways being built in every part of the country. More and more blast furnaces were opened in the vicinity of Middlesbrough to meet this demand and by the end of the century Teesside was producing about a third of the nation's iron output.

The status of Bolckow and Vaughan reached great heights in Middlesbrough and in 1853 Bolckow became the town's first mayor and fifteen years later became its first Member of Parliament. The development of Middlesbrough as an 'Iron Town' spurred on its continuous growth and by 1860 its population had increased to an incredible 19,000. Two years later, the town was visited by the Victorian minister Gladstone who remarked;

> "This remarkable place, the youngest child of England's enterprise, is an infant, but if an infant, an infant Hercules."

By the 1870s, steel, a much stronger and more resilient metal was in big demand and Middlesbrough had to compete with Sheffield. In 1875 Bolckow and Vaughan opened the first Bessemer Steel plant in Middlesbrough. At first phosphorous ores had to be imported from Spain for the making of the steel, but by 1879 methods were developed which could use local iron ores.

In 1881 one commentator described how the ironstone of the Eston Hills processed at Middlesbrough, had been used in the building of structures throughout the world.

> "The iron of Eston has diffused itself all over the world. It furnishes the railways of the world; it runs by Neapolitan and papal dungeons; it startles the bandit in his haunt in Cicilia; it crosses over the plains of Africa; it stretches over the plains of India. It has crept out of the Cleveland Hills where it has slept since Roman days, and now like a strong and invincible serpent, coils itself around the world."

Sir H. G Reid.

Bridge Building

Associated with the making of steel on Teesside is the construction of bridges, one of the industries for which the area has achieved international recognition. Chief among the bridge building firms was Dorman Long, a firm which began as an iron and steel works in 1875 manufacturing bars and angles for ships.

A natural progression from this was to become involved in the construction of bridges particularly when Dorman Long took over the concerns of Bell Brothers and Bolckow and Vaughan in the late 1920s.

The most famous bridge ever constructed on Teesside was Dorman Long's Sydney Harbour Bridge of 1932. This was partly modelled on the 1929 Tyne Bridge, a construction regarded as the symbol of

Tyneside's Geordie pride, but also a product of Dorman Long's Teesside workmanship. The great example of Dorman Long's work on Teesside itself is the single span Newport Lifting Bridge.

Opened by the Duke of York in February 1934 it was England's first vertical lifting bridge. With a lifting span of 270 feet and 66 feet in length it is constructed from 8,000 tons of Teesside steel and 28,000 tons of concrete with towers 170 feet high.

The electrically operated lifting mechanism allowed the road to be lifted 100 feet in one and a half minutes by means of ropes passing through sheaves in the four corner towers.

The Transporter Bridge

The most notable Teesside Bridge is the Transporter Bridge, which was designed by the Cleveland Bridge and Engineering Company of Darlington and opened on 17th October 1911, by Prince Arthur of Connaught.

A kind of a cross between a ferry and a bridge, vehicles are transported across the river by means of a moving car which is capable of carrying 600 persons or 9 vehicles across the Tees to Port Clarence in two and a half minutes. Like the later Newport Bridge it was designed to facilitate the movement of ships along the River Tees. It has a 160 feet clearance above the river.

The Transporter Bridge.

The Incredible Growth of Middlesbrough

The expanding iron and steel industry of Middlesbrough in the 1860s and 1870s spurred on the growth of Middlesbrough with a population of 19,000 in 1861 increasing to 40,000 only ten years later. The residents of this early town came mainly from neighbouring Yorkshire and the North East, but later from Cheshire, Ireland, Scotland, Wales and even some European countries.

Middlesbrough Town Hall.

At the turn of the century Middlesbrough's population had more than doubled to 90,000 and it must have been hard to believe that only seventy years earlier the town did not exist. Today Middlesbrough has a population of 150,000 and is undoubtedly the heart of the Teesside conurbation and the modern 'Capital' of the area. In English history nothing compares to Middlesbrough's rapid growth. It is no wonder that Middlesbrough has been described as the 'oldest new town' in England.

Middlesbrough's town centre today is quite different from the original town planned by Joseph Pease and Partners in 1829. By the later part of the nineteenth century Middlesbrough's centre had moved away from the river with the grand town hall of 1899 forming a centrepiece for the new town.

At the beginning of the twentieth century, Linthorpe Road had become the main shopping street following the course of an old country route from Linthorpe to Middlesbrough called Linthorpe Lane.

Guisborough

Guisborough is an attractive market town in rural surroundings and lies just outside the Tees valley on the northern edge of the Cleveland Hills south of Middlesbrough. Anciently Guisborough was the capital of that part of Yorkshire known as Cleveland and is certainly one of the most historic towns in the area.

At Guisborough the main street is called Westgate in which we can find a curious eighteenth century market cross decorated with a sundial and weather vane. Guisborough's beautiful ruined abbey which is the most notable feature

of the town can cause confusion to tourists who notice that the name of this building is spelled 'Gisborough' without the 'u' that appears in the name of the town.

Originating from the twelfth century, the abbey was built by Robert, a member of the De Brus or Bruce family who were important landowners on both sides of the River Tees. Robert De Brus of Skelton was an ancestor of the famous Scottish king Robert the Bruce (1290-1329).

What is Cleveland?

Cleveland means the cliffland or hilly district, as the word cliff in its old sense referred to rolling hills rather than steep cliffs. Cleveland is an ancient name and is not to be confused with the County of Cleveland created in 1974. Cleveland was a district of northern Yorkshire situated entirely south of the River Tees. The County of Cleveland was quite different and took in towns like Eaglescliffe, Stockton, Billingham and Hartlepool which were originally part of County Durham. Ironically some parts of northern Yorkshire that anciently belonged to Cleveland were excluded from the short-lived County of Cleveland. The Cleveland Hills were never included in the County of Cleveland.

Roseberry Topping

Roseberry Topping is undoubtedly the best known natural landmark in Cleveland and is steeped in local folklore. It can be clearly seen from many parts of rural Cleveland and industrial Teesside and has a distinctive outline. Known as 'The Cleveland Matterhorn'. Roseberry Topping was once used by sailors out at sea as an indicator of changing weather, as the following rhyme records:

"When Roseberry Topping wears a cap,
Let Cleveland then beware of a clap!"

Roseberry Topping was connected with the Vikings, as the word 'Topping', from 'Toppen', is one of a number of old Viking words for a hill, but the original Viking name for Roseberry Topping was 'Odins-Beorge' meaning 'Odin's Hill'. Roseberry may have been a centre for the worship of the Viking god Odin in Pagan times.

The Tees Estuary

The entrance to the Tees estuary is clearly marked on the coast by the pier breakwaters on either side of the river estuary. These are the half mile long North Gare and the two and a half mile long South Gare.

The gares were built following a great storm in 1861 in which 50 vessels were wrecked on the sand bars between Redcar and Hartlepool in the vicinity of the estuary. Both Gares are under the management of the Tees and Hartlepool Port Authority and the South Gare is the sight of a coast guard station which monitors the busy shipping activity of the estuary.

The Tees estuary is one of the biggest on the North Eastern coast and is dominated on either side by the large areas of reclaimed industrial land called Seal Sands on the northern bank and Bran Sands on the southern bank. Seal Sands is the site of an Oil Refinery and Chemical Works.

The two hundred and twenty mile long Ekofisk oil pipeline has its terminus at

Seal Sands by which oil and gas liquids are piped ashore from the Ekofisk oilfield for processing at one of the largest plants of its kind in the world. Today oil is one of Teesside's most important industries.

Despite all the heavy industry the Tees estuary is surprisingly important for its wildlife. Seal Sands, now only half its original size due to land reclamation is still the winter home to thousands of wildfowl and waders.

Seals may still be seen 'basking' in these industrial surroundings. Autumn and Winter is the best time of the year for viewing wildlife at the Tees estuary. The main species are Little Stints, Curlew Sandpipers, Ruffs, Greenshanks, Wood Sandpipers, Bar-Tailed Godwits and Whimbrels.

In Winter time Golden Plovers may also be seen but Winter is best for Duck-Watching when the main species are Shoveler Ducks, Widgeon, Long-Tailed Ducks, Goldeneye and Teal.

Redcar

Redcar, situated on the Cleveland coast just to the south of the River Tees was in early times a 'poore fishing toune', overshadowed by its neighbour Coatham, which held a market and fair from 1257. The extension of the railway to Redcar from Teesside in 1846 brought industry and growth to Redcar's doorstep and brought tourists into the neighbourhood. Like nearby Saltburn, Redcar is still frequented by day trippers in search of the sea but the biggest attraction is undoubtedly the Race Course which the town encircles.

Redcar is less known as the home of the world's oldest lifeboat called The Zetland. It was built around 1810 by Henry Greathead of South Shields and worked at Spurn Head until it was bought by Redcar fishermen in 1802.

The Zetland was built twenty years after the first ever lifeboat which was also built at South Shields

---

A Tiny Church

At the village of Upleatham on the Guisborough to Marske road south of Redcar we find St. Andrew's, a church measuring 17 feet 9 inches by thirteen feet. It is reputedly the smallest church in England.

Saltburn and the Cleveland Coast

Saltburn was an important Victorian bathing resort and home to the North East's only pleasure pier which juts out 600 feet from Saltburn beach. Originally the pier was 1,400 ft long but its length was severely reduced during a storm in 1924 when it was rammed by a ship called the Ovenberg. Another intriguing feature related to Saltburn's role as a Victorian resort lies directly above the pier. Here we find the oldest working water balanced inclined tramway in Britain.

Dating from the 1870s this was specially designed to transport visitors back and forth from Saltburn town to the pier and beach. Although the town's most obvious features are of Victorian origin, its history goes back much further as we know that in the thirteenth century it was inhabited by a hermit.

In even earlier times it was the site of a fortified Roman signalling station. The earthworks of this fort are situated on Hunt Cliff, a vertical sea cliff 365 ft above sea level, only a mile down the coast from Saltburn. Huntcliff was one of a number of Roman signalling stations situated along the Yorkshire coast which were built as watchtowers against the threat of Anglo-Saxon raids from Denmark and Germany. It was eventually overrun by the raiders in the fourth century AD when its occupants were murdered and reputedly dumped in a nearby well.

Smuggling on the Cleveland Coast

The cliffs at Boulby to the north of Staithes are 679 feet high, which makes them the highest on the whole eastern coast of England. Their rugged recesses once provided shelter for smugglers who were especially active on the Cleveland coast during the eighteenth century.

The steeple of a nearby church was one of the places where illicit kegs of wine, gin and whisky were once hidden. Smuggling was a highly profitable business and was a common activity on the North East coast.

Staithes

Staithes is one of the most picturesque places on the old Cleveland coast. It is situated in a deep narrow creek formed by the Roxby Beck which cuts its way through the steep cliffs. This is undoubtedly one of the prettiest coastal villages in England. Romantics claim that the village owes its origins to a French shipwreck whose survivors settled ashore. The headless ghost of a young girl reputedly haunts the coast hereabouts.

James Cook, later Captain Cook worked at Staithes as a boy where he was apprenticed to a local grocer. It was at Staithes that Cook acquired the love of the sea that set him on course for his long and eventful career. Indeed upon leaving Staithes Cook headed straight for Whitby and from 1775 he worked for a Whitby ship owner employed on colliers shipping coals from the River Tyne to London.

Captain Cook

Great Ayton, near Roseberry Topping is the place where the budding young sailor James Cook went to school when he lived as a boy at the nearby Aireyholme Farm at the foot of the hill. On Easby Moor to the south east of Great Ayton there is an imposing monument to his honour.

Captain Cook.

James Cook was actually born a little further north at Marton, now a suburb of Middlesbrough on the 27th October 1728 and moved to Staithes at a later date. It was as a young man that he began working for a Whitby ship owner and was employed on Colliers

shipping coals from the River Tyne to London. After learning basic seamanship, he joined the navy at the age of 27 and soon gained a reputation for his chart making skills.

Cook had a desire to explore new lands and in 1769 he was asked to command HM Bark Endeavour on an expedition that took him to Tahiti, New Zealand and Australia, where he named the territory of New South Wales.

On his return to England in 1771 Cook was promoted from lieutenant to captain and set sail the following year in search of the great southern continent, voyaging as far as the Antarctic Circle. This was a journey that took him further south than anyone else had ever been before. He then returned home to England.

Cook's last voyage was to prove fatal. Leaving England on the 25th June 1776 on board the Resolution and accompanied by the Discovery, Cook went on to discover Hawaii and the Cook Inlet of Alaska. On return to Hawaii where his ship stopped for provisions, Cook unfortunately lost his life on the 14th February 1779, following an affray between local tribesmen and members of his crew. There is a legend recited by local tourist guides on the island of Hawaii that the place where Cook met his death is the only part of the United States of America which still belongs to Great Britain as a mark of respect to the great explorer.

Stewart Park, Marton, Middlesbrough, is today the site of the Captain Cook Birthplace Museum, which has a number of displays connected with the life of the great sailor and the places he visited. A vase made of Granite from Point Hicks, Australia, stands close to the museum marking the site of the thatched cottage where Cook was born.

Staithes.

Part Three
Hartlepool and East Durham

Historic view of Hartlepool

Part Three
Hartlepool and East Durham

The Hartlepool Headland

Surrounded on three sides by the sea, the Magnesian Limestone headland or peninsula called the Heugh at Hartlepool is familiarly known as Old Hartlepool.

In prehistoric times Hartlepool's headland is thought to have been an isolated tidal island covered by thick forests.

In the nineteenth century during excavation of the adjacent marshy area called the Slake, trunks of trees from the ancient forest were found embedded in the clay along with antlers and the teeth from deer that seem to have inhabited the area in large numbers many years ago.

Hartlepool forest is still recorded in existence in the thirteenth century. In fact the ancient Anglo Saxon name for Hartlepool was 'Heret eu' meaning 'Stag Island' which is a reference to either the stag's head shape of the headland or perhaps an indication that the area was inhabited by forest deer.

Hereteu was later known as 'Hart' or 'Hartness' and was in fact the name of a whole district that included the Heugh headland and the villages of Hart and Billingham to the west.

At an early stage the coastal headland was distinguished from Hart by the addition of the word 'pool', a reference to the sheltered coastal bay adjacent to the headland.

St. Hilda of Hartlepool

Hartlepool's headland is of course the site of the original Hartlepool and was to form the natural harbour for the old fishing town for many centuries. In earlier times this area had been the site of a monastery associated with St. Hilda.

The Anglo-Saxon monastery at Hartlepool was founded in 640 AD by St. Aidan for both men and women and its first abbess was an Irish princess by the name of Hieu. Some say that Hieu gave her name to Heugh, the name of the headland. In 649 AD Hieu was succeeded by St. Hilda who was here until 657 AD when she left to establish the monastery at Whitby.

In its later days the monastery at Hartlepool seems to have declined in importance until it was finally destroyed by the Danes in the ninth century. Scandinavian invaders may have continued to be a problem for Hartlepool in following centuries as there is a record of an attack upon this place by Norwegian pirates under King Eystein in 1153 when ships and goods were carried off from the port.

The location of the old Anglo-Saxon monastery at Hartlepool is marked by the beautiful church of St. Hilda. In 1833 a cemetery thought to be associated with the old monastery was discovered nearby.

The present church of St. Hilda dates from the thirteenth century and was built as a burial place for the Norman De Brus (Bruce) family who owned much land hereabouts.

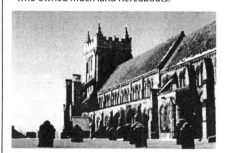

St. Hilda's Church, Hartlepool.

Bruce's Port

In the thirteenth century the coastal port and fishing town of Hartlepool became a fortified place with defensive walls constructed around the Headland. The defences were instigated by Robert Bruce the first, who was grandfather of the famous King of Scotland of that name.

The Bruces acquired Hartlepool after the Norman Conquest although their period of ownership was characterised by disputes with the Bishops of Durham over who exactly owned the place.

Hartlepool Town Walls.

Some parts of Hartlepool's town wall date from the 14th century including the historic Sandwell Gate which can still be seen. Here the wall is eight feet three inches thick.

Hartlepool needed to be well defended as it was the chief seaport of the powerful Prince Bishops of Durham and was a regular target for Scottish and sea-borne attacks.

One notable Scottish raid on Hartlepool occurred in 1315, the year after King Edward II had been defeated by King Robert the Bruce at the Battle of Bannockburn.

Robert the Bruce may have had a particular grudge against Hartlepool as it was the place to which the English King

Edward had fled following the battle. Furthermore Robert the Bruce had once been the owner of Hartlepool, but it was confiscated from him by the English, when he was enthroned as King of the Scots.

A Medieval Port

Throughout the Middle Ages Hartlepool virtually monopolised the shipping of the Durham Bishopric and was one of the busiest places on the eastern coast. Such was its importance that it regularly attracted pirates who hampered its trade.

In the sixteenth and seventeenth centuries Hartlepool was recognised for its strategic importance during rebellions and in times of religious conflict. In the conflicts of the sixteenth century for example it was recognised by all sides as a potential landing place for the enemy.

At the Siege of Dunbar in 1650 it was said that the French had come into the possession of a detailed map of Hartlepool and hoped to set men ashore to fortify the place as a base for seizing the whole of northern England.

In August 1561 Hartlepool was again asked to remain vigilant when the activities of Mary Queen of Scots came under close scrutiny.

The Hartlepudlians were advised to keep a watch out for foreign ships entering the town. Eight years later during the Rising of the North in 1569 the Spanish ambassador had instructed northern rebels to capture Hartlepool in order that the Duke of Alva might land troops from the Netherlands to lend their support.

As a defensive measure the Earl of Sussex ordered that Hartlepool be garrisoned by 200 men to prevent the landing. The order was not obeyed and Lord Neville, leader of the northern rebels seized the town instead.

The foreign support for the rebels at Hartlepool never arrived and on the seventeenth of December 1569 a Royal ship sailing from Scarborough to Tynemouth fired upon the rebels in the town.

The rebels returned fire but the ship managed to capture a Hartlepool fishing coble with three very poor half naked men on board.

In the following century Hartlepool was occupied by the Scots during the Civil War. During the Dutch Wars (1644-67) a report and map of the place was drawn up because vessels pursued by the Dutch frequently took refuge here.

By the eighteenth century Hartlepool's importance as a port had fallen into considerable decline and its harbour had fallen into disrepair. As Hartlepool entered the nineteenth century it was redundant as a port and was known primarily as a health resort and not a very successful one at that.

A final nail seemed to have been hammered into the coffin of Hartlepool as a port when the natural harbour was enclosed for agricultural purposes and corn was grown on the slake.

Fortunately in 1813 a petition was made that aimed to redevelop the port. The enclosure was reversed and the harbour was saved.

If the enclosure had been given a few more years to take effect, irreversible damage may have been done to the harbour.

Old Hartlepool.

West Hartlepool - Jackson's Town

At the beginning of the nineteenth century it was hard to believe that Old Hartlepool, with its small population of only 993 consisting almost entirely of fishermen had been one of the busiest ports on the eastern coast.

It was realised that trade had to be brought into the town in order to save it from oblivion and in 1823 it was suggested that railways be built to connect with local collieries in eastern Durham, so that Hartlepool could be developed as a coal port.

One of the main parties involved in the development of railways and docks at Hartlepool was a Stockton solicitor called Ralph Ward Jackson who established the West Hartlepool Dock Company to the south west of the old town. This signified the birth of West Hartlepool, a town which came to overshadow Old Hartlepool by its shear size.

By 1881 Old Hartlepool's population had grown from 993 to 12,361, but the newly born West Hartlepool now had a population of 28,000. By 1900 the two Hartlepools were one of the four busiest ports in the country and West Hartlepool alone had a population of 63,000.

For many years West Hartlepool and Old Hartlepool were separate towns but merged together as one town, under the Hartlepool Order of 1966. Today the modern town centre of Hartlepool is in the former West Hartlepool where we find many interesting features including the unusual Victorian church called Christchurch, now occupied by an art gallery. The most significant developments at Hartlepool of more recent times include the Hartlepool Marina and Hartlepool Historic Quay where a complete eighteenth century seaport has been created in part of a West Hartlepool dock. Nearby, the Museum of Hartlepool has an interactive museum portraying Hartlepool's historic past.

Seaton Carew

Seaton Carew to the south of Hartlepool near the mouth of the River Tees is Hartlepool's local coastal resort and is named after a Norman French family called Carou. Like many places on the neighbouring coast it was a small fishing town but grew in the eighteenth and nineteenth centuries with the rising popularity of health resorts. Seaton was especially popular in the bathing season with members of the Quaker fraternity from Darlington.

Sedgefield

Hartlepool is surrounded by rolling countryside formed by the magnesian limestone escarpment that dominates much of eastern Durham and its coast.

Further inland the often flat and occasionally poorly drained landscape of south east Durham is among the least populated parts of lowland Durham.

Much of the area around Sedgefield half way between Durham City and Stockton lay outside the Durham coalfield and as a result there are few colliery villages in the locality until we reach Fishburn and Trimdon in the north and Ferryhill further to the west.

Apart from a few tiny rural villages, the most prominent feature in the area is an old Roman road called Cade's Road, which runs northwards from Dinsdale on the Tees through the village of Sadberge towards the outskirts of Sedgefield on its way to Chester-le-Street.

Sedgefield is a small market town, with the pleasant appearance of a very large village. The town is at the heart of south east Durham and in days gone by was fortunate enough to lie just outside the now largely redundant Durham coalfield.

The town is the home of County Durham's only racecourse and is situated close to two notable parkland estates, namely Hardwick Hall (and Country Park), to the west and Wynyard Hall (a private residence) to the south.

Sedgefield is only six miles north of Stockton-on-Tees and many of its residents are commuters who work on Teesside.

The church at Sedgefield is of particular interest. It contains good examples of the beautiful woodwork of John Cosin, Bishop of Durham (1660 - 1672). Sir Nikolaus Pevsner, the architectural historian, has described the work of John Cosin as "one of the most remarkable contributions" of County Durham to the history of architecture and decoration in England.

Sedgefield Church.

Bishop Middleham

A mile to the north west of Sedgefield, is the village of Bishop Middleham, where the remains of a castle earthwork can be seen. The castle was once an important residence of the Prince Bishops of Durham.

Two little known Durham Bishops, Robert De Insula (1274-1283) and Richard Kellaw (1311-1316) are known to have died at the Middleham residence. De Insula was described as "a jolly monk, whose mother complained of too many servants" while Richard Kellaw's reign was troubled by Scottish raids and problems with local robbers and bandits, although he tried very hard to suppress them.

To the west of Bishop Middleham, on the other side of the Durham motorway and back into former colliery country is the small hamlet of Mainsforth near Ferryhill. This was the site of Mainsforth Hall, home of Robert Surtees (1779-1834), author of the History and Antiquities of the County Palatine of Durham. His four volume work is the classic pre-industrial history of the County.

Mainsforth Hall was demolished in 1962, but the Surtees Society was set up after the death of Robert, aiming to continue his work through the publication of historical manuscripts relating to Northumberland, Durham and the North Riding of Yorkshire.

Trimdon

Trimdon lies three miles north of Sedgefield and approximately six miles west of Hartlepool near the source of the River Skerne. It is closely associated with Tony Blair, the British Prime Minister and MP for Sedgefield.

According to legend Trimdon was the place where King Canute shaved his head and trimmed his beard before donning a cloak at the beginning of a bare foot pilgrimage from Garmondsway near Coxhoe to St. Cuthbert's shrine at Durham. Sadly there is no evidence to support the claim that Trimdon means 'trimming and donning' as early forms of the name are quite different.

Historic forms of the name include Tremeldona in 1196 and Trembledon in 1339 and the present form Trimdon did not come into use until 1539. The 'don'

in Trimdon is almost certainly an Anglo-Saxon word for a hill and is perhaps a reference to the nearby ridge which stretches west to Cornforth.

'Tremel', the first part of the early name Tremeldon is thought to mean a wooden cross or sign. It has been argued that the name referred to a wooden post erected by Anglo-Saxons and that a Christian church was later established on the site.

Today the original village of Trimdon is the site of a medieval church. The nearby villages of Trimdon Grange, Trimdon Colliery and Trimdon Station are more recent settlements with coal mining origins.

Trimdon Grange Explosion

Mining disasters and colliery explosions were a feature of life in the coal mining days of County Durham history. The Trimdon Grange Colliery Explosion which took place on February 16 1883 is especially famous because it was recorded in a song by the County Durham miners' poet Tommy Armstrong of Tanfield Lea (1848-1920). Tommy's song was composed to raise money in aid of the widows and orphans.

"Let us not think of tomorrow,
Lest we disappointed be;
All our joys may turn to sorrow,
As we all may daily see.

Today we may be strong and healthy,
But how soon there comes a change
As we may learn from the explosion.
That has been at Trimdon Grange.

Men and boys left home that morning
For to earn their daily bread.
Little thought before that evening
That they'd be numbered
with the dead.

Let us think of Mrs Burnett,
Once had sons but now has none.
By the Trimdon Grange explosion.
Joseph George and James are gone.

February left behind it
What will never be forgot;
Weeping widows, helpless children,
May be found in many a cot.

Homes that once were blest with
comfort,
Guarded by a father's care,
Now are solemn, sad and gloomy,
Since the father is not there.

Little children, kind and loving,
From their homes each day would run
For to meet their father's coming,
As each hard day's work was done.

Now they ask if father's left them.
Then the mother hangs her head
With a weeping widow's feelings.
Tells the child that father's dead.

God protect the lonely widow,
Help to raise each drooping head;
Be a father to the orphans,
Never let them cry for bread.

Death will pay us all a visit,
They have only gone before;
We may meet the Trimdon victims
where explosions are no more."

Kelloe And Cassop Vale

Coxhoe, Cornforth, Kelloe and Quarrington Hill lie in limestone quarry country to the north of Trimdon. Some of the quarries are now protected as nature reserves. The creamy coloured limestone is Magnesian Limestone or 'Dolomite' and contains calcium and magnesian deposits. It has been used in the past as building material most notably to cement together the bricks of Durham Cathedral.

The village of Kelloe had eight small coal mines in its vicinity during the nineteenth century but its history goes back well before the days of mining. Kelloe Law nearby is the site of a burial cist dating from the Bronze age where the skeletons of an ancient family were once found consisting of a father and mother aged about thirty and three children aged about four, eight and twelve.

A little to the east of Kelloe we are at the site of a deserted medieval village called Church Kelloe. The only remains of the settlement is the Norman church of St. Helen noted for the well preserved and beautifully detailed Norman cross dedicated to St. Helena.

A tablet inside the church is also of interest. It commemorates the birth of Elizabeth Barrett Browning who was born nearby at Coxhoe Hall in 1806. Elizabeth's family of course provided the model for the 'Barretts of Wimpole Street' but the hall where she was born was demolished in 1952.

One of the Bishops of Durham, Richard De Kellaw (1311) is known to have originated from Kelloe. He was much troubled by Scottish invasions which were fought off by the forces of the bishopric under the leadership of the bishop's brother Patrick.

Another resident of Kelloe was John Lively the seventeenth century vicar of Kelloe who was noted for the fact that he had no male heir:

"Here lies John Lively,
Vicar of Kelloe
who had seven daughters
but never a fellow."

Not far from Kelloe is Beacon Hill, the site of a Napoleonic warning beacon, and also nearby is Signing Bank where pilgrims traditionally first encountered Durham Cathedral. A little further to the north is the pretty Cassop Vale. In early times this was a hunting area for Durham's Prince Bishops. Its name derives from 'Cat's Hop' meaning valley of the wild cats.

Pittington and Sherburn

To the north of Cassop are the little villages of Shadforth and Ludworth with names that mean 'Shallow Ford' and 'Ludda's Farm'. Ludworth is noted for the ruins of a Pele Tower, a feature very common in Northumberland but much rarer in County Durham.

Peles are tower houses built to protect local people from the invasions of the Scots. The fortification at Ludworth was constructed in 1422 by the Holden family on the site of their manor.

A large part of the building collapsed in 1890 but one wall remains along with

the foundations of a tight spiral staircase which is a typical feature of a pele tower.

To the north west of Shadforth is the village of Sherburn (from Scir Burn meaning 'Bright Stream') and the nearby Sherburn Hospital which was founded in 1181 by Bishop Pudsey as an asylum for lepers. Most of Pudsey's buildings were destroyed by an invasion of Scots and today the only original part of the building is the chapel.

Sherburn Hospital lies on the banks of the Old Durham Beck which joins the River Wear near Old Durham. In times gone by this stream was also known as the 'Sher Burn' or the 'River Pitting'. Upstream the beck leads to Pittington, the site of the historic Norman Church of St. Lawrence.

Pittington church underwent some restoration by Ignatius Bonomi in the nineteenth century but it has some notable surviving medieval features in the form of the nave, the tower and the north arcade. The Norman arches and zigzag decorated pillars in the church are strikingly similar to those found in Durham Cathedral.

Some of the features of the church interior are particularly similar to the cathedral's Galilee chapel. The reason is that both were built by Christian, the master architect of Hugh Pudsey, the twelfth century Bishop of Durham. Christian had been granted land in the Pittington area by the bishop.

The interior of Pittington Church.

The Hallgarth Murder

In the nineteenth century Hallgarth near Pittington was the scene of a famous northern murder. Thomas Clarke, a nineteen year old servant boy at a local mill was accused of murdering Ann Westropp, a servant girl of the same age. The murder occurred on the evening of Sunday 14th August 1831 while the mill owners were away. It was recalled in a local ballad:

"Eighteen hundred three times ten,
August the eighth that day
Let not that Sunday and that year
From memory pass away.

At Hallgarth Mill near Pittington
Was done a murder foul
The female weak- the murderer strong
No pity for her soul.

Her skull was broke, her throat was cut,
Her struggle was soon o'er;
And down she fell, and fetched a sigh,
And weltered in her gore.

Her fellow servant, Thomas Clarke,
To Sherburn slowly sped,
And told a tale that strangers six
Had done the dreadful deed.

Now, woe betide thee, Thomas Clarke!
For this thy coward lie;
A youth like thee for girl like her
Would fight till he did die.

"They've killed the lass," it was his tale,
"and nearly have killed me";
But when upon him folk did look,
No bruises could they see."

West Rainton

There are two notable old mansions in the vicinity of Pittington one of which is the eighteenth century Elemore Hall, birthplace of Ann Isabella Milbanke the wife of the poet Lord Byron. The other is a hotel called Ramside Hall. a building originally called Belmont Hall by Thomas Pemberton the coal owner who constructed it as a mansion in 1820.

To the north of Ramside is the village of West Rainton, which was once an important coal mining area where former colliery owners included John Duck, 'Durham's Dick Whittington' and the third Marquess of Londonderry who had a reputation as a very hard hearted employer.

The spire of the Victorian church at Rainton is a very prominent feature and can be seen from miles around. It was donated to the church by a local MP called Sir George Eliott in 1877. A large granite tablet records the donation of the spire by the MP - this tablet being of special interest in that it is a piece of stone taken from the great pyramid of Ghizeh in Egypt. It was removed from the pyramid with the permission of the Khedive of Egypt.

Easington Church.

Peterlee

Peterlee on the Durham coast is one of the North East's new towns, though few know it is also the site of a deserted medieval village called Yoden. The modern town was created in 1948, to re-house growing populations from nearby mining villages.

Peterlee is named after Mr Peter Lee, an important miner's leader who became the chairman of England's first all Labour council at Durham in 1909. Lee was born in 1864 at Trimdon Grange, a colliery village in eastern Durham and at the age of ten he started work as a pony driver at Littletown Colliery, just outside Durham City.

By the age of sixteen he had achieved the status of a coal hewer. In 1886 Lee emigrated to the United States, where he worked in the mines of Ohio, Kentucky and Pennsylvania, before returning to County Durham in 1887. He died in 1935 at the age of seventy.

The Coastal Denes

Much of the short Durham coast is dominated by a series of small wooded valleys called 'Denes'. The best known of these is the attractive Castle Eden Dene, which joins the sea to the north of the cave infested Blackhall Rocks. The Castle Eden Dene, formed by the wooded ravine of the Castle Eden Burn, provides an ideal nature reserve for the town of Peterlee.

In prehistoric times, a large area of County Durham was a glacial lake that cut its way through the limestone escarpment of the coast during a melting period to form Denes at Crimdon, Castle Eden, Easington, Hawthorn, Dawdon, Seaham and Ryhope.

Seaham - Byron's Wedding

The town of Seaham Harbour lies on the County Durham coast between Easington and Sunderland. The harbour was created in 1828 by the Marquess of Londonderry, whose family name of Vane Tempest was also the name of a local colliery.

Londonderry built the harbour for the shipping of coals from the collieries he owned at Rainton near Durham City.

The poet Lord Byron (1770-1845), was married at Seaham in 1815. His bride was Lady Ann Isabella Milbanke, the daughter of a local squire.

The marriage was not a happy one and the unfortunate wife was later ridiculed in one of Byron's poems as 'Lady Millpond'. Byron does not seem to have enjoyed his time at Seaham as in a letter to his friend Moore he complained;

"Upon this dreary coast we have nothing but county meetings and shipwrecks; and I have this day dined upon fish, which probably dined upon the crews of several colliers lost in the late gales".

East Durham Coal

Until the mid nineteenth century most coal mines in Durham were in the northern and central area of the county and were especially numerous around the Tyne and Wear where the seams were relatively shallow and accessible.

By comparison the coal of east Durham was inaccessible and lay deep below the Magnesian Limestone escarpment which dominates this part of the county.

Coal was first proved to exist in eastern Durham by the sinking of a pit at

Haswell in 1811 but the first great deep pit in the region was sunk at Hetton in 1821. Sunk to a depth of over 1,000 ft, it became one of the most productive pits in the region as well as a focus for some of Stephenson's important locomotive developments.

Monkwearmouth Colliery near Sunderland followed shortly afterwards and was shipping coal from 1835 with a seam 1,590 feet below the surface. Monkwearmouth, 1,700 ft in 1846 was the deepest coal mine in the country. It would be these deeper coastal pits that would be the last to survive the colliery closures of the late twentieth century.

Hetton Colliery.

Part Four
The Wear Valley

Stanhope Church

Part Four
The Wear Valley

Source of the Wear

Upper Weardale, beyond the village of Westgate has some of the highest primary roads in England, most notably in the vicinity of the small village of Wearhead.

Close to here the River Wear begins, formed by the confluence of the Kilhope, Welhope and Burnhope Burns which make up the westerly frontier of County Durham and Cumbria. The word 'hope' which occurs in the names of these streams is of Anglo-Saxon origin and means 'side valley'.

Ancient Man in Weardale

In 1859 a great archaeological discovery was made in the hills above Stanhope in Weardale in which a huge collection of Bronze Age items were uncovered. It included evidence of the earliest use of wheeled vehicles in the British Isles. The items found at the Heathery Burn cave belonged to a particularly wealthy Bronze Age family, whose skeletons were also uncovered. For some unknown reason, perhaps a flash flood, the family had become trapped in this cave some 3,000 years ago. Today the findings of the Heathery Burn Cave are kept in the British Museum, London.

The Bishops' Hunting Park

Of the three Durham Dales - Teesdale, Weardale and Derwentdale, Weardale was historically most closely associated with the Prince Bishops. Eastgate and Westgate, two small villages in the upper part of the valley once marked the boundary of Stanhope Park, the Prince Bishop's hunting ground and it was here that the famous 'Great Chases' were held.

The Great Chases were the hunting expeditions, led by the Prince Bishops and were by all accounts grand occasions, celebrated with much pomp and pageantry.

Such was the scale of the Great Chases, that all the folk of Weardale were required to provide hounds for the hunt, along with enormous quantities of food, wine and beer for the hunters.

The Weardale people were also required to assist with the construction of a large temporary hunting lodge, a chapel, a kitchen and a larder, which were all purposely built for the 'Great Chase'.

Waterfalls or 'Linns' near Eastgate.

Bishop Pudsey's Boldon Buke of 1183, (Durham's equivalent of the Domesday Book), gives a good insight into the preparation for a Great Chase, most notably under entries for West Auckland and Stanhope.

The following two passages from the Boldon Buke refer to the Great Chases and are translated from the original Latin.

The first relates to West Auckland;

"All the villeins of Aucklandshire, that is North Auckland and West Auckland and Escomb and Newton, provide 1 rope at the Great Chases of the Bishop for each bovate and make the hall of the Bishop in the forest 60 feet in length and in breadth within the posts 16 feet, with a butchery and a store house and chamber and a privy. Moreover they make a chapel 40 feet in length and 15 feet in breadth, and they have 2s as a favour and they make their part of the enclosure around the lodges and on the Bishop's departure a full barrel of ale or half if he should remain away. And they look after the hawk eyries in the bailiwick of Ralph the Crafty and they make 18 booths at St. Cuthbert's fair. Moreover, all the villeins and lease holders go on the roe hunt on the summons of the Bishop."

and under the entry for Stanhope

". . . all the villeins build a kitchen, and larder and a dog kennel at the Great Chases and they provide straw for the hall, chapel and chamber, and they lead all the Bishop's supplies from Wolsingham to the lodges."

Weardale made up the second largest hunting ground in England after the New Forest in Hampshire which of course belonged to the King.

Stanhope Park and the forest surrounding it were well stocked with game, deer, wolves, and wild boar and the bishops jealously guarded their right to hunting in the area. A forest court was held at nearby Stanhope, for the trial of poachers.

It is known that hunting had a long history in Weardale as a Roman altar found near Stanhope records the capture of a wild boar in the area.

Lead Mining in Weardale

While the central and eastern parts of County Durham were part of the Great Northern coalfield, the dales in the western part of the county were important for their lead.

Since Roman times, this lead had been exploited in Weardale and the northern Pennines and perhaps it is worth noting that Hadrian's Wall divides the northern fringe of the North Pennine lead field, from the less mineral rich Northumbrian hills to the north. From the thirteenth century lead mining in the Durham dales was encouraged by the Prince Bishops who profited from the mining of the ore.

The heyday of lead mining in the region was not however until the late eighteenth to mid nineteenth centuries, when the North Pennine lead field was arguably the most important in the world.

The North Pennine lead field was bordered in the east by the Durham coalfield, in the south by the Stainmore

Gap and in the north by the Tyne Gap. The main valleys of this area were Teesdale, South Tynedale, the Allendales, Derwentdale and at the centre, Weardale. Collectively they were known as the 'Lead Dales'.

Relics of lead mining can be found in all the 'lead dales' but the most imposing reminder is the great lead crushing mill known as Killhope wheel, on the remote Killhope Burn in upper Weardale. Killhope wheel is now part of a lead mining museum and is the most impressive lead mining site in Britain. The museum includes a lead mine and a 'mine shop' where there is a reconstruction of the lead miners' sleeping quarters.

Miners would have slept in these quarters for the whole of the working week and would only have returned to their homes further down the dale at weekends.

Rookhope Chimney

In the Weardale side valley of Rookhope we may trace the course and remains of the two mile long Rookhope Chimney. This was a massive stone flue which carried dangerous toxic fumes across the moors away from the lead smelter at Lintzgarth near Rookhope village.

Rookhope Chimney.

A great stone arch can be seen nearby, which once supported the chimney. It resembles a ruined stone bridge that leads to nowhere and crosses nothing at all.

The Rookhope Ryde

On December 8th, 1569, the Weardale valley of Rookhope was the setting for a border fray in which a large group of cattle raiders from Tynedale made a raid upon Weardale. The raiders had decided to plunder the Wear valley for its livestock while many of the Weardale men were away in Teesdale, plotting against the Queen in the 'Rising of the North'.

Resistance to the raid was expected to be low, but a number of Weardale men remained to defend the dale. The raiders were pursued north into the Rookhope valley as they made off with Weardale cattle and sheep. When the Weardale men caught up with the mosstroopers, a fray ensued in which four of the Tynedalers lost their lives. The event is remembered in the 'Rookhope Ryde', a 24 verse Weardale ballad dating from 1579.

"Rookhope is a pleasant place,
If the false thieves would let it be.
But away they steal our goods apace,
And ever an ill death may they dee.

Then in at Rookhope Heed they came,
They ran the forest but a miles;
They gathered together in four hours
Six hundred sheep within a while.

But all that was in Rookhope Heed,
And all that was in Neukton Cleugh,
Where Weardale men overtook the thieves,
And gave them fighting eneugh.

About that time the fray began,
I trow it lasted but an hour,
Till many a man lay weaponless,
And was sore wounded in that stour.

And before that hour was done
Four of the thieves were slain,
Besides all those that wounded were,
Eleven prisoners were tae'n."

Stanhope

Stanhope is the 'capital' of Weardale and its Anglo-Saxon name, meaning 'stony valley', is a good description of the Wear and the burns in the area. Like many towns in the North Pennine dales,

Stanhope prospered in the nineteenth century as a lead mining centre, but is unmistakably a dales town. It is the site of a castle built in 1798 as a residence for a Gateshead MP by the name of Cuthbert Rippon.

A 250 million year old fossilized tree stump is proudly on display in Stanhope's churchyard. It was actually brought here from Edmunbyers in the Derwent valley.

Stanhope Church.

A Battle with the Bishop

In 1818 Stanhope was the site of a most unusual battle which involved the local lead miners and the Prince Bishop of Durham. When times got hard, the lead miners of Weardale had come to regard it as their right to shoot the game which was so plentiful in their valley.

The Bishop of Durham had a different view and regarded such activities as poaching. He warned the lead miners that it would have to stop. When the poaching continued the bishop brought an army of his men into the Wear valley, arrested the suspected poaching ring leaders and temporarily imprisoned them in a local inn.

Hearing of the arrests, a large and angry crowd of lead miners quickly gathered outside the inn and demanded the release of the men. It was not long before a violent 'battle' broke out, in which the Bishop's men were heavily defeated by the lead miners. Although no one was actually killed, much blood was shed and one man is said to have lost an eye.

The bloody event known as 'The Battle of Stanhope' is remembered in a lengthy folk ballad called The Bonny Moor Hen, a few verses can be found below;

"You brave lads of Weardale,
I pray lend an ear
The account of a battle
you quickly shall hear
That was fought by the miners,
so well you may ken
By claiming a right
to the bonny moor hen.

Oh this bonny moor hen,
as it plainly appears,
She belonged to their fathers
some hundreds of years;
But the miners of Weardale
are all valiant men,
They will fight till they die
for their bonny moor hen.

Oh the miners in Weardale,
they are bred to the game
They level their pieces
and make sure of their aim;
When the shot it goes off -
Oh, the powder doth sing,
They are sure to take off
a leg or a wing.

Now, the times being
hard and provisions being dear,
The miners were starving
almost we do hear;
They had nought to
depend on, so well you may ken,
But to make what they could
of their bonny moor hen.

There's the fat man of Auckland
and Durham the same
Lay claim to the moors
and likewise the game
They send word to the miners
they would have them to ken
They would stop them from
shooting the bonny moor hen.

Of these words they were carried
to Weardale with speed
Which made the poor miners
hang down their heeds
But then sent an answer
they would have them to ken
They would fight till they
died for their bonny moor hen.

When this answer it came
to the gentlemen's ears,
An army was risen,
it quickly appears;
Land stewards, bum bailiffs,
and game-keepers too,
Were all ordered to Weardale
to fight their way through.

Oh this battle was fought
all in Stanhope town,
When the chimneys did reek
and the soot it fell down
Such a battle was ne'er
fought in Stanhope before
And I hope such a battle
will ne'er be fought more."

Frosterley and Wolsingham

Weardale is noted for a unique form of marble, which can be found in the vicinity of the attractive stone village of Frosterley.

The 'marble' is actually a black, carboniferous limestone speckled with the remains of prehistoric plants and marine creatures. These tiny beasts appear in the form of sea shells and for this reason Frosterley marble is known to local quarrymen as 'Cockle'.

Frosterley marble can be found as a decoration in churches throughout the world and some of the best examples of the marble may be seen in Durham Cathedral.

To the west of Frosterley is the town of Wolsingham, where the Bishop of Durham's beekeeper lived in the days of the Boldon Buke. Today Wolsingham is a picturesque dales town and the annual home to England's oldest agricultural show. To the north of the town is a pretty little valley, formed by the Waskerley Beck and Tunstall Burn, within which we find the beautiful Tunstall Reservoir that was constructed in 1897.

All of the streams in upper Weardale are called 'Burns', from an old Anglo-Saxon word, but curiously streams joining the Wear east of Wolsingham towards Durham City are generally called 'Becks' (from the Old Norse word Bekk). The reason may be that this particular stretch of the Wear deviates south into the part of County Durham which had formed the Viking settled territory called Sadberge.

Witton-le-Wear and Hamsterley Forest

Witton Castle at Witton-le-Wear is often regarded as being at the entrance to Weardale. It was once the seat of the Eure family but, later passed into the hands of the Lambtons.

For many years the castle was the home of the famous 'Red Boy' portrait by Sir Thomas Lawrence, a painting of the only son of John George Lambton, the first Earl of Durham.

Over the river to the west of Witton-le-Wear, we find the village of Hamsterley, which is not to be confused with the village of the same name on the River Derwent in North West Durham. Nearby occupying the valley of a substantial stream called the Bed-Burn Beck we find Hamsterley Forest, the largest forest in County Durham.

Not far from Hamsterley forest we may find the remains of an overgrown ancient fort called 'the Castles'; it may be of Iron Age origin.

Auckland Gatehouse.

Bishop Auckland

The town of Bishop Auckland is situated at the confluence of the River Wear and the River Gaunless and has been the site of an important market since medieval times. 'Bishop', as it is sometimes known to the locals, grew most rapidly in the nineteenth century as a colliery town, but was important in much earlier times. Its earlier history is centred around the park and Castle of Auckland, the principal residence of the Bishops of Durham since the twelfth century.

Auckland Castle.

Auckland Castle, also known as Auckland Palace, began as a manor house, built around 1183 by Bishop Pudsey, but was converted into a castle by Bishop Anthony Bek in the fourteenth century. It is the last remaining of fourteen country seats belonging to the Bishops of Durham.

Shildon's Railway History

The town of Shildon across the River Gaunless, a mile to the south east of Bishop Auckland will be forever associated with the history of the railways as it was from here on the 26th September 1825 that George Stephenson's famous Locomotion Number One', made its historic journey to Darlington for the opening of the world's first public railway.

Shildon, rather than Darlington was the western terminus for locomotives on the Stockton and Darlington railway and in fact the railway itself, extended further west still, beyond Shildon towards Etherley and Witton Park Collieries near the River Wear. This part of the railway was operated by means of stationary engines.

Binchester Fort

One of the main streets in Bishop Auckland is called Watling Road and follows the course of the Roman Dere Street. This led to the Roman fort of Binchester, the site of which lies near Auckland park, just to the north of the town.

In Roman times, Binchester was called Vinovia which meant 'a pleasant spot'. The remains of the fort, which cover an area of 10 acres have been excavated and there is a small museum displaying one of the best examples of a Roman hypocaust (a central heating system) to be found in Britain.

Escomb Church

Many of the stones from the Roman fort at Binchester were used in the construction of what may be Britain's oldest church at Escomb, a mile to the west of Bishop Auckland.

A pretty, but somewhat humble looking building of Anglo-Saxon origin it has been described by the great architectural authority, Sir Nicholas Pevsner as 'one of the most important and moving survivals of the architecture of the time of Bede'. The early history of Escomb and why it should have survived is a mystery.

Brancepeth and the Brawn

At Bishop Auckland the River Wear makes a sudden and unexpected detour northward towards Durham. It passes the eastern outskirts of the town of Willington and then on through a quiet rural stretch of land between Brancepeth and Spennymoor.

The surroundings of Brancepeth are quite pleasant and the ivy covered cottages which lead up to its castle are particularly attractive. The Brancepeth area caught the attention of both William Wordsworth who visited the place and featured Brancepeth in a poem and Albert Lord Tennyson who wrote 'Come into the Garden Maud' at Brancepeth.

Bobby Shafto Country

Spennymoor is a town with industrial origins, but the countryside nearby has an unexpected romantic connection. The connection is with Whitworth Hall, not far from the River Wear to the north of the town. Here once lived none other than a certain Mr Robert Shafto, whose name is immortalised in the well known North Country Ballad;

"Bobby Shafto's gone to sea,
Silver buckles on his knee,
He'll come back and marry me,
Bonny Bobby Shafto.

Bobby Shafto's bright and fair,
Combing down his yellow hair;
He's my ain for ever mair
Bonny Bobby Shafto.

Bobby Shafto went to court
All in gold and silver wrought
Like a grandee as he ought
Bonny Bobby Shafto.

Bobby Shafto rode a race
Well I mind his bonny face
Won it in a tearing pace
Bonny Bobby Shafto.

Bobby Shafto throws his gold
Right and left like knights of old
Now he's left out in the cold
Bonny Bobby Shafto.

Bobby Shafto's gettin' a bairn
For to dangle on his airm
In his airm and on his knee
Bonny Bobby Shafto."

Bobby Shafto was in fact a County Durham MP, who was elected in 1761, when the song was used as an election jingle. A sweetheart of Bobby Shafto, to whom the ballad is often attributed is believed to have lived at Brancepeth Castle across the River Wear, three miles north of Whitworth. She died of a broken heart!

Brancepeth Castle.

Brancepeth is said to acquire its name from being the 'Brawn's Peth', an area frequented by a notorious brawn (or wild boar) many centuries ago. The brawn roamed the marshy forests that once existed south of Durham in Saxon and Norman times and is said to have terrorised the local people. There is no doubt such beasts actually lived in the Durham area and we know that there is another brawn legend associated with Bishop Auckland.

A young man by the name of Hodge from Ferryhill was employed in the pursuit of the Brancepeth Brawn and he took careful note of the paths that it frequently used.

He then constructed a deep pit on the brawn's highway and covered it with boughs and earth. Hodge was successful in his pursuit. The brawn came tumbling along and went head first into the depths of the pit.

Its nauseating screeches echoed throughout the countryside. No doubt the beast later ended up on someone's dinner plate.

It has been suggested that the nearby village of Brandon was anciently the site of the Brawn's lair or den but this may also be claimed by an ancient iron age site to the north west of Brancepeth called the Brawn's Den.

Brandon to the north of Brancepeth was a colliery village and was the setting for Frederick Grice's delightful children's novel about growing up in the old Durham coalfield entitled 'The Bonnie Pit Laddie'.

Croxdale

From Brandon a road leads a little way south to the junction with the Great North Road near to the point where the River Browney joins the River Wear at Croxdale. There are two great halls in this area to the east and west of the River Wear.

One is Croxdale Hall which has been the seat of the Salvin Family since the fifteenth century. The other is Burn Hall which was built to the designs of the Durham architect Ignatius Bonomi in 1821. For a time it also belonged to the Salvins.

Burn Hall, Croxdale.

Shincliffe

To the north of Croxdale, the River Wear is densely covered on its eastern side by Croxdale wood. This leads north to the river crossing of Shincliffe bridge and the nearby village of Shincliffe. Shincliffe is the last village on the River Wear before the river enters Durham City.

The village derives its name from the Anglo-Saxon 'Scinna Cliffe' meaning 'the hill of the ghost or demon' although it is a pleasant old village which seems an unlikely setting for demonic activities.

In medieval times Shincliffe belonged to the priors of Durham Cathedral monastery who seemed to have got involved in several quarrels with the bishop in this area.

It is recorded that in 1300 the prior was attacked by the bishop's retainers on Shincliffe Bridge and five years later the same prior complained that one of the bishop's servants had stolen a horse from him at Shincliffe and taken it off to Durham Castle. The priors' park lay just to the north of Shincliffe.

High Shincliffe lies just to the south of Shincliffe itself. It is now a modern estate but occupies the site of an old mining settlement called Bank Top. The pitmen who once lived here came from all parts of Northumberland and Durham but surprisingly few if any actually originated from Shincliffe.

Shincliffe.

The pit had been sunk around 1837 and one of its later owners was Joseph Love a former pitman who married into wealth and became a coal owner. Despite his charitable donations to the church he had a reputation for undue harshness in his behaviour towards the miners.

Love is said to have made a fortune from fining miners who in his opinion were not working hard enough and would also occasionally stop credit to miners at the local shops which he owned.

Love's colliery village had a population of around 1,000 but in 1874 the seams had been worked and the pit was closed. Poverty quickly followed and gradually all the residents were forced to move away. The modern High Shincliffe stands on the site of the old Bank Top Colliery village.

Part Five
The City of Durham

Framwellgate Bridge

Part Five
The City of Durham

The City of Durham.

Durham's Legendary Origins

In 995 AD after years of wandering the north, the carriers of St. Cuthbert's coffin came to a halt at a hill called Warden Law to the east of Durham. Here the vehicle on which the coffin was transported came to a standstill and despite the efforts of the whole congregation the coffin would not move.

Aldhun, Bishop of Chester-le-Street, the leader of the congregation, committed the monks to three days of fasting and prayer until St. Cuthbert appeared in a vision to a monk called Eadmer. St. Cuthbert instructed Eadmer that the coffin should be taken to Dun Holm. Suddenly, the coffin could be moved.

Dun was an Anglo-Saxon word meaning 'hill', Holm meaning 'island' is a word of Scandinavian origin. Dun Holm was later called 'Duresme' by the Normans and was known in Latin as 'Dunelm'. Over the years the name has been simplified to the modern form - Durham.

According to legend the monks had not heard of Durham. Luckily by chance in an area later known as Mount Joy, a milkmaid was overheard asking another milkmaid if she had seen her Dun Cow - a grey coloured beast that had wandered off on its own.

The other maid answered that she had seen the cow roaming about near Dun Holm. When the monks heard mention of Dun Holm they were filled with joy and followed the footsteps of the milkmaid as she searched for her cow.

By this stroke of luck or Divine Providence, they were able to find the site of Dunholm - a wooded 'Hill - Island' peninsula formed by a tight gorge-like meander of the River Wear. The legend of how Durham was first discovered is remembered in an eighteenth century carving on the north wall of Durham Cathedral, which depicts the milk maid and her Dun Cow.

The White Church

Dun Holm provided an ideally defended site for the resting place of St. Cuthbert. It was on high ground protected on three sides by the steep wooded gorge of the River Wear. Firstly however the site had to be cleared of its thick woodland and the wood provided ideal building material for the first houses in the newly born City of Durham.

A small temporary church was built from the boughs of the trees to house St. Cuthbert's coffin and this building is said to have occupied the site of the present church of St. Mary le Bow. The church of boughs was replaced a few days later by a white-washed wooden building called 'The White Church' or 'Alba Ecclesia', built in the centre of the Dun Holm peninsula. The White Church remained in use until September 4th 998 ADwhen it was replaced by a second 'White Church', an Anglo-Saxon minster built of stone.

The people who constructed the new minster came from all parts of Northumbria from the Coquet to the River Tees and were employed by Uchted, a powerful Anglo-Saxon earl who ruled the whole region. The minster was presided over by the Bishop called Aldhun who was Uchted's Father-in-Law. Aldhun was the first Bishop of Durham but had previously been the Bishop of nearby Chester-le-Street where he was still an important landowner.

Fortress against the Scots

The carriers of St. Cuthbert's coffin had fled to Durham to escape Viking raids but by the time the monks settled at Durham the Vikings were not so great an enemy as the Scots, who were to pose a threat to the wealthy shrine of St. Cuthbert at Durham for many years to come.

Durham's defensive position was clearly going to be of importance.

Durham's natural assets were fully demonstrated in 1006 when the Scots

made their first attack on the small city. They were quickly repelled and many of the invaders lost their heads to an army of English comprised of Northumbrians and Yorkshiremen.

The captured Scottish heads were displayed around the Durham City walls as a menacing warning against further attack. Four of the city's women were each presented with the generous gift of a cow for washing the heads and combing the hair of the best looking Scots which were displayed around the city.

A Place of Pilgrimage

As well as being an important defensive site Durham was also an important place of pilgrimage. The early cathedral and shrine at Durham were visited by many pilgrims who came to visit Durham in the same way as the pilgrims who had visited St. Cuthbert's shrine at Lindisfarne a century before.

Among the visitors to Durham was King Canute the Dane (1017 - 1035), who as a mark of respect, walked six miles bare footed to the site from Garmondsway. As a gift King Canute returned some of the land that had been taken from the Bishops of Durham by his Viking ancestors. The land included the large estate owned by King Canute in the Tees valley, centred upon Staindrop and Gainford, near Darlington.

The Conqueror's Visit

When the Normans invaded Britain in 1066 under William the Conqueror they may have been aware of the fatal defeat of the Scots at Durham years before but were not deterred in their aim to take control of the city. William the Conqueror is said to have visited Durham with the intention of viewing the remains of St. Cuthbert.

William ordered his men to open St. Cuthbert's tomb. Mysteriously before the king had even looked at the saint's coffin he found himself breathless and panic stricken by a sudden burning fever. Thinking himself to be possessed by some strange force, he fled from Durham and would not dismount until he had crossed the Tees into Yorkshire, seemingly outside the limits of St. Cuthbert's mysterious powers.

The lane by which the king made his hasty retreat from Durham acquired the name of 'King's Ride' or 'Kingsgate'. In those days the lane led to a ford across the River Wear. Today, called Bow Lane, it leads across the River Wear by means of the Kingsgate Foot Bridge.

Massacre of the Normans

King William had good reason to fear Durham as the people of the city had little love for the Norman invaders. This was proved when a Norman army of seven-hundred men stormed into the city on the January 30th 1069 under the command of an aggressive Norman earl by the name of Robert Comine.

His men had distributed themselves throughout the narrow streets of the city and were confident they could take control of the place despite strong warnings from the Bishop of Durham called Aegelwine, who predicted their defeat.

The following morning the Bishop's prediction proved true as the Norman occupants of the city were set upon by the Durham people aided by a large Northumbrian army from the north who broke open all gates of the town and stormed through the narrow streets of the city, slaughtering the Normans as they went.

Some of the Normans, including Comine fled for safety to the bishop's palace but this was set alight causing a fierce blaze which posed a threat to the western tower of Durham's early stone minster. This caused the local people to fall to their knees;

"with eyes filled with tears and elevated hands, petitioning heaven, that by some assistance of the holy saint the structure might be saved from damage."

Miraculously the wind changed direction and diverted the flames away from the minster's tower. Comine and the occupants of the bishop's palace were burnt to death and the snow covered streets of the city, filled with the carcasses of dead soldiers are said to have ran with Norman blood.

All but one of the Norman occupants lost their lives in the massacre. King William was extremely angered by this event and by other rebellions in York. He sent north an army to burn and plunder the land between York and Durham. This was known as the 'Harrying of the North'. It demonstrated the might of the Norman army to the people of northern England and forced them to recognise Norman control.

Durham Cathedral and the Prince Bishops

When William the Conqueror finally took control of Durham he appointed a Norman called William Walcher as Durham's first Prince Bishop by combining the powers of the Bishop with those of the Earl of Northumbria. The term 'Prince Bishop' did not actually come into use until many centuries later but it is a good description of the political and ecclesiastical powers of Walcher and succeeding Bishops of Durham.

Walcher's time as a Prince Bishop was characterised by weak leadership which ultimately resulted in him being murdered at Gateshead in 1081.

He was replaced by a new bishop called William St. Carileph who was the man responsible for building the present cathedral. Carileph designed the greater part of the Cathedral of Durham as it stands today and began its construction in the year 1093.

Occupying the site of the old stone minster built by Uchted, the new building was completed to the bishop's designs in more or less forty years. Unfortunately Carileph did not live to see the completion of his cathedral in 1135.

Architectural Innovations

Durham Cathedral's Nave, Choir and the accompanying aisles form the central body of the cathedral and it is these that were largely built to Bishop Carileph's designs in the period 1093 to 1135.

Inside the cathedral, the nave is particularly striking for its massive spiral and zigzag decorated cylindrical piers (or columns) and the multiple columned compound piers which support the impressive diamond ribbed vaulting of the ceiling high above.

Durham Cathedral Nave.

The ribbed vaulting at Durham was in its time technically far more advanced than any vaulting to be found anywhere else in Britain or on the continent. It was at Durham that the transition from the rounded arches of Norman architecture to the pointed arches of Gothic architecture took place. This is demonstrated in the illustration above. The Cathedral at Durham is also important for the flying buttresses, a feature invented by the Norman masons at Durham. Situated in the Triforium or upper storey of the cathedral they can not be seen by visitors.

The Galilee Chapel

In later years two major additions were made to the cathedral of William St. Carileph. One was the Galilee Chapel built by Bishop Hugh Le Puiset, who is known more affectionately as Bishop Pudsey (1153-1195). Pudsey's Galilee Chapel is at the western end of the cathedral and is situated right at the top of the gorge formed by the River Wear, where it is overshadowed by the cathedral's twin towers.

Durham Cathedral: The Galilee Chapel.

The Galilee Chapel is famous as the home of the black marble-topped tomb of The Venerable Bede (673-735 A.D), who was the first historian of England. Bede lived most of his life at Jarrow near the River Tyne. His bones were brought to Durham from the ruins of Jarrow monastery in 1020 A.D. Bede's tomb is inscribed with the following words

*'Hac sunt in fossa Baedae
Venerabilis Ossa'*

which translated means 'in this tomb are of Bede the bones'. Legend tells us that the use of the word Venerable is said to have been inspired into the mind of the writer of this poetic epitaph by an angel who told him how to complete the rhyme. The inscription dates from 1830.

The Galilee Chapel is also known as the Lady Chapel as it was once the only part of the cathedral that could be entered by women according to the rules of the Benedictine order of monks. A little way inside the main cathedral building we can see a line of black Frosterley Marble in the cathedral floor which marked the point beyond which women were not allowed to pass. So strict was the rule against women entering the cathedral that in 1333 when Queen Philippa, wife of Edward III crossed the line to find sleeping quarters in the cathedral, she was forced to sleep elsewhere. The Durham monks petitioned the King and insisted that she find sleeping accommodation in the castle to avoid upsetting St. Cuthbert.

Lady Chapels are normally constructed at the eastern end of cathedrals and not at the west so Durham is quite unusual in this respect. Initially there had been an attempt to build the Lady Chapel at the eastern end but problems with crumbling masonry forced Bishop Hugh Pudsey to transfer the building work to the west end. The building problems at the east end arose from the nature of the ground here, but legend attributes the damage to St. Cuthbert who is said to have disliked the idea of a Lady Chapel so close to the site of his tomb. At a later stage another chapel called the Chapel of the Nine Altars was built at the cathedral's east end - mysteriously this seems to have had no major structural problems.

Chapel of the Nine Altars

The huge Chapel of the Nine Altars at the eastern end of the cathedral was begun during the episcopacy of Bishop Richard Le Poore (1228-1237) who was also associated with the building of Salisbury Cathedral. This new chapel provided more space for the increasing number of visiting pilgrims who packed the aisles and choir of the cathedral to view the shrine of St. Cuthbert.

A number of interesting features can be seen in this chapel including some elegant piers of Frosterley Marble, a decorative black substance originating from the Durham valley of Weardale. It is embedded with the white shells of ancient sea creatures.

Another prominent feature in the chapel is a large white statue of Bishop William Van Mildert who died in 1836. Van Mildert, the last Prince Bishop of Durham was the man largely responsible for the foundation of Durham University in 1832. The University is of course the third oldest in England after Oxford and Cambridge.

Without doubt the most beautiful feature of the Chapel of the Nine Altars is the huge Rose Window which was originally made in the fifteenth century by Richard Pickering of Hemingbrough and reconstructed in the eighteenth century by James Wyatt. The Rose is ninety feet in circumference with a central core depicting Christ surrounded by the twelve apostles. Inside the cathedral the Chapel of the Nine Altars lies just to the east of an elevated Feretory (a chapel for saint's relics) in which we find the tomb of St. Cuthbert.

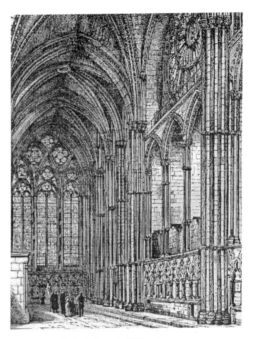

Durham Cathedral: Chapel of Nine Altars.

The Tomb of St. Cuthbert

In medieval times Durham Cathedral was one of the greatest centres of pilgrimage in England and the chief reason for pilgrimage was the rich and glorious shrine of St. Cuthbert.

Today the simple grey stone tomb inscribed 'Cuthbertus' is all that remains of the shrine, but prior to the Dissolution of the Monasteries in the sixteenth century the whole area around the tomb was an elaborately decorated shrine described as one of the richest monuments in England. Once decorated with an "ingeniously made structure of costly green marble and gilded with gold" the shrine was bestowed with an incredible number of gifts and jewels including contributions from kings, queens, churchmen and wealthy nobles.

These gifts were stored in beautifully decorated wainscot lockers that were situated on the north and south sides of the feretory.

The lockers which also contained relics associated with St. Cuthbert and other saints were opened for viewing on special occasions such as the feast day of St. Cuthbert.

The magnificent shrine of St. Cuthbert was destroyed in the sixteenth century along with many others throughout the land by the order of King Henry VIII. The men who opened St. Cuthbert's tomb found a number of precious jewels and a wand of gold which were all confiscated by the crown.

A Screen and a Throne

St. Cuthbert's tomb and feretory are hidden from the Choir and Nave by the magnificent fourteenth century Neville Screen which was once decorated with 107 alabaster figures. The screen was donated to the cathedral by John The 5th Lord Neville (died 1388) and is constructed from Caen limestone originating from a quarry in France.

The massive screen was constructed in London and shipped north to Newcastle from where it was carried across land by cart to Durham. John Neville's tomb lies in the south aisle of the Nave where he is accompanied by his wife Matilda. The tomb of John's father Ralph Neville is also in the cathedral. It was Ralph who successfully led the English into victory over the Scots at the Battle of Nevilles Cross just outside Durham in 1346. As an honour for the victory he became the

first layman to be allowed burial in the cathedral.

The south aisle of the cathedral choir contains the tomb of Bishop Thomas Hatfield (1345-1381) who was bishop at the time of the aforementioned battle. His tomb is covered by his alabaster effigy which lies snugly tucked under a decorated arch formed by a short stairway leading to the Bishop's Throne or 'Cathedra' directly above. The Bishop's throne at Durham is the highest in Christendom.

To the west of the choir we stand directly beneath the Central Tower which was built in the fifteenth century. An earlier tower had been destroyed by lightning in 1429. The entrance to the cathedral tower is in the South Transept where we find the sixteenth century decorated Cathedral Clock.

During the Civil War when 4,000 Scottish prisoners were held in the cathedral following the Battle of Dunbar (1650) nearly all the woodwork in the great church was destroyed by the Scottish prisoners for firewood. The clock was spared, seemingly because it has a carving of the sacred Scottish thistle upon it.

The Cathedral Monastery

To the south of, but adjoining the cathedral are the buildings of the Cloisters which are clustered around a small square green called the Cloister Garth. The buildings surrounding the garth were the monastic priory buildings of the cathedral and included the Chapter House, the Monk's Dormitory, the Refectory and the Great Kitchen. Around the square green are four covered Cloister walkways where the monks spent considerable periods of time during the heyday of the Durham priory.

One of the walkways on the northern side of the cloisters by the main cathedral wall was formerly the monk's Scriptorium. This contained a number of reading chambers in which the monks could study. At the western end of this walkway a plaque can be seen informing American tourists that an ancestor of George Washington was a prior at Durham Cathedral. The Washingtons were an old County Durham family originating from Washington near Sunderland.

Above the western walkway of the Cloister is the Monk's Dormitory, the site of the sleeping quarters. It dates from the fourteenth century and has an impressive roof of wooden oak beams. It now houses a library belonging to the Dean and Chapter and has a collection of Anglo-Saxon and Viking crosses from throughout the ancient kingdom of Northumbria.

On the opposite side of the cloisters we find the Chapter House where meetings are held to discuss the day to day running of the cathedral. The building contains the tombs of three very important Bishops of Durham - William St. Carileph, Ranulf Flambard and Hugh le Puiset. Above the southern walkway of the cloisters was situated the Refectory or eating area. This is now a private library belonging to the Dean and Chapter. Behind the refectory is the peculiar octagonal shaped building of the Kitchen.

Relics of a Saint

Today most visitors to the cloisters are drawn to the cathedral's restaurant, the bookshop and the Treasury Museum which all lie in the south western corner of the cloisters. The Treasury Museum is one of the most important museums in the north of England and contains many relics of the 'Golden Age of Northumbria'.

The museum's ancient exhibits include the 7th century wooden coffin of St. Cuthbert which has been carefully pieced together and the pectoral cross of St. Cuthbert. Some very impressive silver plate may also be seen in the museum which belonged to the Prince Bishops of Durham. Other interesting items include some ancient books and the sword called the Conyer's Falchion which is said to have been used by Sir John Conyers in the killing of the legendary 'Sockburn Worm'.

Sanctuary Knocker

Most visitors to the Cathedral will have entered the building from Palace Green by the North Door on which we find the imposing bronze Sanctuary Knocker. This is a near perfect replica of the twelfth century original which can be seen in the Treasury Museum. It features the face of a hideous lion-like beast and represents the ancient privilege of sanctuary once granted to criminal offenders at Durham cathedral. Criminals could seek refuge at Durham by loudly banging the knocker to alert the attentions of the watchers who resided in two small chambers overlooking the door.

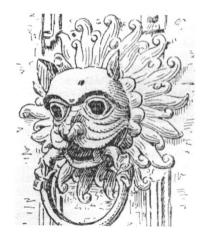

The Sanctuary Knocker.

A watcher would then invite the criminal inside the cathedral. Upon entering the cathedral the criminal had to exchange his clothes for a black robe with a yellow cross of St. Cuthbert imprinted on the left shoulder. He would then confess the details of his crime before a coroner and was allowed to remain inside the cathedral for a period of thirty seven days. Here he was provided with food and water paid for by the church.

Before or on the thirty seventh day the criminal was expected to leave the country by an assigned port or else face execution. In the case of Durham the assigned port was usually Hartlepool. The criminals were escorted to the sea port by the constables of each parish they passed through. On no account was the criminal allowed to stray from the king's highway during the journey as this was punishable by death. Offenders seeking sanctuary at Durham came from every part of the country and included burglars, cattle stealers and horse thieves. More usually the offence was Murder.

Durham Castle and University

Durham Castle is the ancient palace of the Prince Bishops of Durham and lies at the northern end of Palace Green opposite the cathedral. It is situated on the site of a fortress built to the orders of William the Conqueror on his return from Scotland in 1072.

Waltheof, the Saxon Earl of Northumberland undertook the work of building the castle for William but over the years a succession of Prince Bishops have added important sections to the great building.

The present castle is dominated by the Keep which although the most imposing part of the castle is in fact the least historic. In the tradition of the Norman Motte and Bailey castles the keep is situated on a mound and was first erected in the fourteenth century during the episcopacy of Bishop Thomas Hatfield.

Over the centuries the keep fell into a ruinous state but was rebuilt in the 1840s as a sleeping quarters for students when the castle became Durham's University College.

The older and greater part of the castle is situated around a courtyard to the west of the keep. The courtyard is entered from the Gatehouse near to the site of the castle moat.

The moat was crossed by means of a drawbridge just outside the Gatehouse. This is primarily the work of Bishop Pudsey (1153-1195). The castle's thirteenth and fourteenth century Great

Hall was built by Bishop Anthony Bek (1284-1311) and Bishop Thomas Hatfield (1345-1381).

Durham Castle: Gatehouse.

Palace Green

Palace Green separates the castle from the cathedral at the southern end of the green. Until the twelfth century this area was the centre of Durham and the site of the old market place. It contained a mass of wooden houses huddled together between the castle and the cathedral until Bishop Flambard cleared them all to remove the potential fire hazard which threatened his castle and cathedral.

It thus became an open area as it is today. Today the green is flanked on its east and west sides by a number of historic

buildings dating mainly from the eighteenth century. Most of these now belong to Durham University. They include a former Grammar School on the western side near the cathedral towers. It is reputedly haunted by a young pupil who suffered a fatal punishment from one of his masters who apparently threw him from a balcony in a fit of anger.

From the western side of Palace Green a narrow lane called Windy Gap leads to the wooded river bank and the famous Fulling Mill. Once the property of the Priors of Durham, the Fulling Mill was known historically as the Jesus Mill.

Today it is the home of the University's Museum of Archaeology which houses relics of the region's Anglo-Saxon and Roman past. A little to the south of the Fulling Mill is the Prebends Bridge of 1777 from where the view inspired Sir Walter Scott to write;

"Grey towers of Durham- yet well
I love thy mixed and massive piles -
half church of God;
half castle 'gainst the Scot;
And long to roam those venerable aisles,
with records of deeds long since forgot."

The Baileys

In days gone by the fifty-eight acre Durham river peninsula was surrounded by the defensive city walls linked to the castle. Throughout the Middle Ages the whole peninsula was known as 'the castle' so that the cathedral arguably lay within the castle. Just enclosed within the castle walls on the eastern side was the castle bailey which took the form of a street. The street still exists - part is called the

South Bailey, the other part the North Bailey. The North and South Baileys are among the most historic and most attractive streets of Durham City and are described by the architectural historian Sir Nicholas Pevsner as the best streets in Durham. In Early times the houses in the North and South Bailey were of extreme importance as they were held by military tenants employed to defend the city of Durham from attack.

Most of the present houses of the North and South Bailey are of Georgian origin as in the eighteenth century these two streets were very fashionable town houses for County Durham's wealthiest landowners. The residents included the Earls of Strathmore, (the Bowes Family) who are ancestors of the present Royal family and the coal owning Liddell Family whose relatives included Alice Liddell, the inspiration for Alice in Wonderland.

Other former residents of the Bailey included a certain Captain Boulby who fought at Waterloo, Sir Robert Kerr Porter, an artist to the Tsar who later married a Russian princess and the little Polish Count called Joseph Borruwlaski.

The Champion Boxer

One famous nineteenth century resident of the Bailey was John Gully who settled at Durham in the later part of his life. A one time champion pugilist of all England, Gully learned to fight during a period of imprisonment for debt at Bristol. He had the good fortune to be bought out of prison by a group of wealthy sportsmen on condition that he agreed to box against a notorious

undefeated champion fighter called Henry the 'Game Chicken' Pearce.

Gully was defeated in the match against Pearce but only after the fight had gone a staggering fifty-nine rounds on October 8th 1805. It was not long afterward that Pearce retired and Gully went on to become the champion of all England by defeating another great boxer called 'The Lancashire Giant'. During his eventful life Gully not only established himself as a great boxer but was for a time a Member of Parliament and was also a very successful horse owner, winning the Derby on two occasions.

In County Durham he invested his winnings in collieries at Trimdon, Hetton and Thornley. It was in 1863 at his house at number 7 the North Bailey, that Gully finally died at the age of 80. He left behind him twenty-four children from two successive marriages.

Statues in the Market Place

Durham Market Place, the focal point of the city has medieval origins but the present Market Square is largely of Victorian origin. The most imposing features of the market place are the Town Hall and Guildhall, the city church of St. Nicholas and the statues of Neptune and the 3rd Marquess of Londonderry. The Victorian church of St. Nicholas replaced an earlier church of St. Nicholas which dated from the early part of the twelfth century.

The bare-bottomed statue of Neptune was originally placed in the Market Square in 1729 to cover a 'pant' – a fountain of drinking water. Neptune,

God of the sea, symbolised an ambitious plan of 1720 to turn Durham into a sea port by altering the course of the River Wear. The plan was to construct a canal north to join the Team, a tributary of the Tyne near Gateshead. In 1759 another plan was made to bring ships to Durham by making the river navigable from Durham to Sunderland by altering the river's course, but it became unrealistic due to the increasing size of ships. In 1923 the pant on which Neptune stood was demolished and he was removed to Wharton Park where he remained for most of the century until his return to the market place in 1991 following restoration.

Statue of Lord Londonderry.

Neptune's equestrian neighbour is the electroplated-copper statue of Charles William Vane Tempest Stewart, the 3rd Marquess of Londonderry. He owned collieries in the vicinity of Durham and is principally famous as the builder of Seaham Harbour which he founded in 1828.

The sculptor of Londonderry's statue was Signor Raphael Monti (1818-1881) who did not, as is often thought, commit suicide following the discovery of a flaw in his creation by a blind beggar man. Legend has it that Monti boasted that no one could find fault with his statue until one day a blind man pointed out that the horse had no tongue by feeling inside its mouth.

A Polish Dwarf

Durham Town Hall is modelled on a medieval hall but is actually of Victorian origin. The adjacent Guildhall dates from 1665. The Town Hall contains a case displaying items of clothing and a violin that belonged to the Polish dwarf known as Count Joseph Borruwlaski. He was remarkable for many reasons including the fact that his height from head to toe was only three feet and three inches.

Count Borruwlaski.

He had travelled widely throughout Europe in his early life and his admirers had included the young Marie Antoinette who gave him a diamond ring while he entertained the court of the Austrian empire in Vienna. Borruwlaski retired to Durham in 1790 which he described as his "quiet place". Count Borruwlaski died on the 5th September 1837 at the old age of ninety and was buried in the cathedral where his grave is simply marked 'J.B'.

Durham Mustard

In the eighteenth century Saddler Street, to the east of the market place, was the site of a factory which produced the famous Durham Mustard which was highly esteemed. In 1720 a Durham woman called Mrs Clements discovered a method for extracting the full flavour from mustard seed by grinding the seed in a mill and subjecting it to similar processes used in the making of flour from wheat. Mrs Clement's mustard gained huge popularity and she travelled to all the great towns of England collecting orders for her product, visiting London twice a year. Mustard is no longer produced in Durham today and the production of the original Durham mustard has passed into the hands of Colmans of Norwich.

Saddler Street and Fleshergate

Saddler Street was known historically as Saddlergate. The lower part of the street which joins the market place was originally called 'Fleshergate' or 'Flesh-Hewer-Rawe'. This was the street that contained the Butcher's shambles as 'Flesh Hewer' was an old name for a 'Butcher'. The offshoot of the street leading down to Elvet Bridge was historically called 'Souter Peth' – 'the shoemaker's steep street'.

Silver Street

The western side of Durham Market Place is joined by Silver Street, one of the busiest shopping streets in the town. Its narrowness is a reminder of its medieval origins. The part of the street that joins Framwellgate Bridge was once known as Smithgate.

Silver Street.

Silver Street was the home of John Duck, 'Durham's Dick Whittington'. He arrived in Durham in 1655 with the intention of becoming a Butcher's apprentice. He approached every butcher in Durham but was refused work because he had no details of his place of birth.

The concern seemed to be that he may be a Scot, and the employment of such was forbidden by the Butcher's guild. When one butcher finally accepted to take Duck on, the Butcher's Guild persuaded him to change his mind. Legend states that the dejected Mr Duck in a state of misery was wandering by the river side in Durham pondering over his failure to gain an apprenticeship when a passing Raven dropped a coin of gold at his feet.

With this gold coin John Duck went on to make his fortune, though how exactly is not altogether clear. Evidence suggests Duck was not always law abiding in the way he accumulated his wealth and is known to have bought cattle from a livestock thief. Mr Duck went on to become one of the wealthiest men in Durham, owning both land and collieries in the area. In 1680 he became the Mayor of Durham and ultimately progressed to the rank of a baronet when he became Sir John Duck of Haswell on the Hill.

Elvet and its Bridge

Elvet lies across the River Wear to the east of the Durham peninsula and is bounded by the river on its western, northern and eastern sides so that like 'Dun Holm' it forms an 'island', although flatter in appearance.

Records of Elvet's existence actually predate the settlement of Dunholm in 995 A.D. It was once called Aelfet Ee an old name meaning 'Swan Island'. It was the place where a certain Peotwine was consecrated Bishop of Whithorn in the year 762 A.D.

In the twelfth century during the time of Bishop Pudsey (1153-1195) the growth of Elvet was stimulated by the construction of Elvet Bridge linking Elvet to Saddler Street on the Durham peninsula.

Elvet Bridge.

Elvet Bridge has seven arches of which three are dry 'land arches' Two of the arches are hidden by buildings. In medieval times a number of buildings were situated upon this bridge including two chapels which stood at either end. One building still exists on the bridge today above a dry arch and can be identified by its Dutch gabled exterior. It is situated at the Elvet end of the bridge on the site of the medieval chapel of St. Andrew. Elvet bridge is one of only three bridges in England with houses situated upon them.

The Ghost of a Gypsy Piper

At the Saddler Street end of Elvet Bridge stood St. James's Chapel replaced by a house of correction in 1632. Two former prison cells can be seen beneath the western land arch of Elvet Bridge. They are reputedly haunted by the ghost of Jimmy Allen, a gypsy piper who was one of the most notorious and colourful characters in the history of Northumbria.

Jimmy was an adopted member of the Faas, a famous gypsy clan who inhabited the Cheviot Hills on the border between England and Scotland. His father Wull Faa had taught him to play the

Northumbrian pipes at a young age and his musical talents caught the attention of the Duchess of Northumberland to whom became the official piper.

Jimmy had a great love for drinking and gambling and an eye for pretty women, many of whom he conned out of purse. Cattle stealing was another of Jimmy's vices but his favourite pastime seems to have been enlisting and deserting from British and Foreign armies.

On the run for most of his life, Jimmy was pursued far and wide for desertion and other crimes. He was locked up twice and escaped twice, running off to Edinburgh and Dublin where he amused the residents of those cities with his musical abilities. His journeys took him much further still to the Dutch East Indies via India and to the Baltic "without any passport but his pipes".

In 1803 Jimmy was finally arrested at Jedburgh for stealing a horse from Gateshead. He was taken to Durham and sentenced to death. Luckily for him someone intervened and his sentence was reduced to life imprisonment.

He remained in the Durham cell for seven years where he died in the year 1810 aged 77. He was unfortunate because a pardon had been granted but it arrived a few days after his death. It is said that if you listen carefully beneath Elvet Bridge you may still be able to hear the eerie, haunting musical sounds of Jimmy's ghost playing the Northumbrian pipes.

Old and new Elvet

Elvet Bridge leads directly into the street of Old Elvet, once the site of the city's horse fair. Many buildings in Old Elvet are 18th century in origin with the obvious exception being the Old Shire Hall, a Victorian red brick building. Built in 1895 it was formerly the County Hall for Durham. Britain's first all Labour council assembled here in 1909. It has been the administrative headquarters of the University since 1963.

The other prominent building in Old Elvet after the Shire Hall is the Royal County Hotel, created from four existing buildings in the 1970s one of which was already known as the Royal County. Parts of the building date from the eighteenth century.

Old Elvet leads towards the riverside area once known as the 'Smiddy Haughs' – 'the smooth meadow'. It is commonly known as the Racecourse but races have not been held here for many decades. The Durham Miners' Gala or 'Big Meeting' is traditionally held here on the third Saturday in July.

Framwellgate Bridge

Framwellgate Bridge links Silver Street to the 'Old Borough' of Framwellgate on the western side of the river and was known for many years as 'Old Bridge' as it was built more than forty years before Elvet Bridge. The bridge was erected in 1120 on the orders of Bishop Ranulf Flambard (1099-1128).

Framwellgate Bridge.

Over the years Flambard's bridge witnessed many notable events in Durham's history such as the murder in 1318 of the Bishop's steward Richard Fitzmarmaduke by his cousin Ralph Neville 'the Peacock of the North'. The murder took place on the bridge itself and was the final result of a long standing quarrel between these two wealthy men.

Until the 1970s when the neighbouring Millburngate Bridge was built, nearly all the city centre traffic including buses and lorries had to pass through the narrow Silver Street and over Framwellgate Bridge to get from one part of the city to the other. The bridge leads into the Victorian street called North Road and a much older offshoot called Crossgate.

The Crossgate Peth Ghost

The climbing street of Crossgate or Crossgate Peth as it is called higher up, leads to the site of the Battle of Nevilles Cross. In days gone by when carriages, horses and carts made their journey up Crossgate Peth they would often stop for a drink along the way. Occasionally during their periods of rest, the drivers would become aware of a peculiar unexplainable fall in temperature.

As they continued up the bank they noticed the presence of a grey sombre looking young woman with a young newly born child in her arms. She would remain sad and silent in the cart or carriage for the course of the journey and then upon reaching Neville's Cross at the top of the bank would mysteriously disappear.

Legend suggests that the grey lady is the ghost of a young woman who lost her husband at the Battle of Nevilles Cross in the year 1346. It is said that her husband had gone to fight in the battle without receiving her farewell. Perhaps her ghostly journeys were undertaken in the hope of finding his body on that old battlefield at the top of Crossgate Peth.

Battle of Neville's Cross

In 1346 the greater part of the English army of Edward III were away at war fighting against the French with the assistance of among others Thomas Hatfield, the Bishop of Durham who took along his own private army. The French were desperate for the English to be diverted and called upon King David II of Scotland to attack the English border.

King David gladly obliged and headed into England with 20,000 men who wrecked and plundered parts of Cumberland and Northumberland before entering Durham where they made camp at Bearpark. The Scots were comprised of three factions under the respective commands of King David, the Earl of Moray and Sir William Douglas.

On the 17th October the men of Sir William Douglas went on a rampage throughout Durham straying as far south as Ferryhill where to their surprise they encountered part of an English army of some 15,000 which pursued them north. Under the leadership of Sir Ralph Neville and supported by the men of Thomas Rokeby and Lord Percy, the English were successful in this initial encounter and a number of Scots lost their lives.

Moving north the real battle took place on the Red Hills in the vicinity of a stone cross called Nevilles Cross (which existed before the battle). Arrows were fired, axes began hacking, swords were thrusting and as the blood bath continued the indication was that the Scots were going to lose. David, the Scottish king fled from the scene. In the far distance praying monks watched from the Cathedral's central tower while nearby on a hill called the Maiden's Bower at Crossgate Moor other monks watched at closer quarters. Here they held high the holy cloth of St. Cuthbert, which was a call for the support of God in this battle.

The call seemed on this occasion to be answered as the Scots were easily defeated. Meanwhile in the vicinity of Aldin Grange where the road from Crossgate to Bearpark crosses a tributary of the Wear called the River Browney, a Northumbrian soldier by the name of Copeland came across a rather exciting discovery, for there beneath the arch of Aldin Grange Bridge lay hiding none other than David, King of the Scots who was badly injured from two spears that had pierced his body. Copeland quickly captured the Scottish monarch and for a time the English held on to him for ransom.

Eventually a fee was agreed for the return of King David to Scotland and he was released. The canny Scots never paid the fee! The Victory at Nevilles Cross was long commemorated in Durham City folklore by local children. Boys of the city traditionally claimed that if you walked nine times around the Nevilles Cross and then put your head to the ground you could hear the sound of battle and the clash of arms.

Claypath and Gilesgate

From St. Nicholas Church in the market place the street of Claypath leads out to the east and was historically the only route into the city that did not require crossing the River Wear.

The long, steeply banked street of Gilesgate is a continuation of Claypath and is occasionally known by its medieval name of 'Gillygate', meaning the street of St. Giles. It is named after the nearby St. Giles Church, an attractive little building which claims to be the second oldest church in the City after the cathedral.

St. Giles Church is well situated back from the street of Gilesgate with commanding views from its graveyard of the Cathedral, Pelaw Wood, Maiden Castle and Old Durham. Built in 1112 by Bishop Ranulf Flambard the church was constructed as a chapel for a hospital dedicated to St. Giles.

The hospital stood close to the church but was burned down in the 1140s. The trouble was caused by William Cumin, a notorious usurper who had falsely appointed himself as the Prince Bishop of Durham with the encouragement of

King David of Scotland. Cumin took up residence at Durham Castle and terrorised the neighbourhood.

When the rightful bishop was elected Cumin could not to be removed. Cumin would not allow the new bishop anywhere near the castle and he was forced to take refuge at St. Giles Church for the night. The following morning Cumin's men broke down the doors of the church and a pitched sword battle broke out between the supporters of the real bishop and the usurper.

On this occasion the real bishop was forced to accept defeat but Cumin was ousted at a later date. During these troubles the Hospital of St. Giles was burned down and was relocated a little further to the north by the River Wear at Kepier. This medieval hospital remains as a farmhouse with a large vaulted gateway.

Kepier Hospital.

Kepier, Frankland and Finchale

A mile or so to the east of Kepier Hospital the River Wear forms a steep gorge which is occupied on the south bank by Kepier Wood. This wood is of great importance in the history of Durham City as it is the site of the Kepier Quarries. The remains of quarrying can still be seen in the steep riverside escarpments occupied by pleasant woodland. Kepier's ancient quarries are significant as this was the area from where most of the sandstone used in the building of Durham Cathedral was quarried many centuries ago.

Some of the stone also came from the area now occupied by Quarryheads Lane a little nearer to the cathedral. It is likely that the stone from Kepier was ferried upstream for the construction of the great church.

On the northern side of the river from Kepier Wood is Frankland Wood and further west Frankland Farm. This was the site of Frankland Park, an old deer park belonging to the Bishops of Durham. Today a large part of this area is occupied by the Newton Hall Housing Estate, one of the largest private housing estates in Europe. It takes its name from the original Newton Hall, a Georgian mansion demolished in 1926.

Finchale Priory stands on a beautiful secluded spot by the River Wear near the outskirts of Newton Hall, where the river winds its way north towards Chester-le-Street. The priory was formerly a holiday retreat for the monks of Durham Cathedral and dates from 1196. A hermit called St. Godric had lived at Finchale during the earlier part of the twelfth century. He was a former sea pirate who turned to Christianity and lived to 105. His grave lies within the priory ruins.

Part Six
Chester-le-Street to Sunderland

Historic view of Sunderland

Part Six
Chester-le-Street to Sunderland

Chester-le-Street

In 793 AD the Vikings made their first attack upon the coast of Britain with a raid upon Lindisfarne and by the end of the following century the threat of further raids was such that the monks of the island fled with the body of Saint Cuthbert to seek refuge on the mainland.

> *"How when the rude Dane burn'd their pile*
> *The monks fled forth from Holy Isle:*
> *O'er northern mountain, marsh, and moor,*
> *From sea to sea, from shore to shore,*
> *Seven years St. Cuthbert's corpse they bore."*

Sir Walter Scott.

In 882 AD, after several years of wandering the north the monks were granted land at Chester-le-Street where Eardwulf, the last Bishop of Lindisfarne became the first Bishop of Chester-le-Street. There were a succession of nine bishops at Chester-le-Street until 995 AD, when the threat of further raids caused the bishop's see to be moved again. After more wandering, St. Cuthbert's carriers would eventually settle at Durham.

Chester-le-Street Church

The eleventh century church of St. Mary and St. Cuthbert is the most historic feature of Chester-le-Street. It is built on the site of a Roman fort called Concangium. Here once stood an Anglo-Saxon Minster, where the shrine of St. Cuthbert was housed. The present church has an interesting museum called the Anker's House, with displays concerning Chester-le-Street's Roman and Anglo-Saxon history.

The Anglo-Saxon minster that stood at Chester-le-Street many centuries ago was the place where the first ever English translation of the Gospels was made. The translations were added to the Latin text of the famous Lindisfarne Gospels which had been brought from Lindisfarne to Chester-le-Street with St. Cuthbert's coffin. This great book can now be seen in the British Museum, London. English speaking visitors to the museum will however, have difficulty understanding the translations, since they are written in an old Anglo-Saxon language called Northumbrian, a language from which the modern dialect of North East England derives.

Chester-le-Street Church.

Lumley and Lambton

Inside the church at Chester-le-Street, are fourteen Elizabethan effigies of Durham's famous Lumley family. When James, the first king of England and Scotland visited Chester-le-Street in 1603 he is supposed to have viewed the Lumley effigies and remarked:

> *"I did nae ken Adam's name was Lumley"*

The first of the effigies is not in fact of Adam but Liulf of Great Lumley, an Anglo-Saxon noble, from whom the Lumley family claim descent. Liulf was killed in the eleventh century by one of William Walcher's men in an incident that led to that Bishop's murder at Gateshead in 1081.

Lumley Castle, which dominates the countryside across the River Wear, to the east of Chester-le-Street was for centuries the seat of the Lumley family. It was begun in 1389 by Sir Ralph Lumley, whose descendants include 'Lily of Lumley', now a ghost who reputedly haunts the castle. Today Lumley castle, situated by a pretty wooded valley adjoining the River Wear is a hotel where popular 'Elizabethan Banquets' are occasionally held. Here guests are entertained by people in period costume, as they enjoy a hearty feast of food, wine and mead. Across the A1(M) motorway to the north of Lumley is Lambton Castle which commemorates another of County Durham's great families. Dating from 1797 Lambton Castle is not as historic as Lumley.

Lambton Castle.

Penshaw Monument

Two miles north east of Lambton Castle, is the famous Penshaw Monument, a far more imposing reminder of the Lambton family. It is a copy of the temple of Theseum in Athens, though half its size. It can be seen clearly from parts of west Durham, North Tyneside and as far south as the Stang Forest in Teesdale. The monument was erected in 1848 in honour of John George Lambton, first Earl of Durham (1792 - 1840), known to Durham pitmen as 'Radical Jack', because of his democratic views.

Penshaw Monument.

The Earl was a chief instigator of the 1832 Reform Bill, which abolished the so called 'Rotten Boroughs', an undemocratic feature of British politics. Such Boroughs included Old Sarum in Wiltshire, where two MPs were elected by the owner of a 'green mound and a well'. This Reform Bill also gave MPs to large towns like Manchester, Birmingham and Leeds, which previously had none at all.

Other government reforms of the 1830s brought about the abolishment of the County Palatinate of Durham, terminating the last remaining vestiges of power held by the 'Prince Bishops'. The Prime Minister at the time of the 1830 reforms was of course the Northumbrian, Earl Grey to whom another famous northern monument was erected at Newcastle upon Tyne. Both Penshaw and Grey's Monument were designed by Benjamin Green.

The Legend of the Lambton Worm

Penshaw Hill and Worm Hill near Washington are both closely associated with one of the North East's best known folk tales; The Legend of the Lambton Worm. The hero of this legend was a certain young man called John Lambton, who on one particular Sunday morning decided to go fishing in the River Wear rather than attend the local church, as he was expected to do.

His truancy was rather a waste of time, as he did not have a very successful morning's sport. The only thing he had been able to catch, was a tiny worm-like creature which he despondently threw into a nearby well before returning home for lunch.

In later life John Lambton became a knight and crusader and left England to fight in the Middle East, where he soon forgot about the strange little worm caught on that otherwise uneventful Sunday morning.

Unbeknown to John, while he was away abroad, this tiny creature had grown into an enormous hideous serpent, that began to terrorise the local neighbourhood.

It is said that the worm would feed off the udders of cows and swallow little children alive and after feasting, would fall asleep and lazily lap its tail around the crest of Penshaw Hill.

Naturally, many attempts were made to slaughter this beast, but even when it was cut into many pieces the parts would rejoin and the worm remained alive. John Lambton, perhaps feeling partly responsible for the activities of the worm, decided to return home to England, where he consulted the advice of a wise old witch.

He asked her how he should go about killing such a creature. The old lady explained that the only way to kill the beast was by standing in the middle of the River Wear, wearing a suit of armour coated with blades of steel, and wait patiently for the worm to arrive.

However a warning was given to Lambton, that upon defeating the worm, he must then kill the first living thing he set eyes upon. Otherwise a curse would be placed upon nine generations of the Lambtons so that none would die in their bed. Lambton, obeying the words of the old lady put on the appropriate armour and instructed his father to send one of the family hounds to him, so he could complete the deed in accordance with her wishes.

Making his way to the banks of the Wear he stood in the centre of the river, where he didn't have to wait for long. The worm came darting towards its adversary of long ago and proceeded to viciously wrap itself around the armoured knight. After a short struggle the creature was gradually sliced up into many tiny pieces by the steel blades of Lambton's armour. Bit by bit each piece of the worm was carried away by the current of the river before they had time to rejoin.

At last the worm was dead. The victorious but exhausted Lambton, made his way back to the bank of the river, remembering that he must now kill the first living thing he set eyes upon. As he emerged from the river he looked up with shock and horror to see his excited father, who had evidently forgotten the hound. Lambton could not kill his own Dad!

Would the curse prove true? Well history seems to suggest it did. Several Lambtons met violent deaths and indeed one General Lambton, confined to his bed by a terrible illness, pleaded and pleaded with his servants to release him. When they finally lifted him from his bed - he died. That is the twist in the tale of the legend of the Lambton Worm!

The Lambton Worm Song

The Legend of the Lambton Worm is the subject of a famous local folk song, which was once a great favourite in the old Victorian music halls of Tyneside;

"One Sunday Mornin' Lambton
went a 'fishin' in the Wear,
And cowt a fish upon his heuk
He thowt leukt varry queer.

But whatn't kind of fish it waas
Young Lambton couldn't tell
He waddn't fash te carry it hyem,
So he hoyed it doon a well.

(Chrorus) Whisht! lads, haad yer gobbs,
An' aa'l tell yer aa'l an aaful story,
Whisht! lads, haad yer gobbs
An' aa'll tell yer boot the worm.

Noo Lambton felt inclined te' gan,
An' fight in foreign wars
He joined a troop of knights that cared
For nowther wounds nor scars.

An' of he went te' Palestine
Where queer things him befel,
An' varry seun forgat aboot
The queer worm i' the well.

But the worm got fat and growed an
growed An' growed an aaful size
He'd greet big teeth, a greet big gob,
An' greet big goggly eyes.

An' when at neet he craaled aboot
Te' pick up bits o' news
If he felt dry upon the road,
He milked a dozen coos.

This fearful worm wad often feed
On calves an' lambs and sheep,
An' swally little bairns alive
When they laid doon te' sleep.

An' when he'd eaten aal he could
An' he had had his fill,
He craaled away an' lapped his tail
Seven times roond Penshaw Hill.

The news of this myest aaful worm
An' his queer gannins on
Seun crossed the seas, an gat te' the ears
Of brave and bold Sir John.

So hyem he cam an' catched the beast
An' cut him in twe halves,
An' that seun stopped his eatin' bairns
An' sheep an' lambs and calves.

So noo ye knaa hoo aal the folks
On byeth sides o' the Wear
Lost lots o sheep and lots o sleep
An' lived in mortal fear.

So lets hev one te brave Sir John
That kept the bairns frae harm,
Saved coos an' calves by myekin' halves
O' the famous Lambton worm.

Noo lads Aa'll had me gob
That's aal Aa knaa aboot the story
Of Sir John's clivvor job
Wi' the aaful Lambton worm."

Washington
an American Connection

To the north of Lambton within the boundaries of the city of Sunderland is the new town of Washington. The town is divided into sixteen districts or 'villages'. Eight of the districts are built on the sites of existing villages, of which the most historic is Washington itself.

Washington village, is the site of Washington Old Hall, now a National Trust property. The Hall is important in that it was once the home of the ancestors of George Washington, the first president of the United States.

The connection dates from 1180 AD when William De Hartburn (Hartburn near Stockton-on-Tees), bought the manor of Washington from Hugh Pudsey, Bishop of Durham and changed his name to William De Washington (or Wessyngton as it was then spelled).

William became the first member of the family which ultimately gave its name to the capital city of the U. S. A. Washington, District of Columbia therefore acquired its name from Washington County of Durham (or Washington, City of Sunderland as it is now).

It is amusing to speculate that if history had taken a different course, the seat of the American president could perhaps have been called Hartburn DC.

Elsie Marley

South of the Washington village of Rickleton, close to the edge of the motorway near Chester-le-Street is a rather undistinguished little place called Picktree, once the home to two quite different characters from local folklore. One was a mysterious little Goblin called the 'Picktree Brag' who used to get up to all kinds of mischief in the area, the other was a local landlady called Elsie Marley, known to children and adults alike as the subject of a well known folk song;

"Di' yer ken Elsie Marley Hinny?
The wife that sells the barley hinny
She's lost her pocket and all of her money
A' back o' the bush in the garden hinny.

Elsie Marley's grown so fine
She cannot get up to serve the swine
But lays in bed till eight or nine
And surely she does take her time.

Elsie Marley wore a straw hat
Noo she's gettin' a velvet cap
Lambton lads mun pay for that
Di' yer ken Elsie Marley Hinny?

The pitmen and the keelmen trim
They drink bumbo made of gin
An' when te' dance they de begin
The tune is Elsie Marley Hinny."

Alice Marley was the wife of the innkeeper at Picktree and was very popular with her customers. In her later years this unfortunate lady was confined to bed with a terrible illness, and became completely delirious. After escaping unnoticed from her sick bed one night, poor 'Elsie' went running across a field nearby. She fell into a disused coal pit and drowned. Sadly the inn where Elsie worked has long since gone.

Bernard Gilpin the Apostle of Houghton-le-Spring

Houghton-le-Spring, is a former mining town within the City of Sunderland, four miles to the east of Lumley and Chester-le-Street. Like Chester-le-Street, the name Houghton-le-Spring contains the

Norman-French element 'le', which also occurs in the name of nearby Hetton-le-Hole.

The history of Houghton-le-Spring is centred around the attractive Norman church of St. Michael and All Angels, within which we find the tomb of Bernard Gilpin (1517-1583), who was known as 'the Apostle of the North'. Gilpin, a member of an important Westmorland family, was the great nephew of Cuthbert Tunstall, Bishop of Durham (1530-1559) and in 1552 this bishop appointed Bernard as vicar to the historic parish of Norton-on-Tees.

Later, Gilpin was appointed Archdeacon of Durham and in 1557 he became the rector at Houghton-le-Spring, then one of the largest parishes in England. Despite his important status, Gilpin was a generous man who always had the interests of his parish at heart.

On all Sundays between Michaelmas and Easter he declared his rectory an 'open house' and gave free dinners to all who visited, whether they were rich or poor.

Most residents of Houghton today commemorate Bernard Gilpin's generosity in the annual 'Houghton Feast', a fair which he is said to have inaugurated. The tradition is that an ox was once donated by Gilpin, to be roasted and distributed amongst the members of his parish. Houghton Fair is now a more modern fairground attraction that takes place on the first Friday of each October. Gilpin was a scholarly man, and was keen to see that the humble and poor received a good education. He even sent some of his

brightest young parish residents to university at his own expense.

With the financial help of a Londoner named John Heath (who owned land at Kepier near Durham), Gilpin founded the Kepier Grammar School at Houghton-le-Spring in 1557 and this considerably helped to improve the educational standards of the district.

Among the famous students to attend Kepier School in later centuries was Robert Surtees (1779-1834), the great Durham historian. Bernard Gilpin's good works extended beyond his parish and he is perhaps best known for his journeys into the rough border country of Northumberland where he preached among the Northumbrian people in the same way as St. Aidan and St. Cuthbert many centuries earlier. Spreading the word of God was not an easy task for Gilpin in the North East of England, during a period of time when the local people were often ignorant and violent in nature. Indeed a sixteenth century Bishop of Carlisle observed of Durham and Northumberland;

"There is more theft, more extortion here by English thieves than by all the Scots in Scotland."

Described as 'tall and lean in person, with a hawk like nose and of charming and tactful manners' Bernard Gilpin was perhaps an ideal match for such a race of people and his efforts were met with some success. Even the roughest of Border folk looked upon Gilpin with awe and respect. Bernard's long and adventurous life came to a tragic and rather unexpected end on the 4th of March 1583, when he was unfortunately knocked down by an oxen in the market place at Durham. He was aged sixty six. If it had not been for the fact that Gilpin lived in an age of religious controversy (with which he refused to be involved), this 'Apostle of the North' could well have been venerated as one of Northumbria's most famous saints.

Sunderland

Although the greater part of the city of Sunderland lies to the south of the Wear some of the oldest and most historic parts of the modern city are on the northern bank of this river. Undoubtedly the most historic part of Sunderland is that area on the north bank by the coast called Monkwearmouth. Sunderland was originally part of Monkwearmouth and the name Sunderland derives from 'Sundered Land', that is land that was sundered or separated by the River Wear, from the monastic estates of Monkwearmouth in Anglo-Saxon times.

For centuries Sunderland was only a part of Wearmouth and although the name Sunderland was commonly used for the whole area, it was not until 1719 that Sunderland itself achieved the status of a separate parish. In 1897 roles were finally reversed and Monkwearmouth officially became part of the town of Sunderland.

Sunderland High Street.

Monkwearmouth

Monkwearmouth is where Sunderland's history really begins. In 674 AD the land on the northern bank of the river overlooking the coast at Wearmouth was granted by Ecgfrith, King of Northumbria to a noble called Benedict Biscop who used the land to build a monastery.

All that remains of the monastery today is the Anglo-Saxon church of St. Peter which is one of the most historic churches in England. Biscop had great ambitions for his monastery at Wearmouth and brought in masons and glaziers from France and even employed an Archchanter, from St. Peter's cathedral in Rome.

The Venerable Bede (675-735) who was born in the vicinity of Sunderland, began his monastic life at Monkwearmouth before moving on to Biscop's other later monastery at Jarrow on Tyne.

The ancient churches of St. Pauls, Jarrow and St. Peters Monkwearmouth, were described by Bede as "one monastery in two places". Both still stand today in what are strikingly similar industrial, riverside settings. Monkwearmouth and Jarrow, were two of the most important centres of Northumbrian culture and learning, in that period of history which today we call the 'Dark Ages'.

Sir Timothy Eden in his History of Durham (1948) beautifully explains the former importance of these two venerable places:

"It was not long before, round these two last communities all the light and learning of England was to revolve, and not only England, but of the whole of Europe, during one of the darkest periods in the history of man."

Sadly the Anglo-Saxon life of St. Peters Monkwearmouth was brought to an end in the ninth century by Viking raids when it was sacked by the Danish pirates Hubba and Hingmar.

Fortunately the Monkwearmouth and Jarrow churches were re-established in Norman times when they became monastic cells of the great cathedral of Durham.

St. Peters, Monkwearmouth.

The Civil War - Sunderland Versus Newcastle

Sunderland, the largest place on the eastern coast of England, grew primarily as a result of its development as a coal exporting harbour at the mouth of the River Wear. Its growth took place despite centuries of fierce resistance from the wealthy and powerful town of Newcastle upon Tyne, which possessed a Royal Charter, restricting the shipment of coal from nearby ports like Sunderland.

During the Civil War the rivalry between the ports of Sunderland and Newcastle was intensified, when Newcastle became a staunchly Royalist City.

Sunderland had a significant number of Parliamentarian supporters amongst its population. In 1642 Sunderland received a garrison of Parliamentarians from Cromwell composed mainly of Scots or 'Blew Caps' as they were nicknamed.

Sunderland became a centre for Parliamentarian offensives against Royalist strongholds of North Eastern England like Durham City and Newcastle upon Tyne.

The most significant of the Parliamentarian attacks upon a North Eastern town was the siege of Newcastle in 1644, where for a time the walled Tyneside town held out against parliamentarian forces comprised mainly of Scots.

Sunderland's stance in the Civil War aroused much bitterness from the Newcastle Royalists. The role of Sunderland and Newcastle in the Civil

War was of extreme importance, as Newcastle was the major supplier of coal to London.

Historic view of Sunderland.

If Sunderland had followed Newcastle and supported the Royalist cause the essential supply of coal to Cromwell's London would have been virtually cut off and perhaps the outcome of the Civil War may even have been different.

In fairness to Sunderland, it was perhaps not surprising that its sympathies lay with the Parliamentarians rather than the Royalists as after all it was a Royal Charter that restricted Sunderland's trade and gave Newcastle a somewhat unfair advantage in any competition between the two ports.

One result of the Civil War, was that Sunderland and its coal trade began to rapidly expand while Newcastle, though remaining the major coal port of Britain, gradually lost its monopolistic hold on the export of local coal.

A Shipbuilding Tradition

Sunderland was long an important coal port, but the industry for which the town was until recently better known was shipbuilding.

Since 1346 when a certain Thomas Menville was recorded as building vessels here, Sunderland has had a shipbuilding industry and it is claimed that shipbuilding had taken place in even earlier times

In 1885 a primitive 2,000 year old canoe, was found in the River Wear at Sunderland near Hylton, in the north west of the town. This is claimed to be the first example of Sunderland boat building workmanship.

Whatever the origins of shipbuilding on Wearside, by 1814 Sunderland had 24 shipyards, a figure which had risen to 65 in 1840. By the mid twentieth century, when the town produced more than a quarter of the nation's total tonnage of merchant and naval ships for World War Two, Sunderland was widely regarded as the largest shipbuilding town in the world.

Sadly, despite strong opposition from workers and community leaders, Sunderland's last shipyards were closed down in 1988.

Wearmouth Shipbuilding 1842.

The Cauld Lad of Hylton

Today the two sides of the River Wear at Sunderland are linked by the steel arched Wearmouth Bridge of 1929 and the Queen Alexandra Bridge of 1909, though until the eighteenth century Sunderland was only linked to Hylton and Monkwearmouth on the north side of the Wear by means of a ferry. Hylton Castle, one of Sunderland's most historic buildings stood guard over an important ferry crossing of the Wear. It was built by one William De Hylton around 1400 and is most famous for its ghost called the 'Cauld Lad o' Hylton'. This ghost is said to be the spirit of a stable boy who was slain by a baron of Hylton in the sixteenth century. The unfortunate young man had been caught napping by the temperamental lord, who in a fit of rage brutally struck the boy with a pitch fork, killing him instantly.

The ghost who may or may not carry his own head under his arm, was occasionally seen and often heard by the domestic servants of Hylton Castle. Like all good poltergeists the Cauld Lad's favourite pastime was throwing dishes, plates and pewter, but this only happened if the Hylton kitchen had been left in a tidy state. Curiously if the servants left the kitchen untidy, the Cauld Lad would tidy it up. Naturally the servants took advantage and always left the kitchen untidy. The castle building was not the only place to be haunted by this mischievous ghost, for on occasions the Cauld Lad is known to have impersonated the boatman on the Hylton ferry, where after accepting fares he would leave his passengers stranded in the centre of the river.

Hylton Castle.

The pranks of the 'Cauld Lad' were finally ended by presenting him with a green cloak and hood which were laid before the kitchen fire. The Hylton servants sat up watching until midnight when the ghost appeared took the garments and then suddenly disappeared with the last words:

"Here's a cloak and here's a hood,
The Cauld Lad o' Hylton
will do no more good."

Though Hylton was occupied until the early twentieth century all that remains of the Castle today is largely a ruined shell hidden in the north western suburbs of Sunderland. One of the notable features of the castle are the stone carved coats of arms of various local families, which can be seen on its walls. They include the shields of the Hyltons, Lumleys, Percys, Greys Eures and Washingtons who lived nearby. The Washington coat of arms consists of two bars and three stars and is believed to have been adapted by George Washington for the 'stars and stripes' flag of the United States.

Part Seven
The Derwent Valley

Blanchland

Part Seven
The Derwent Valley

Blanchland

To the west of the Derwent Reservoir on the Northumberland side of the River Derwent, is the attractive village of Blanchland. Its name is Norman-French and means the 'White Lands'. This is probably a reference to the white habits worn by the Premonstratensian monks of the old Blanchland abbey which was founded in 1165 by a Norman baron called Walter De Bolbec. A well-known legend relates how Blanchland abbey fell victim to a Scottish raid due to the foolishness of the monks.

The story is that Scots were raiding the Derwent valley hoping to plunder the Blanchland monastery for its riches. Fearful of what the raiders might do, the monks of Blanchland began to pray. Prayers seemed to have been answered, when suddenly a thick mist engulfed the Derwent valley and caused the raiding party to lose their way.

Crossing the Derwent into County Durham the raiders, unable to locate the abbey, continued to look for livestock or anything else they could thieve from this north western part of the Durham Bishopric.

It was then that the monks made a fatal mistake, for upon hearing that the Scots had passed them by they began to joyfully ring the abbey bells in celebration.

The raiders still in County Durham at a place later named Dead Friars Hill, were of course able to hear the bells, which enabled them to make their way back towards Blanchland.

Many of the monks lost their lives in the ensuing raid. The abbey was severely burnt. Did the bell ringers, live to regret their actions? We do not know. All that remains of the old abbey today is Blanchland's church of St. Mary.

Blanchland.

Most of present day Blanchland is a well planned stone village dating from 1752. Using stone taken from the ruined Blanchland abbey the village was built largely by the Trustees of Nathaniel Lord Crewe, an eighteenth century Bishop of Durham.

The charming village is built around an L shaped piazza, with a gateway that gives it an Italian appearance. Lord Crewe's name is commemorated in the name of an inn called the Lord Crewe Arms, in the centre of the village.

The Muggleswick Plot

The village of Muggleswick lies to the
east of the Derwent Reservoir. This was
the site of the hunting lodge for
Muggleswick Park, which belonged to
the priors of Durham. Muggleswick park
was enclosed by prior Hugh De
Darlington in the thirteenth century as
an alternative to the Prince Bishop's
hunting park at Stanhope, in Weardale.
In 1662 a rather mysterious event took
place at Muggleswick.

The bishop's association with the
Blanchland area resulted from his
marriage to a member of a local family
called the Forsters, who also owned land
at Bamburgh, (where we find another
Lord Crewe Arms). The Forster family
were strongly associated with the Jacobite
rising of 1715 that was led by the
Northumbrian Tom Forster.

On March 22nd of that particular year,
news came to the Bishop of Durham that
a huge army of Quakers, and religious
reformers were gathering on
Muggleswick Common. It was said that
they were preparing to murder the
Bishop, Dean and Prior, and overthrow
the parliament of all England.

The part played in the rising by Bishop
Crewe's niece, Dorothy Forster is
commemorated in the Sir Walter Beasant
novel Dorothy Forster (1884). Scenes
from the novel feature Blanchland.

Bishop John Cosin, along with the High
Sheriff of Durham, quickly collected
together their retainers and set off for
Muggleswick to put down the rising.
When they finally arrived at
Muggleswick there was however, no trace
of the rebels.

To the west of Blanchland is the source of
the River Derwent, at a point called
'Gibraltar Rock'. Here the river is formed
by the confluence of the Nookton and
Beldon Burns. To the south are the valleys
of Weardale and the Rookhope Burn.

In fact, there was no evidence that any
large group of people had ever been
anywhere near Muggleswick Common.
The Bishop of Durham had clearly been
the victim of a practical joke. Either that
or the rising was mysteriously
abandoned.

Blanchland.

Shotley Bridge

Shotley Bridge, a village in the Derwent valley near the town of Consett was once the heart of Britain's sword making industry. The origins of sword making here dated from 1691, when a group of Lutheran sword makers from Solingen in Germany settled at Shotley after leaving their homeland to escape religious persecution.

Shotley had probably been chosen because of the rich iron deposits in the area and because of the fast flowing waters of the River Derwent which were ideal for tempering swords. Another factor may have been the remoteness of the area, as the sword makers were keen to preserve their trade secrets.

It is also worth noting that the sword makers were able to employ the services of the famous local engraver Thomas Bewick. Swords are no longer made in the Shotley district.

The iron ore deposits in the vicinity of Shotley also encouraged the growth of the nearby town of Consett. Consett began to grow after the establishment of the Consett Iron and Steel works here in 1837. The works dominated the local skyline until their closure in 1980.

A Sword Maker's Challenge

There is a story that one of the Shotley sword making fraternity, a certain William Oley was once challenged by two other sword makers to see who could make the sharpest and most resilient sword. On the day of the challenge the three men turned up but it seemed that Oley had forgotten to bring an example of his work.

The two other sword makers, assuming that he had been unable to make a sword of a suitable standard began to boastfully demonstrate the strength, sharpness and resiliency of their work pieces.

Eventually their curiosity got the better of them and they asked Oley why he had not brought a sword. With a mischievous grin, Oley removed his stiff hat to reveal a super-resilient sword coiled up inside. He challenged the other two sword makers to remove the sword from the hat, but their attempts nearly resulted in the loss of their fingers. In the end the sword could only be removed by means of a vice. For strength, sharpness and resiliency Oley's sword was undoubtedly the winner.

St. Ebbe and Ebchester

Ebchester was the place where the Roman road called Dere Street once crossed the River Derwent en route between York and Hadrian's Wall. It was also the site of a Roman fort called

Vindomara , whose name meant 'Edge of the Black Moor'.

The site of the Roman fort has undergone very little excavation, as it is largely built over, but some Roman remains, including an altar are incorporated into the stonework of the village church. Ebchester church, dedicated to St. Ebbe stands at what would have been the south west corner of the Roman fort. It is a Norman church with nineteenth century alterations and is supposed to occupy the site of an Anglo-Saxon monastery founded by St. Ebbe in the seventh century. St. Ebbe was the daughter of Aethelfrith, the first King of Northumbria, but there is no proof of the existence of her monastery at Ebchester. It may have been destroyed by the Vikings.

The Wooded Derwent

In its upper stretches, the river Derwent forms the Pennine dale of the Derwent while further downstream, close to the outskirts of industrial Tyneside, the lower parts of the valley are the setting for attractive wooded countryside. The Derwent valley may always been well wooded hereabouts, as its ancient British name 'Dere Went' means 'river where oaks grew'.

One notable feature of the lower Derwent valley is the attractive Derwent Walk Country Park, which follows the course of the old Derwent valley railway between Swalwell on Tyne and the town of Consett.

Chopwell - 'Little Moscow'

On the north bank of the River Derwent, in view from the country walk, is the beautiful Chopwell Wood and nearby, the village of Chopwell, which was known in the 1920's as 'Little Moscow' because of the extreme political views of its miners. During the General Strike of 1926, the residents of this former mining town went to the extremes of replacing the Union Jack at the local council offices with that of the 'Hammer and Sickle'. They are also said to have removed a copy of the Bible from the church and replaced it with the works of Karl Marx. Even the streets of Chopwell were named after Lenin, Marx and Engels.

Jorrocks

Hamsterley Hall near Chopwell, on the south side of the Derwent was the home of Robert Smith Surtees (1803-1864), a character of a quite different nature to the once militant miners of Chopwell. Not to be confused with Robert Surtees the Durham historian, this author was more famous for his novels on fox hunting and country pursuits. He was the founder of the New Sporting Magazine of 1831, which featured his best known creation Jorrocks 'the Sporting grocer'. Surtees is buried in the churchyard at Ebchester, a village further upstream.

Tommy Armstrong

Tanfield Lea, a former mining village to the north of Beamish was the home of Thomas Armstrong (1848-1919) who was known as the 'Pitman Poet' or the 'Bard of the northern coalfield'. His songs were written in the Northumbrian style and reflected life in the Durham coalfield at the turn of the century.

They were primarily written to keep him in beer money. With fourteen children to support, Tommy's ability to write good folk songs proved invaluable. He had them printed and sold around the local public houses at a penny a time. Armstrong's best known pieces include 'Wor Nanny's a Maizor', 'The Trimdon Grange Disaster', 'The Oakey Strike Evictions' and 'Durham Gaol'.

Tommy Armstrong.

'The Oakey Strike Evictions' are a reminder of a particularly nasty aspect of life in the Durham coalfield in the nineteenth century:

> *"It was in November*
> *and aw never will forget*
> *How the polisses*
> *and the candymen*
> *at Oakey Houses met.*

> *Johnny the Bellman*
> *he was there*
> *squintin' roond aboot*
> *And he put three men*
> *at ivvery door*
> *te' torn the miners oot.*

> *And what would a dee*
> *if aw had the power mesel'*
> *Aw would hang the twenty candymen*
> *and Johnny whe carries the bell."*

Despite poor and dangerous working conditions, low pay and long hours, the often tyrannical coal owners of the nineteenth century would not hesitate to resort to such measures as eviction to deal with miners' strikes.

The 'candymen' employed by the coal owners to evict the miners were disreputable characters of the lowest order, brought in from the docksides of the large towns in the region.

Described as "low, mean ragged fellows", the "yelling, shouting, and tin panning together with the pitiful cries of children had no effect on these inhuman beings employed to do this work".

The Tanfield Railway and Causey Arch

In the seventeenth century colliery railways were beginning to develop in the North East called 'Newcastle Roads' which enabled coal mines to be opened further away from the rivers Tyne and Wear. This enabled more mines to open up in North West Durham.

The 'Newcastle Roads' were built first of wood and later of iron. They were the first railways in the world and were operated by horse drawn wagons called 'Chaldrons' which were filled with coal. Some examples of Chaldron wagons can be seen at Beamish Museum in County Durham.

The Tanfield railway dates from 1725 and claims to be the oldest existing railway in the world. It was originally eight miles long and terminated at Dunston on the Tyne. Only a short stretch remains as a museum with a small collection of carriages, wagons and active colliery locomotives. Nearby we find the historic stone bridge known as Causey Arch which crosses the Causey Burn Dene. The bridge was historically part of the Tanfield Railway and dates from 1727. It is the world's oldest surviving railway bridge.

Causey Arch.

Beamish Museum

Four miles west of Chester-le-Street, near the town of Stanley in the County Durham district of Derwentside we find one of the North East's biggest tourist attractions; the North of England Open Air Museum at Beamish which achieved the status of European Museum of the Year in 1987.

The museum was opened in 1970 with the aim of bringing to life the social and industrial life of the North East of England at the turn of the century.

The main features of the museum are a colliery, a drift mine, pit cottages, a working farm, a railway station with steam engines and a signal box. Most popular of the attractions at Beamish is the old fashioned town, complete with its own print works, stationers, dentist, co-operative store, brewery stables and public house. The co-operative store has drapery, hardware and grocery departments with brand names long since forgot. Individual parts of the museum are linked together by means of real old fashioned electric tram cars.

Beamish museum is built near the grounds of the 17th century Beamish Hall, a former residence of the Shafto and Eden families. The name Beamish derives from the old French 'Bew Mys' meaning 'Beautiful Mansion'.

Lanchester

From Ebchester, the course of the Roman Dere Street leads six miles south to Lanchester village, site of the Roman fort of Longovicium. Lanchester is in the valley of the River Browney, which joins the River Wear near Durham City.

Longovicium means the 'long settlement', and there seems to have been a large Roman civilian settlement or vicus at Lanchester in addition to the fort. The fort which is in fact half a mile south west of Lanchester was built around the time of Hadrian's Wall (AD 122).

It superseded the earlier Vindomara (Ebchester) and Vinovia (Binchester), which are the neighbouring forts on Dere Street. Longovicium was in use until the 4th century AD.

Some of the stones from the ruins of Longovicium are incorporated into local farm buildings and into Lanchester's attractive Norman church of All Saints. Inside the south porch of the church, a Roman altar can be seen dedicated to a goddess called Garmangabis.

Lanchester Church.

Such Roman remains were of great interest to Canon William Greenwell (1822-1919), the historian, archaeologist and archivist who is buried in Lanchester churchyard. Greenwell was for forty six years a librarian at Durham cathedral and was noted for his studies of archaeological sites, like ancient barrows.

Greenwell was also a keen angler and is perhaps best remembered in the name of Greenwell's Glory, a type of fishing fly, which he invented. Greenwell's father had been a great friend of the Durham historian Robert Surtees, but Lanchester is more closely associated with the principal historian of Northumberland, the Reverend John Hodgson, who lived here between 1804 and 1806. In his time at Lanchester, Hodgson made extensive studies of the fort of Longovicium.

Part Eight
Tynedale and the Roman Wall

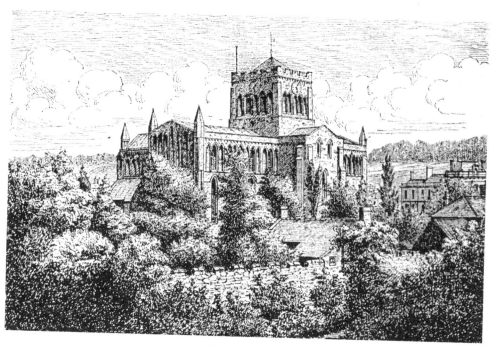

Hexham Abbey

Part Eight
Tynedale and the Roman Wall

Source of the South Tyne

The Tyne is formed by the confluence of two rivers - the South Tyne and North Tyne near Hexham. The North Tyne rises in the Cheviot Hills near the border with Scotland whilst the South Tyne rises near the Cumbrian town of Alston in the vicinity of Cross Fell, the highest point in the Pennines.

Cross Fell is also the source of the River Tees and the streams that feed the two rivers almost merge in the boggy moorland of the mountain.

The Cumbrian town of Alston is an attractive little place with a cobbled market square, 1,000 feet above sea level. From Alston, the South Tyne flows north into Northumberland through the remote and beautiful scenery of South Tynedale. An ancient Roman road called the Maiden Way follows the course of the valley here towards Haltwhistle, where we first enter the 'Roman Wall Country'. Here the South Tyne changes its course and heads east towards Tyneside. For much of its course Hadrian's ancient frontier is never far to the north of the river.

Hadrian's Vale

Stretching 80 Roman miles (73 modern miles), from Bowness on the Solway Firth to Wallsend on Tyne, Hadrian's Wall crosses the shortest east to west coast distance in England. It runs along the northern fringe of the naturally formed route way through the hills called the 'Tyne Gap'.

When Hadrian became Emperor in 117 AD, the Tyne Gap was already the site of a number of Roman forts associated with a Roman military road called the Stanegate. This road ran from Corbridge on Tyne (Corsiotopitum) to Carlisle (Luguvalium) and was more or less a frontier in itself. On completion of Hadrian's Wall the Stanegate's defensive role was relegated to that of a supply route for the new frontier.

"For Hadrian's pride shall open lie
To bittern's boom and curlew's call;
From Solway sands to mouth of Tyne
Vale is whispered on the wall."

Howard Pease

Gilsland

Gilsland, situated near the Cumbrian border is the most westerly village in Northumberland where Hadrian's Wall enters North East England. The boundary between Cumbria and Northumberland here is at the centre of an east-west watershed as nearly all streams to the west enter the Cumbrian River Irthing destined for the Irish Sea, while streams to the east of Gilsland are tributaries of the Tyne ultimately destined for the North Sea.

Even the names of the streams differ from one side of the county boundary to the other. Those on the Northumbrian side are called 'Burns', those in Cumbria to the west are called 'Becks'. Burn is an Anglo-Saxon word, Beck is a word of Viking origin.

The course of Hadrian's Wall can be traced in the village of Gilsland where it runs through the vicarage garden. A number of former Roman camps may be seen in the locality of Gilsland, which were probably occupied during the construction of Hadrian's Wall.

Gilsland was the place where the famous romantic border poet, Sir Walter Scott, first met his future wife, Charlotte Carpenter and it was to Miss Carpenter that he dedicated the verses 'To a Lady, with Flowers from the Roman Wall', written nearby at Thirlwall in 1797:

> *"Take these flowers,*
> *which purple waving,*
> *On the ruined rampart grew,*
> *Where, the sons of freedom braving,*
> *Rome's imperial standard flew.*
> *Warriors from the breach of danger*
> *Pluck no longer laurels there;*
> *They but yield the passing stranger*
> *Wild-flower wreaths for Beauty's hair."*

A Flaw in the Wall

The ruins of Thirlwall Castle, to the east of Gilsland lie close to what was arguably the weakest part of Hadrian's Wall. It was here that the Caledonians 'thirled', or threw down part of the wall, during a Barbarian raid in Roman times. The castle at Thirlwall was constructed in the thirteenth century, long after the Roman period, but was built using Roman stones taken from the ruins of the nearby fort of Carvoran.

For many years Thirlwall was the home of a notorious Border family called the Thirlwalls, who in 1550 were recorded as "prone and inclined to theft". The family were immortalised in a well known local ballad, commemorating a border fray in which Albany Featherstonehaugh, a High Sheriff of Northumberland was murdered;

> *"Hoot awa', lads Hoot awa',*
> *Ha'ye heard how the Ridleys*
> *and Thirlwalls and a'*
> *Ha' set upon Albany*
> *Featherstonehaugh*
> *And taken his life at the*
> *Deadmanshaw?*
> *There was Williemontswick*
> *And Hardriding Dick,*
> *And Hughie of Hawden and Will of*
> *the wa'*
> *I canno' tell a', I canno' tell a'*
> *And mony a mair that the De'il may*
> *knaw."*

These verses were part of a ballad sent to Sir Walter Scott by his great friend, the Durham historian Robert Surtees, who claimed he had heard it recited by an old woman on the moors near Alston in South Tynedale. In truth the ballad had been composed by Surtees himself. It was enough to fool Sir Walter, who included it in his lengthy poem called 'Marmion'.

Magna - Carvoran

South of Thirlwall, Hadrian's Wall crossed a tributary of the River Tyne, called the Tipalt Burn, by which lie the villages of Greenhead and Glenwelt. The remains of a Roman fort at Carvoran, known in Roman times as Magna, lie to the north east of Greenhead. It is situated at the junction of two Roman route ways known as the Stanegate and the Maiden Way, both of which predate Hadrian's Wall.

Magna was built many years before Hadrian's Wall and is probably associated with Julius Agricola's attempted conquest of Caledonia. Today, Carvoran is the site of an interesting Roman Museum.

The Blenkinsopp Ghost

Between the village of Greenhead and the town of Haltwhistle, on the South Tyne, we may find the ruins of Blenkinsopp Castle, which are said to be linked to those at Thirlwall by a secret passage. Blenkinsopp is associated with a legend and ghost story, concerning one Bryan Blenkinsopp who lived here many centuries ago.

Blenkinsopp Castle.

As a young man Blenkinsopp boasted he would not marry until he met with a lady possessing a chest of gold heavier than ten of his strongest men could carry. Remarkably, later in his life, Bryan's wishes were fulfilled when he met with such a lady while abroad fighting in the Crusades. Bryan brought her back to England where they were married but the lord did not, as expected, live happily ever after.

When the new bride learned of her husband's youthful boasts, she became worried he had only married her for her wealth, so she secretly hid her treasure chest in the Blenkinsopp grounds, where Bryan could not find them. Bryan responded to this bitterly and either heartbroken or humiliated by his bride's lack of trust, mysteriously left his wife and castle and was never to return again.

The Lady came to regret her actions, but despite strenuous efforts to find her husband, he could not be traced. She died a lonely and remorseful woman. It is said that her ghost may occasionally be seen haunting the grounds of the ruined castle where she waits, ready to guide the way to the spot where her chest of treasure is hidden. Some believe that the spirit will not lay to rest until the treasure is discovered and removed.

Haltwhistle - The Wall Country Town

Haltwhistle is the nearest town to Hadrian's Wall and is the largest town in South Tynedale, 12 moorland miles north of Alston.

Haltwhistle grew most rapidly as a coal mining settlement in the nineteenth century, which may lead one to think that its name has something to do with it being the site of a Victorian railway station.

In fact the delightful name Haltwhistle, is of very old Anglo-French origin deriving from 'Haut-Twisla' meaning 'high fork in the river', a reference to the confluence of the Haltwhistle Burn and the South Tyne.

This burn, called the Caw Burn in its upper stretches, runs close to the site of two Roman forts; namely the little known Haltwhistle Burn fort and the fort of Great Chesters, which both lie just to the north of the town.

A Roman Aqueduct

Aesica, is the name the Romans gave to the fort at Great Chesters, the remains of which can be seen north of Haltwhistle. As late as 1724, this fort was recorded as being exceptionally large, standing at a height of thirteen feet. It is probably for this reason that it acquired the name Great Chesters.

Like other forts along Hadrian's Wall, Aesica had a civilian settlement and a bath-house outside its walls, but perhaps its most interesting feature, was a six mile long Roman aqueduct used to supply water to the fort. The aqueduct's course can be traced in the hills to the north. There were also Roman aqueducts in the region at South Shields, Chester-le-Street and at Lanchester.

When the word 'Chester' occurs in place names like Great Chesters it usually signifies the former site of a Roman fort. The name 'Chester' was given to such places not by the Romans, but by the later Anglo-Saxons. Nevertheless the word is of Roman origin deriving from the Latin 'Caistra', meaning fort or city. In some parts of Britain the alternative word 'Caster' is found in place names like Lancaster or Doncaster. Caster has exactly the same meaning as Chester.

The Great Whin Sill

Some of the most spectacular views of Hadrian's Wall can be seen in the vicinity of Great Chesters, where it runs along the crest of the rocky crags formed by the 'Great Whin Sill'. This is a cliff-like band of hard black basaltic rock called Dolerite which was formed by a volcanic intrusion 280 million years ago.

The Great Whin Sill can be traced as far south as Teesdale (where it forms the famous waterfalls), and stretches north towards the sea near Berwick, where it forms the Farne Islands and the solid coastal foundations of Bamburgh, Dunstanburgh and Lindisfarne Castles.

The imposing inland cliffs formed by the Great Whin Sill which run in an east-west direction a few miles to the north of the River Tyne would have been a very important consideration by the Emperor Hadrian in the siting of his great defensive wall.

Vindolanda and its Vicus

Without a doubt, the two best known Roman sites of the Northumbrian 'Wall country', are the fort of Vindolanda at Chesterholm and the fort of Vercovicum, better known by its English name - Housesteads. Both forts are just off the B6318 Newcastle to Gilsland road, in the vicinity of the hamlets called Once Brewed and Twice Brewed. The B6318 follows the course of a Roman military road.

Vindolanda is not actually on the Roman wall, but like the fort of Carvoran near Haltwhistle it was built forty years earlier as an important military garrison on the Stanegate Roman road between Corbridge and Carlisle.

The fort of Vindolanda is strategically situated on a 'holm', a section of land formed by the junction of two streams. Hence the name Chester-holm.

Vindolanda, the Roman name, means 'white enclosed land'.

The fort itself is of considerable interest, but archaeologically Vindolanda is best known for the remains of the 'Vicus', or civilian settlement just outside the fort. Excavations on the vicus have revealed a number of houses, shops, a cemetery and a hoard of leather shoes, but the most interesting discovery was that of a Roman Mansio or Inn containing rest rooms, kitchen, courtyard, a bath house, and a latrine.

Many of the items from the vicus are displayed in Vindolanda's museum and research centre which was built by an archaeologist in the nineteenth century using Roman stones. The museum houses replicas of a Roman and a Celtic chariot and displays a recreated Roman kitchen.

A full-scale replica reconstruction of a small section of Hadrian's Wall has also been made at Vindolanda. It gives a good insight into what the wall would have looked like in Hadrian's time.

Housesteads

Hadrian's Wall runs along the crags to the north of Vindolanda in the vicinity of which are five small shallow lakes called 'Loughs' (Loffs) in a fashion curious to Northumberland and Ireland. Hadrian's Wall overlooks a lake called the Crag Lough, a mile to the west of the fort of Housesteads.

When Hadrian's Wall was built in AD 122, Housesteads, known to the Romans as Vercovicum, succeeded Vindolanda as the most important garrison in the area Like Vindolanda it had an important civilian settlement. The vicus at Housesteads suffered considerably from raids by native 'Barbarians' and eventually the civilian inhabitants were forced to move permanently into the fort for refuge.

Housesteads.

Arthur's Secret Hideaway?

North of Housesteads is the shallow Broomlee Lough and further north still are the Kings and Queens Crags, which are supposedly named after Arthur and Guenevere. Nearby, a mile to the south east are the Sewingshields Crags, once the site of an old castle near Hadrian's Wall where King Arthur is said to have held court.

Arthur, a legendary Celtic king is said to have fought in battle against the invading Anglo-Saxons in the vicinity of Hadrian's Wall.

Legend has it that in the nineteenth century, a shepherd sat knitting on the ruins of Sewingshields castle when he accidentally dropped a ball of wool. Chasing it through the mass of weeds and nettles that covered the overgrown ruin, the shepherd stumbled upon a secret passage infested with bats lizards and toads.

Looking towards the end of the passage the shepherd noticed a bright and distant light. He entered the passage to investigate further, until he eventually discovered a blazing but fuel-free fire emitting from the centre of a great subterranean hall. Close to the fire, stood a table upon which lay a bugle, a garter and a sword. Around the table were seated King Arthur, his queen, his knights and his hounds. All of them lay in a deep, deep sleep.

Instinctively the shepherd removed the sword from its scabbard and proceeded to cut the garter. This astonishingly caused Arthur and his knights to awaken. The startled shepherd quickly returned the sword to its sheath, causing all but the king to instantly return to their sleeping state. In terror the shepherd returned to the passage and ran from the hall as quickly as he could, his heart beating faster and faster. As he ran he heard the growling snores of King Arthur echo along the passageway as he fell back into his slumbering sleep. In the distance the king was heard to mutter these last angry words;

"O, woe betide that evil day
On which this witless wight was born,
Who drew the sword the garter cut,
But never blew the bugle horn."

The shepherd returned to Sewingshields on a number of occasions, but no matter how hard he tried, he could not find the entrance to the secret passage. Some say that King Arthur will be found at Sewingshields once again and that next time the bugle will be blown, freeing

Arthur and his knights, from their sleepy spell to fight for Britain in the hour of its greatest need. This legend of King Arthur is similar to the Legend of Sir Guy the Seeker associated with Dunstanburgh Castle.

Admittedly King Arthur is usually associated with south western England and throughout the country there are many Arthurian legends of a similar nature to the Sewingshields story. Many historians do however agree, that if such a figure as King Arthur ever existed, he seems most likely to have lived in the vicinity of Hadrian's Wall, probably in the region of Carlisle in Cumbria.

The Allendales

Five miles to the east of Haltwhistle, the River South Tyne is joined by the River Allen, which forms one of the least known valleys of the Pennines.

The River Allen itself is in fact a comparatively short ravine that can be followed only four miles upstream to where it is formed by the confluence of the much longer valleys of the Rivers East and West Allen. The Allendales have only two main settlements, the small village of Allenheads and Allendale Town, both of which are in the valley of East Allendale.

Allendale Town, once known as Allenton, is a former lead mining settlement, which claims to be the geographical centre of Great Britain. This claim is also made by Hexham, but a glance at a map shows Allendale to have a particularly strong case.

A Pagan Ceremony

Allendale Town is best known as the site of an annual 'Baal festival', a custom with mysterious Pagan origins.

The Baal Ceremony takes place here every New Years Eve and the celebration involves a procession of 'Guisers', or local men in costume who parade through the town, carefully carrying blazing tar barrels above their heads.

Upon reaching Allendale's market place the 'Guisers', throw the contents of their barrels onto a huge bonfire which they dance around in the manner of an ancient ritual.

The precise origins of the Allendale festival are not known, but it is most likely to have developed from some ancient pagan celebration of the Winter Solstice. Allendale's baal festival is a great spectacle and attracts visitors from near and far.

The Allendale Horse Thief

Two miles north of Allendale Town, the East and West Allen merge where the valley becomes thickly wooded as it approaches the River Tyne. This part of Allendale was once the home of a notorious livestock thief or 'mosstrooper' called Dickie of Kingswood, who operated in the area long after the time of the violent Border Reivers, who carried out similar activities in the border dales during the Tudor period.

Legend has it that Dickie once stole some oxen from a farm at Denton Burn, on the outskirts of Newcastle and then drove them across the country to Lanercost in Cumberland where he sold them to a farmer for a good price.

While at Lanercost, Dickie had become attracted to a particularly fine horse, belonging to the farmer to whom he had sold the stolen oxen. Dickie asked if he could buy the horse but the farmer explained that the mare was one of the finest in England and under no circumstances would he part with such an animal. Dickie accepted the farmer's refusal to sell and advised him to look after his mare and keep it well protected from horse thieves. He then departed with the money he had received for the oxen.

The temptation to steal the valuable horse from the farmer was too much for Dickie and later that night he returned to Lanercost, broke into the sleeping farmer's stable and made off with the horse.

While on his way home to Allendale, who should Dickie meet but the Denton Burn farmer, from whom he had stolen the oxen. Naturally the farmer asked Dickie if he had seen the oxen, the description of which Dickie immediately recognised. "Aye" said Dickie, "I'm sure I saw them up on a farm at Lanercost". Dickie did not of course tell the farmer that it was he who had stolen the oxen and delivered them to Lanercost.

The farmer was now in very good spirits in the hope of regaining his oxen. He gratefully thanked Dickie and complimented him on his fine looking mare.

Dickie immediately recognised that here was an opportunity to return the horse to its Lanercost owner so he told the farmer that if he liked the mare so much he would gladly sell it to him for a reasonable price. A price was agreed and the horse was handed over to the delighted farmer who set off for Lanercost to reclaim his oxen. It is not known what happened when the two farmers met up with each other at Lanercost but one thing is certain, Dickie returned to Allendale a wealthier man.

Hexham

Despite its important status as the largest town in Tynedale and its role as the main centre for touring Hadrian's Wall, Hexham surprisingly does not seem to have Roman origins. One suggestion is that the town was once the site of a number of Roman villas belonging to prominent Roman officers but this has never been proved.

Hexham's recorded history does not begin until 674 AD, three centuries after the Roman departure, when in Anglo-Saxon times an abbey was founded here by the Northumbrian saint and bishop, called Wilfrid.

Educated on the holy Island of Lindisfarne, St. Wilfrid (634 - 709 AD) had travelled to Rome and was impressed by the lifestyle and magnificence of European churches. He decided that something of a similar nature needed to be built in Northumbria.

Hexham Abbey.

The results were the great churches at Hexham and Ripon. Hexham Abbey was one of the first buildings in Anglo-Saxon Britain to make full use of stone. Wilfrid's abbey at Hexham was regarded as one of the finest in the country and its beauty was particularly enhanced by the use of Roman stones taken from the ruins of Hadrian's Wall and the nearby Roman fort at Corbridge.

Wilfrid was a flamboyant, highly educated and persuasive man but his talents brought him into inevitable conflict with the King of Northumbria, who threw him into prison for nine months. On release, Wilfrid was banished from Northumbria and fled to Sussex, where he played a very important part in converting the South Saxons to Christianity.

For a time Wilfrid's abbey at Hexham had the status of a cathedral and was the centre of a see stretching from the Tees to the River Aln. The cathedral and see of Hexham was later superseded by Lindisfarne and Chester-le-Street and even later by Durham.

By the time of the Norman Conquest Hexham and its abbey were part of the see of Durham but in the reign of Henry I it regained a degree of independence, when the town and its surrounding district known as Hexhamshire', were confiscated from the Prince Bishops of Durham and given to the Archbishops of York, to whom it belonged until 1837.

"Hey for the buff and the blue,
Hey for the cap and the feather
Hey for the bonny lass true,
That lives in Hexhamshire."

The Hexhamshire Lass'.

A Victim of Scottish Raids

In 875 AD, Hexham and its abbey were severely destroyed by the Vikings, under the leadership of Halfdene the Dane but historically Hexham is better known as a long suffering target for Scottish raids.

A most notable raid was that of 1296, when the Scots laid the town to waste, burning the abbey and the Hexham grammar school. Another great raid took place in 1346 when King David of Scotland plundered and burned the abbey prior to the Battle of Nevilles Cross, near Durham.

Hexham abbey suffered badly at the hands of many Scottish raids but centuries of continuous rebuilding, have ensured that a complete historic abbey, or more accurately, a priory church, still stand at Hexham today.

Sadly of the work of St. Wilfrid, only the Saxon crypt remains beneath the abbey floor. There is however one other reminder of St. Wilfrid's time, namely a thirteen hundred year old Anglo-Saxon 'Frith' or 'Frid' stool, which is found in the abbey choir. Carved from a block of stone, it was at one time used as a symbol of the sanctuary provided for criminals and refugees at Hexham. The 'stool' or 'stol', is said to have been the throne on which Northumbrian kings were once crowned but is more likely to be a primitive example of a bishop's throne.

The Hexham Massacre

The abbey dominates Hexham's busy market place, which has witnessed much of the town's turbulent past. It is however, somewhat surprising to discover that one of the bloodiest events of Hexham's history took place in this market place as late as the eighteenth century, long after the days of the border warfare.

Hexham Market.

The incident occurred on the 9th March 1761, during a protest against methods of conscription into the local militia. Objection was to the election of men to the militia by balloting, instead of the selection of recruits by landowners as had previously been the case. The introduction of this new system met fierce resistance in other parts of Northumberland and in Durham so there was a large military presence for the balloting of men at Hexham.

Around 5,000 men attended the meeting, mostly to protest and as their anger increased the Riot Act was read and they were asked to disperse. The protesters made it clear they would not give in, so magistrates ordered soldiers from the North Yorkshire Militia to open fire on the crowd. At least forty people were killed and over three hundred injured in the resulting chaos. The event became known as the 'Hexham Massacre' and for many years later the North York Militia were labelled the 'Hexham Butchers'.

The story has a rather sad and gruesome ending - on the 17th August of the same year, a seventy four year old man called Patterson was arrested for his alleged involvement in the Hexham 'riot'. It is said that he was sentenced to be hanged, cut down alive, disembowelled, have his entrails burnt in front of his eyes and then to be beheaded and quartered. In the event it was decided that the old man's sentence be reduced to a straight forward hanging.

Straight forward it was not, Patterson's rope snapped before he died and in the tradition of a martyr, he was able to utter his last words 'innocent blood is hard to spill'. It was later discovered that Patterson had not been in Hexham on the day of the riot!

A Temple to Mithras

There are a number of interesting Roman sites to visit in the vicinity of Hexham and a few miles north west of the town near Carrawborough we may see the remains of the fort of Brocolitia, the next major Roman site on Hadrian's Wall to the east of Housesteads. In 1949 an important Roman find was made here when the ruin of a Mithraeum or temple to Mithras was discovered. Comprised of three inscribed altars dedicated to a god called Mithras by Roman officers. It is one of the best preserved in Britain.

Mithraism, the disciplined worship of the Persian god of life, was encouraged by the Roman army and involved secret initiation ceremonies. It was strongly opposed by Christians in later centuries and they were probably responsible for the eventual destruction of the temple at Carrawbrough.

Mithras was by no means the only god worshipped on the Roman Wall and at Carrawbrough, a shrine called Coventina's Well, has also been found. Coventina was a Celtic water goddess worshipped by the native inhabitants of the wall country. The Well was excavated in 1876 by the archaeologist John Clayton, who also discovered thirteen thousand Roman coins on the site.

"Mithras, God of morning
Our trumpets waken the wall!
"Rome is above the nations,
But thou are over all!"
Now as the names are answered
And the guards are marched away,
Mithras, also a soldier,
Give us strength for the day!"

Rudyard Kipling.

Temple of Mithras.

A Roman Bath House

A mile to the north west of Hexham the River Tyne is formed by the confluence of the South Tyne with the North Tyne. The South Tyne is normally more closely associated with Hadrian's Wall but at Chesters to the north of Hexham, Hadrian's Wall actually crossed the North Tyne by means of a bridge.

The North Tyne has its origins in the Border Country of the Cheviot Hills many miles to the north of Hadrian's Wall and is covered in Part Ten of this book.

The ruins of the fort of Chesters, known to the Romans as Cilurnum lie close to the western bank of the North Tyne in attractive surroundings. This fort was one of the biggest in the Wall Country and was originally built to house a cavalry regiment.

The site is best known for the foundations of a Roman Bath House, which is one of the best preserved in Britain. Lying almost right beside the River North Tyne, the Bath House was comprised of Hot Rooms, Cold Rooms, a Sweating Chamber and a large entrance hall. Soldiers would have relaxed and bathed in this bathhouse in much the same way as in a modern Turkish or Swedish bath.

In the nineteenth century Chesters was the home of the amateur archaeologist and classical scholar John Clayton, whose old house is situated in the parkland that surrounds the fort.

Clayton owned most of the Roman Wall forts in Northumberland and successfully protected them from the threat of whinstone quarrying. It is largely to Clayton that we are indebted for the preservation of many central sections of Hadrian's Wall

In earlier centuries many of the forts along the central area of Hadrian's Wall, had been protected by a more unlikely source, namely the Border Reivers and Mosstroopers. Some of these lawless clans, like the Armstrongs at Housesteads, used the wall forts as permanent bases and thus kept souvenir hunters at bay. They also discouraged local farmers from plundering the ancient sites for stone.

Corbridge

Two miles east of Hexham, on the northern bank of the River Tyne, is the village of Corbridge which in Roman times was the site of 'Coriostopitum'. The fort was built around AD 80, by the Roman Governor of Britain, Julius Agricola. The remains of the fort can still be seen, half a mile to the west of Corbridge village.

Coriostopitum guarded an important crossing of the River Tyne, located at the junction of the two important Roman roads known as Dere Street and the Stanegate.

The fort played an important strategic role in Julius Agricola's attempted conquest of Caledonia but when this proved to be an unprofitable use of resources, Hadrian's Wall was built and Coriostopitum fell into temporary decline. Coriostopitum is not located on the Roman Wall.

About AD 160 Coriostopitum regained importance, when it developed into a military supply base serving the whole eastern half of Hadrian's Wall. A large civilian settlement, with tradesmen and merchants grew up around this base and Coriostopitum developed into one of the most important Roman towns in the wall country.

Corbridge.

The Devil's Causeway

The Excavations on Coriostopitum, which began in 1906, have uncovered a number of interesting features, including temples dedicated to a number of different gods. The base of a Roman fountain can also be seen at Coriostopitum. It was originally decorated with statues and was fed by a small aqueduct.

Like a number of other sites along the Roman frontier, Coriostopitum now has a museum with displays of Roman glass, pottery, tools, military equipment and even Roman board games. The 'Corbridge Lion' is one of the museum's best known exhibits. It is a sculpture of a lion devouring a stag and was probably used to decorate a Roman officer's tomb at Coriostopitum.

To the north of Corbridge at a place called Port Gate, the Roman Dere Street crossed Hadrian's Wall, as it continued north into Redesdale on its way to Caledonia. Another Roman road known as the 'Devil's Causeway' joined Dere Street at Portgate. It can be traced north eastwards across Northumberland to the mouth of the River Tweed at Berwick.

Corbridge in the Dark Ages

In the centuries following the Roman departure from Britain, the importance of Corbridge continued and in Anglo-Saxon times it was a capital of Northumbria. In the later Dark Ages, Corbridge was the scene of two important battles in 914 and 918 AD in which Northumbria's Anglo-Saxons, with help from the Scots, fought against the invading Norsemen. These particular Viking invaders did not come, as might be expected from the eastern coast, or from the new Scandinavian kingdom in Yorkshire but came from the west, from the Norse settled kingdom of Dublin.

In the twelfth and thirteenth centuries, Corbridge became one of the wealthiest towns in Northumberland and as a result suffered greatly from Scottish raids. It was occupied by David I of Scotland in 1138, burnt by William Wallace in 1296, by Robert the Bruce in 1312 and also by David II in 1346.

Vicar's Pele, Corbridge.

The Vicar's Pele tower at Corbridge, a fortified ecclesiastical residence is a strong reminder of this violent history. It was built around 1300 using Roman stones taken from the ruins of Coriostopitum.

Wylam on Tyne

Wylam on Tyne , is the last village in the Tyne valley, before we enter built up Tyneside. There is perhaps no other place in the world of comparative size to Wylam that more deserves the title 'Birthplace of the Railways'.

George Stephenson's House, Wylam.

It was here that the great railway pioneer William Hedley, built his Puffing Billy locomotive, which worked at Wylam colliery from 1813.

The Puffing Billy operated from Wylam colliery to the coal staithes on the River Tyne at Lemington on the outskirts of Newcastle, a few miles to the east. Later the Puffing Billy was replaced by Hedley's Wylam Dilly which was in operation until 1862.

Hedley was assisted in much of his work by the Wylam born blacksmith Timothy Hackworth (1786 - 1850) who is another of Wylam's great railway pioneers. Hackworth later went on to assist George Stephenson with the construction of the Stockton and Darlington Railway for which he developed his own engine called 'The Royal George'.

Ultimately Hackworth established his own engine works at Shildon in County Durham, where today we find a museum dedicated to his life and work.

Hackworth was a remarkable man, his last engine The Sans Pariel achieved a speed of 80 mph in 1849 and he was the man who introduced locomotives to Russia in 1837.

Both Hedley and Hackworth deserve to be better known but they are both overshadowed by another Wylam born engineer, George Stephenson who of course built the 'Rocket', the first locomotive to capture the imagination of the world.

Thomas Bewick

At Mickley on the south bank of the River Tyne four miles east of Corbridge we find the birthplace of the famous wood engraver and naturalist, Thomas Bewick (1753-1828). Bewick began his trade as an engraver, apprenticed from 1767 to the Newcastle engraver Ralph Beilby with whom he later formed a partnership. In 1784 he published a number of his beautiful woodcuts in his 'Select Fables' and many of his pictures, often designed for the entertainment of children have their own story to tell.

Thomas Bewick.

As a naturalist, Bewick is best known for the History of British Quadrupeds, a work written and illustrated by him in 1790 and the History of British Birds written and illustrated between 1797 and 1804. He is also noted for giving his name to the Bewick Swan. At Stocksfield, the cottage called 'Cherryburn', where Bewick was born, is the site of a museum dedicated to the work of Northumbria's greatest artist. Set in a beautiful part of the Tyne valley, the museum includes a printing house and many examples of Bewick's work. Visitors are likely to be amazed at the skilled detail of Bewick's engraved vignettes and tail pieces and will be amused by Bewick's sense of humour which is noticeable in a number of his works.

Bewick is buried a little further down the Tyne valley, in the churchyard of the village of Ovingham opposite the town of Prudhoe which is the site of an impressive ruined Norman castle. Dating from 1173 Prudhoe Castle is thought to have the oldest castle keep in Northumberland. It was originally built by the Umfraville family but passed into the hands of the Percys in the fourteenth century.

Part Nine
Newcastle and Tyneside

Grey Street Newcastle

Part Nine
Newcastle and Tyneside

Roman Tyneside

Benwell, in the western suburbs of Newcastle upon Tyne was the site of a fort on Hadrian's Wall called 'Condercum'. The present name is of Anglo-Saxon origin and derives from Beonnam-Wall meaning 'place within the wall'. Today most of what remains of the fort at Benwell is largely buried beneath modern housing, but the defensive Roman ditch called the 'Vallum' can still be clearly seen. The ruins of a Roman temple dedicated to a god called Antenociticus are also nearby.

From Benwell the Roman wall continued east, towards the fort at Newcastle called 'Pons Aelius'. Between Benwell and Newcastle centre, Hadrian's Wall more or less followed the course of the present Westgate Road. Westgate Road is actually built along the site of a Roman defensive ditch that was situated north of Hadrian's Wall.

In Roman times the fort of Pons Aelius at Newcastle was probably not as important as that at Benwell but it had a significant role in guarding a Roman bridge across the Tyne. 'Pons' was the Latin word for bridge, so 'Pons Aelius' was the name of both the fort and the bridge at Newcastle. In fact Pons Aelius can be translated to mean 'the bridge of

Hadrian's family, as Aelius, was the family name of the Emperor who built the Roman Wall.

The Roman bridge at Newcastle was built of timber on stone piers and may have continued in use for many centuries. Records suggest that the bridge may still have stood in Norman times and if this is so then it was not finally destroyed until 1248 during a raging fire. It is highly likely that a medieval bridge which replaced this burned structure still utilised the Roman foundations.

Initially the Roman bridge and fort at Newcastle formed the eastern terminus of Hadrian's Wall but later the wall was extended three miles further to the east where a fort called Segedunum was built at what we now know as Wallsend.

The fort of Segedunum was strategically located at the point where a short northward flowing section of the River Tyne suddenly turns east towards the sea. East of here the Tyne provided a natural continuation of Roman defences. This is demonstrated by the fact that one of the defensive walls of Wallsend fort actually extended into the River Tyne itself.

Newcastle's Castle

In Anglo-Saxon times the old Roman fort at Newcastle came to be known as 'Monkchester' after a small community of monks settled in the area. The later name, Newcastle did not come into existence until Norman times when Robert Curthose, eldest son of William the Conqueror built a castle here on return from a raid into Scotland.

Robert called the building his 'New Castle', and the name has stuck ever since. Robert's castle was built right on the site of the Roman fort of Pons Aelius.

Newcastle Castle.

A medieval walled town grew up around this new castle which became an important stronghold in the northern defences against the Scots. Its military importance stimulated trade and commerce and the expanding town of Newcastle developed into a major sea port. By 1300 Newcastle's importance was such that it was permitted to appoint its own mayor and a century later the town became a county in its own right, independent of Northumberland which lay outside its walls.

Rope making, shipbuilding and glass making were among the early trades to develop in Newcastle but without a doubt the most important of all the industries of the town was the mining and export of coal. The Tyneside pits were among the first to be worked in England and for centuries Newcastle was the most important exporter of coals to London. Thus we have the familiar modern phrase 'To carry coals to Newcastle', an expression of something which is quite needless.

Castle Keep and Blackgate

The 'New Castle' of Robert Curthose was built of earth and timber and was situated on a defended plateau overlooking the River Tyne. It seems to have performed its defensive role well until 1095 when it was seized by Norman barons under Robert De Mowbray Earl of Northumberland, during a rebellion against King William Rufus. The King sent north an army to stop this rebellion and the castle of Newcastle was forced to surrender.

The Blackgate.

In 1172 during the reign of King Henry II the castle at Newcastle was rebuilt in stone by Mauricius Caementarius and most of the stonework of the present keep still dates from this period. Later in about 1250 a barbican was added to the castle called the Black Gate which can still be seen today. The Blackgate was converted into a house in 1618 by the addition of a roof and windows which can be seen in the accompanying drawing. In Victorian times the building was cut off from the castle keep by the construction of a railway which runs between the two.

The Town Walls

In 1265 the burgesses of Newcastle decided to supplement the defences of the castle with the building of town walls to protect them from the raids of invading Scots. When completed the walls extended for over two miles around the town and were never less than 7 feet thick and up to 25 feet high. The castle and its Black Gate were not part of the town walls but were enclosed within them.

The Town Walls.

The Newcastle town wall consisted of six main gateways called Sand Gate, West Gate, New Gate, Pandon Gate, Pilgrim Gate, and Close Gate along with seventeen towers and a number of smaller turrets built as lookout posts situated at intervals between the towers and gates. During the reign of Henry VIII the famous antiquarian John Leland described Newcastle's defences as "far passing all the waulls of the cities of England and most of the cities of

Europe" in their strength and magnificence.

Today the most impressive surviving section of the old town wall is to the west of the city centre in the vicinity of Stowell street where the remains of four towers may be seen. A smaller section of wall survives near Forth Street behind the Newcastle Central Station but nothing remains of the walls to the north of Newcastle. To the east only the remains of three isolated towers remain. One tower in the vicinity of City Road has a small gateway called the 'Sally Port' from where defenders of Newcastle would sally forth against the enemy.

Newcastle's Quayside the Historic Core of Tyneside

The oldest part of Newcastle is the Quayside, which was until the nineteenth century, the commercial hub of all Tyneside. Most historical of the buildings in this area of the town are the keep of the Norman castle and the adjacent fourteenth century church of St. Nicholas with its famous lantern tower. Until the onset of Victorian developments these two buildings were the two most prominent buildings in Newcastle upon Tyne.

In 1882 when the diocese of Newcastle was created from the northern portion of the diocese of Durham, St. Nicholas church became a cathedral and Newcastle subsequently gained the title of a city. However for most of its history Newcastle has been a town and despite its Victorian rise in status, Newcastle is still commonly known to its residents as 'The Toon'.

Staying on the Quayside, not far from the cathedral is a road called the Sandhill where some of the oldest remaining houses of the Newcastle Quayside can still be seen. They date from the sixteenth to eighteenth centuries and were once occupied by wealthy Newcastle merchants.

In one of these houses there once lived a certain Bessie Surtees who in 1772 defied the wishes of her wealthy merchant father and secretly climbed from an upstairs window to elope with a humble young man called John Scott. Scott went on to become a wealthy peer, acquiring the barony of Eldon near Bishop Auckland and later in 1801 he became the Lord Chancellor of England.

Lord Eldon of course gives his name to Eldon Square, the modern commercial centre of Newcastle upon Tyne. Bessie Surtees' house in Sandhill is marked by a plaque which commemorates the famous elopement.

Newcastle Quayside houses.

Sandgate and the Keelmen

At the western end of the Newcastle Quayside is a street called Sandgate which once entered Newcastle by the Sand Gate of the town wall. This street is however better famed as the one time home of that famous Newcastle community, the Keel Men, who were unique to the region. These were the highly skilled boatmen, who handled the movement of coal from the riverside to ships on the River Tyne. The keelmen took their name from their small vessels called Keels which could carry around 20 Tons of coal.

The word 'keel' was the first English word ever to be written down, recorded by a Welsh chronicler in the sixth century. Its etymology is explained by R. J. Charleton in his 'History of Newcastle Upon Tyne' (1882). He reminds us that when the heathen Anglo-Saxons invaded Britain in the fifth and sixth centuries, they sailed across the sea in boats called 'Ceols' which:

> *"after all these centuries... are still to be seen (on the Tyne) as though endowed with the enduring and persistent characteristics of the race that built them".*

Charleton claims that the design of the Keel was very similar to that of the Anglo-Saxon Ceol. The earliest recorded use of Keels for transporting coal on the Tyne is in the early 1300's and it is possible that at this time the Keelmen had already established a community in The Sandgate District.

Boatmen from the Borders

Sandgate of course lay outside the town walls of Newcastle and the Keelmen regarded themselves as the residents of an almost separate town. Intermarriage was a general rule among the Keelmen and they even dressed differently from the other residents of Newcastle both at work and in a social context. A distinctive blue jacket was worn by the Keelmen along with a yellow waistcoat, belled trousers and a black silk hat tied with a ribbon. In fact so keen were the Keelmen to preserve their own identity that they even employed their own tailors.

Newcastle Guildhall and Tyne Bridge.

The Keelmen were as tough, hardworking and as militant as the miners of Northumberland and Durham had to be in the nineteenth century. Like the miners, their toughness may well have been a reflection of their place of origin. In the seventeenth century many of the Keelmen originated from the Scottish and Northumbrian border valleys, like Redesdale and North Tynedale and were often descendants of famous Border raiders or Reiver clans like the Armstrongs, Charltons, Robsons, Turnbulls, Grahams and Dodds.

The Keel Row

With the onset of the Industrial Revolution in the nineteenth century and the development of coal staithes as an alternative method of loading collier ships, the Keel men's trade gradually declined until it became virtually non-existent.

The Keel community of Sandgate, once the most populous part of Newcastle, was also sadly to die.

All that is left to remind us of this bustling Quayside community today are the unique and distinctive collection of Sandgate folk songs, the most notable being 'The Keel Row' of which Rudyard Kipling wrote while in India:

"The man who has never heard the 'Keel Row' rising high and shrill above the sound of the regiment..... has something yet to hear and understand".

The Keel Row is undisputedly a Tyneside song but the song does seem to have a slight Scottish influence - perhaps a reminder of the keelmens' Border origins.

As aa cam' thro' Sandgate,
Thro' Sandgate, thro' Sandgate,
As aa cam' thro' Sandgate'
Aa heard a lassie sing:

Weel may the keel row,
The keel row, the keel row
Weel may the keel row
That ma laddie's in.

He wears a blue bonnet,
Blue bonnet, blue bonnet,
He wears a blue bonnet,
An' a dimple on his chin.

An' weel may the keel row,
The keel row, the keel row
Weel may the keel row
That ma laddie's in.

Seven Great Bridges

All views of the Newcastle riverside are dominated by the seven famous bridges across the Tyne that link the city with Gateshead on the south bank of the river. From west to east they are; the Redheugh bridge, King Edward VII bridge, Queen Elizabeth II bridge, the High Level bridge, the Swing bridge, the George V Bridge and the Millennium Bridge. The George V Bridge is known more commonly as the Tyne Bridge.

The Tyne Bridge was opened in 1929 by King George V and built by Dorman Long of Middlesbrough. It served as a model for the similar but very much larger Sydney Harbour Bridge which was also built at Middlesbrough.

Lowest of the old bridges is the Swing Bridge of 1876, which leads directly into the heart of the Newcastle Quayside below the castle keep. Designed by the famous Tyneside engineer William Armstrong (1810-1900), it is located on the site of the Roman and medieval bridge.

During the construction of this swing bridge, two Roman altars were dredged from the river dedicated to the gods Neptune and Oceanus. They would have belonged to a shrine built to protect the Roman bridge of Pons Aelius from the tidal Tyne.

The King Edward bridge was built in 1906 by Cleveland Bridge of Darlington, while the Redheugh and Queen Elizabeth II bridges are more modern structures, the former built of concrete the latter a steel structure used by the Metro system.

Oldest of Newcastle's Tyne bridges is the High Level Bridge which was erected in 1848 to the designs of Robert Stephenson, it comprises two tiers for road and rail. One of the best views of Newcastle can be obtained from on board a train as it crosses this bridge on the main London to Edinburgh line.

The Millennium Bridge footbridge is the most modern of the seven bridges and was built to commemorate the Millennium, it is sometimes known as the blinking eye because of its tilting mechanism.

A City and its Streets

With the exception of the Millennium Bridge and Armstrong's lower level Swing Bridge all the bridges take you high over the old quayside and into the modern heart of the city, which lies a little further to the north.

Here we find the Eldon Square Shopping complex, the busy Northumberland Street, the Civic Centre, the two Universities, the busy offices and institutions, the banks, museums, libraries, markets, restaurants, night clubs and theatres which make up this vibrant regional centre.

The city life of Newcastle is centred around its fine city centre streets which in many ways set it apart from most other northern cities which grew so rapidly during the industrial revolution.

The classical features of Grainger Street and Clayton Street, are of particular note but most impressive is Grey Street, once described by the Prime Minister, Gladstone in 1862 as 'our best modern street'. Sir John Betjeman went further and wrote;

> "As for the curve of Grey Street, I shall never forget seeing it to perfection, traffic-less on a misty Sunday morning. Not even Regent Street, even old Regent Street London, can compare with that descending subtle curve".

Grey Street.

Grey Street is named after the British Prime minister Earl Grey (1830-34), whose monument stands at the head of the street. Earl Grey, a Northumbrian by birth, was the Prime Minister at the time of the Reform Bill of 1832.

Where Modern Times Began

The industrial developments of the nineteenth century literally changed the world and paved the way for the astonishing technological developments in transport, communications and mass production which today we take so much for granted.

There is no doubt that Britain played a major part in these developments and the northern part of England played a very important role.

But here we may go further and say that there was one particularly small part of Northern England where so many early industrial developments took place that it could easily be described as the place 'where modern times were born' we are of course talking about Tyneside.

The abundance of natural resources were what initially stimulated the growth of

industry on Tyneside. Coal had been mined in the area since medieval times and had directly stimulated the development of the world's earliest railways in the North East by the 1600s.

Coal also played its part in the development of less obvious industries like chemicals. Alkali salts for example could be pumped out from the coal mines to be used in the production of glass and soap which were increasingly demanded by the growing population of industrial Tyneside.

But also significant for Tyneside was the local availability of iron ore which in conjunction with coal provided the lifeblood for the giant nineteenth and early twentieth century industries of shipbuilding, locomotive engineering, civil engineering and armament manufacture.

Industrial Pioneers

The great industrial developments on Tyneside were only made possible by the investment and foresight of some of the greatest industrial pioneers the world as ever seen. Men like George Stephenson, William Armstrong, Charles Parsons and Joseph Swan were all Tynesiders by birth or adoption.

Some of these great industrial figures were great friends and would often meet to discuss their industrial and technological developments at the Literary and Philosophical Society of Newcastle upon Tyne. One of the greatest local institutions of Victorian Britain the 'Lit and Phil' still exists today as a private library with a very famous lecture hall.

It was here at the Lit and Phil that Joseph Swan first demonstrated his electric light bulb and where George Stephenson first showed off the miner's safety lamp which made possible the opening up of ever deeper mines thus ensuring that the industrial revolution on Tyneside would continue uninterrupted.

The Stephensons

Of all the great industrial pioneers of Tyneside, George Stephenson (1781-1848) often referred to as the 'Father of the Railways' is the most widely known. Stephenson was born at the village of Wylam on Tyne where his father was the engine man at the Wylam Colliery winding house. Aged fourteen Stephenson became an assistant to his father and later followed in his footsteps to become the engine man at Killingworth colliery to the north of Newcastle.

It was here that Stephenson developed one of the earliest locomotives called the Blucher which ran on the Killingworth colliery railway in 1814. From the period 1814 to 1826 Stephenson was virtually the only man building and developing new locomotives - proof that he recognised that locomotives had not yet reached their full potential.

In 1819 Stephenson became involved in a project to build a railway for Hetton Colliery near Hetton-le-Hole in County Durham and here the colliery was worked by stationary engines and locomotives.

The Hetton Railway was in its time the largest in the world and served as a prototype for Stephenson's Stockton and Darlington Railway of 1825 which was of course the world's first public railway.

Robert Stephenson.

In 1824 George Stephenson with his son Robert formed an engineering business and workshop in Forth Street Newcastle, specifically for the building of locomotives. A number were built culminating in the construction of Stephenson's most famous locomotive called the Rocket. This locomotive is famed for achieving a world record speed of thirty six miles per hour at the famous Rainhill Trials held near Liverpool in 1829.

Robert Stephenson (1803-1859) was George's only son and played a very important part in many of the developments associated with his father including the construction of the 'Rocket'. Robert is however better known for his work in the field of civil engineering.

Robert Stephenson's best known achievements are the tubular bridges over the Menai Straits in Wales and over the St. Lawrence River in Canada. Closer to home Robert constructed Royal Border

Bridge near Berwick and of course Newcastle's very own High Level Bridge.

William Armstrong

If George Stephenson was primarily associated with steam engineering then William George Armstrong (1810-1900) by comparison was a 'Jack of All Trades'. Armstrong was just as much a scientist as a scholar or an engineer but was also very much an enterprising industrialist with the advantage of an open enquiring mind as demonstrated by the following lines once quoted by the man himself;

"However high we climb in the pursuit of knowledge we shall still see heights above us, and the more we extend our view, the more conscious we shall be of the immensity which lies beyond."

Armstrong was born in the Shieldfield area of Newcastle on the 26 November 1810. His father was the proprietor of a corn merchants business on the Newcastle Quayside and had a strong interest in natural history and mathematics and was a member of the Literary and Philosophical Society.

Young William trained to be a solicitor and although he became a partner in a legal practice he had inherited similar interests to his father, particularly in the field of science and engineering.

Armstrong gave knowledgeable lectures on these subjects at the Newcastle Lit and Phil and in 1842 he constructed a Hydro-Electric generator. This was constructed with the knowledge gained following the accidental discovery of a discharge of static electricity from a colliery boiler by an engine man at a Northumberland coal mine.

Around 1846 Armstrong's interests shifted from Hydro-Electricity to Hydraulics and he persuaded wealthy Newcastle men to back him in the development of hydraulic cranes for Newcastle which were powered with the assistance of the town's Whittle Dene Water Company.

The scheme was such a great success that in 1847 Armstrong gave up his legal practice to establish the Newcastle Cranage company at Elswick which later became known as 'Armstrong's Factory' as immortalised in the 'Blaydon Races'.

William Armstrong.

Following the Crimean War in the 1850s Armstrong became increasingly involved with the manufacture of armaments and his eighteen pound breach loading gun was one of many Armstrong weapons recognised as the best in the world.

Such devices, often tested on the moors of Allendale, were ordered by armies and navies all over the world from Russia and Japan to the United States. In fact Armstrong supplied both armies in the American Civil War.

From 1863 onward Armstrong became less and less involved in the day to day running of his company affairs and began to pursue other interests. He became particularly noted for his successful pursuits in the field of landscape gardening.

This was initially carried out in Newcastle's beautiful Jesmond Dene most of which he owned and where he had built a house for himself and his wife in the 1830s. Jesmond Dene was donated by Armstrong to the people of the city of Newcastle upon Tyne in 1883.

The later years of Armstrong's life were spent in his magnificent parkland mansion of Cragside near Rothbury in Northumberland. Cragside was of course the first house in the world to be lit by Hydro Electric power.

Charles Parsons

Sir Charles Algernon Parsons is another well known industrial pioneer of Tyneside. A son of the Third Earl of Rosse (a famous astronomer), Parsons was an adopted 'Geordie' who began his career as an apprentice to William Armstrong. Later he became a partner in the Tyneside firm of Clarke Chapman and it was here in 1884 that he developed the Steam Turbine for the generation of electricity.

Charles Parsons.

The steam Turbine engine was especially recognised for its potential use in the propulsion of ships. The first vessel to use such an engine was the Turbinia built by the Parson's Marine Steam Turbine Company at Wallsend in 1897.

The vessel was put to the test in marine trials off Spithead in that year and achieved a record speed of 34 knots. Later ships to use the Parsons Turbine included the Wallsend built Mauretania of 1907, a liner which held the Blue Riband for the fastest crossing of the Atlantic for twenty two years.

In terms of the history of shipping Charles Parson's Turbine plays an important part but it has an even greater place in history as one of the greatest steps forward in the development of electric power generators. When we consider that power stations using Parsons turbines are still supplying heat, light and electric power to homes and industries throughout the world we can understand the justification for describing Parsons as 'the man who invented the twentieth Century'.

Joseph Swan

Another great industrial pioneer on Tyneside was Joseph Wilson Swan who was born in Sunderland on October 31st 1828 and began his career as an apprentice to a local chemist. In 1862 Swan moved to Gateshead and as a member of the Newcastle Literary and Philosophical Society he had a strong desire to research and experiment in the field of chemistry.

Some of Swan's earliest developments were in the field of photography where he perfected the carbon process of photographic printing and developed the rapid photographic plate. He also patented the first Bromide paper in 1879. His photographic developments were of immense importance as they turned photography into a practical pastime and greatly spurred on its popularity.

Swan is however better known for his development of the incandescent filament electric lamp. This was the first practical electric light bulb and the first demonstration of this source of electric light was performed by Swan at the Literary and Philosophical Society of Newcastle upon Tyne on February 3rd 1879.

Joseph Swan.

Swan's demonstration proved to be a success and at Benwell in the western suburbs of Newcastle he established the world's first electric light bulb factory. Later Swan went on to light up Mosley Street in Newcastle City Centre reputedly the first street in the world to be lit by electric light. By 1881 Swan's light bulbs had arrived in London where 1,200 of them were used in lighting the Savoy Theatre in front of an astonished audience.

Blaydon and the Races

The town of Blaydon lies on the western fringe of the district of Gateshead but is separated from the rest of the borough by the River Derwent which enters the Tyne nearby.

Blaydon is of course internationally known as the subject of the Geordieland 'National anthem', 'The Blaydon Races', which was originally a Victorian Music

Hall song written by Gateshead's Geordie Ridley (1835-64).

The first public performance of the song by Ridley was on the fifth of June 1862 at a testimonial for the great Tyneside sporting hero Harry Clasper held at Balmbra's Music Hall in Newcastle. The song was composed as an advertisement for a Geordie Ridley concert to be held at Blaydon and describes a coach journey from Newcastle to Blaydon.

In Ridley's time 'The Blaydon Races' song was nothing like as well known as it is today and it was only at the beginning of the twentieth century that it was made popular by a Tyneside comedian called Scatter.

In 1862 the Blaydon Races were to be held on an island in the middle of the River Tyne at Blaydon but they were called off when a heavy storm made it impossible for the horses to make their way across to the race course.

This storm is recorded in the last verse of the 'Blaydon Races' but most of the events referred to in the song actually took place in 1861. The last Blaydon Races were held on the 2nd September 1916. They were abandoned after a riot broke out following the disqualification of a winning horse.

(Chorus)
Oh me lads ye shud a' seen us gannin',
Passin' the folks upon the road,
Just as they were stannin'
Thor wes lots o' lads and lasses there,
All wi' smilin' faces,
Gannin' alang the Scotswood Road
Te' see the Blaydon Races.

Aw went te Blaydon Races,
'twas on the neenth o' Joon,
Eighteen Hundred and Sixty Two,
on a summer's afternoon,
Aw teuk the bus frae Balmbra's an'
she was heavy laden,
Away we went alang Collingwood Street,
That's on the road to Blaydon.

We went past Armstrong's factory,
and up te the 'Robin Adair',
Just gannin' doon te' the railway bridge,
The bus wheel flew off there.
The lasses lost their crinolines off,
An' the veils that hide their faces.
An' aw got two black eyes and a broken
nose
In gan te Blaydon Races.

When we gat the wheel put on
away we went agyen,
But them that got their noses broke,
they cam' back ower hyem.
Some went te the dispensary,
an' others te' Doctor Gibb's,
An' some sought oot the infirmary to mend
their broken ribs.

Noo when we gat te Paradise
thor wes bonny game begun,
Thor wes fower and twenty on the bus,
Man hoo they danced and sung
They called on me to sing a sang, aw sung
them 'Paddy Fagan'
Aw danced a jig and swung me twig,
That day aw went te Blaydon.

We flew across the Chine Bridge
reet into Blaydon toon
The bellman he was callin' there- they call
him Jacky Broon.
Aw saw him talkin' te some chaps,
an them he wes persuadin'

Te' gan an' see Geordie Ridley's concert,
In the Mechanic's Hall at Blaydon.

The rain it poor'd doon aal the day
an' myed the groond quite muddy,
Coffy Johnny had a white hat on,
They were shootin' "whe stole the cuddy?"
There wes spice staals an' monkey shows,
an' aad wives sellin' ciders,
an' a chep wiv a hapeeny roondaboot,
shootin "now me boys", for riders.

Harry Clasper - A Great Tyneside Hero

Across the River Derwent to the east of Blaydon is the town of Whickham which is centred around the attractive village of Whickham and its parish church of St. Mary. In the cemetery of this church we find a memorial to Harry Clasper (1812-1870), one of Tyneside's greatest sporting heroes.

Today the sporting greats of Tyneside tend to be footballers, but in Victorian times rowing was the great cult sport of the area and Harry Clasper, a pitman from Dunston on Tyne was one of the greatest of British oarsman.

Harry who constructed his own boats was a regular champion of all the major regattas in the country and competed as a sculler or in fours and pairs with his equally talented brothers.

In 1845 Harry constructed a boat called The Lord Ravensworth to compete against the best British oarsman in the coxed fours of the Thames Regatta.

Accompanied by three brothers (one as coxswain) and his uncle, Ned Hawks, Harry's team were victorious by one and a half boat lengths to claim the championship of the world.

When Harry died in 1870 his loss was lamented by all Tyneside and his funeral procession was attended by an incredible 130,000 people who crammed the Tyne bridges and the banks of the river to watch as his coffin was carried on board a steam tug to Derwenthaugh near Blaydon from where it was taken ashore for burial at Whickham.

Whickham's Coal Mining History

Although there are no coal mines in this area today, the Whickham district has played a very important part in the mining history of North Eastern England as coal mining is recorded in the district as far back as the fourteenth century. At this time the local mines belonged to the bishop of Durham and were reputedly the largest in Europe. In a later century Queen Elizabeth I obtained the coal mines in the Whickham area from the Bishop of Durham in a 'Grand Lease' which lasted for ninety nine years.

The Queen passed the rights to the Earl of Leicester from whom it ultimately passed into the hands of a group of wealthy Newcastle merchants known as the 'Hostmen'.

Later in the eighteenth and nineteenth centuries most of the coal mines in the Tyneside area were owned by a group of wealthy landowners called the 'Grand Allies'. They included the Bowes family

who lived near Whickham. Originally from Teesdale, the Bowes family came to be associated with the area after Sir William Bowes of Streatlam married Elizabeth Blakiston of Gibside near Whickham.

Many of the mines in the Whickham area owned by the Bowes family were linked together by what is now the world's oldest existing railway at Tanfield. The Tanfield wagonway crossed what is now the world's oldest railway bridge at Causey Arch near Beamish. The wagonway led to coal staithes at Dunston on the River Tyne.

Dunston Staithes

The town of Dunston, between Whickham and Gateshead is located at the point where the little River Team enters the River Tyne adjacent to the impressive pier like structure of Dunston coal staithes. These staithes are reputedly the largest wooden structure in Europe and possibly the world.

Constructed in 1890 by the North Eastern Railway Company for the purpose of loading north Durham coal into ships, the staithes protrude into the River Tyne for 1,709 feet and run parallel to the river bank forming a large tidal basin in which ships once moored.

Several railway lines ran along the top of the coal staithes from the river bank and rose at a gradient of 1 in 96 from the western to the eastern end of the staithes. This enabled locomotives to shunt coal wagons to an appropriate height for loading up ships anchored alongside the staithes.

Coal wagons fitted with trapdoors were shunted along the staithes and lined up with hoppers in the staithes floor. Gangs of men called 'Teemers' would then release these trapdoors and teem the coal into the hoppers.

This was not an easy task as often the coal would jam or freeze in the wagon or hopper so that men would have to jump in to free the coal and run the risk of falling through. Sometimes accidents of this nature would happen and the men could sustain serious injuries.

The hoppers in the staithes were linked to coal chutes called spouts and the teemers had the task of adjusting these spouts according to the height of the ships they were loading. The spouts were adjusted by means of a hand windlass.

Once coal or coke had been loaded from the shute into the holds of the ships, gangs of men called 'Trimmers' were set to work to level out the coal in the ships for stability.

At the peak of its career in the 1920s Dunston staithes were shipping an average of 140,000 tons of coal per week on vessels bound for both London and the continent but by the 1970s this figure had fallen to 3,000. In 1980 the staithes were finally closed. They remain today as a listed building and as the most important monument to the once busy days of the 'Coaly Tyne'.

Around Gateshead

Gateshead Borough on the south side of the River Tyne is the home to over 200,000 people and includes the towns of Whickham, Blaydon, Winlaton and Ryton as well as Gateshead and its suburbs. It is quite a diverse area with a heavily built up centre comprised of blocks of flats and busy roads, while the south west of the borough has much open rolling countryside.

The Angel of the North, Gateshead.

Throughout its history the town of Gateshead has lived in the shadows of the commercially powerful and historically wealthier Newcastle, but despite this strong competition Gateshead has managed to rigidly hold onto its own identity and refuses to become a mere suburb of the Geordie capital. Today Gateshead is widely famed as a venue for top level International Athletics, the home of the Baltic Arts Centre, Metro Centre shopping and leisure complex and of course the famous Angle of the North.

Gateshead 'Goat's Head'

From the earliest times Gateshead has been at the head of an important road or 'gate' from the south and this would suggest that the name of the town is a reference to its location at the head of the 'gate'.

There is however an alternative suggestion that Gateshead means 'Goats

Head' - a headland frequented by wild goats and this is supported by the Venerable Bede who described Gateshead under the Latin name of 'Ad Caprae Caput' meaning 'Goat's Head'. Bede referred to Ad Caprae Caput as the site of a monastery belonging to an abbot called Utta in 653 AD who was described as a 'truthful and serious man'. We know virtually nothing else about Gateshead in Anglo-Saxon times.

Whatever its origins, Gateshead is certainly the site of an ancient route, and in Roman times a 'street' ran here between the Roman forts of Concangium (Chester-le-Street) and Pons Aelius (Newcastle).

The Roman road may partly have followed the course of the modern Gateshead High Street. It crossed the Tyne by means of a Roman bridge upon which some say there was inscribed the emblem of a goat's head!

No evidence has been found for the existence of a fort at Gateshead in Roman times (although one has been discovered at Whickham), but Roman coins and artefacts were discovered in the vicinity of Church Street and Bottle Bank in the eighteenth and early nineteenth centuries.

If there was some kind of Roman outpost fort associated with the Roman bridge the most likely setting would be on the site of the Gateshead parish church of St. Mary close to the edge of the Tyne.

Murder of the Bishop

In Norman times Gateshead passed into the hands of the Prince Bishops of Durham who for centuries virtually ruled the land between the Tyne and the River Tees.

The first Norman Bishop of Durham was William Walcher of Loraine who upset the locals of Gateshead when one of his men murdered a popular Anglo-Saxon noble called Liulf of Lumley in 1081.

The bishop realised that the activities of his men were beginning to get out of hand and called for a meeting with his people to try and make amends.

For some reason the bishop chose Gateshead as the site for this meeting which suggests Gateshead may have been a place of importance in Norman times.

Whatever his reasons for choosing Gateshead, the bishop was not successful in his attempts to make peace. An angry mob had assembled to drown out the words of the bishop.

A cry of "good rede short rede slea ye the Bishop" was heard as the mob sallied forth. The bishop took refuge in a church (on the site of St. Mary's) but the mob set alight to the building causing the bishop to flee once again. He was set upon by the mob and brutally murdered.

Later the bishop's mangled body was found on the site by the monks of Jarrow who conveyed it first to their own monastery and then to Durham for burial.

Prince Bishops in Gateshead

In the twelfth century Gateshead became a favourite place of residence of Hugh Pudsey, a powerful Prince Bishop of Durham, who was attracted by the extensive hunting forests in the vicinity of Gateshead and Heworth.

Disputes over Gateshead

Newcastle's wealthy merchants continuously tried to restrict trade on the south side of the river at Gateshead and several attempts were made to annex Gateshead as a part of Newcastle. On each occasion the king came out in support of the Bishop of Durham. However in March 1553 John Dudley Duke of Northumberland, (who virtually ruled England during the reign of the boy-King Edward VI) finally annexed the town of Gateshead to Newcastle. The annexation only lasted a few months with Gateshead returning to Durham with the accession of Queen Mary to the throne.

In 1574 another attempt was made by Newcastle to annex Gateshead but the Gateshead people fiercely petitioned parliament against such a possibility claiming that the merchants and poor people would suffer. This petition was successful but Newcastle was not to give in and in the reign of Queen Elizabeth I Newcastle finally gained control of Gateshead's coal trade in a grand lease of ninety nine years. The coal mines of Gateshead were worked very heavily during this period and all the wealth from these mines went into the pockets of the Newcastle merchants and not the bishops of Durham.

Despite this attraction, the bishop instigated the clearance of some of these forests which continued into the following centuries. As the forests were cleared subsequent Bishops of Durham gradually lost interest in Gateshead's hunting grounds. They may have preferred to see the use of the forest timber in the construction of Tyneside pits which were an increasing source of wealth for the bishops.

The Prince Bishops seem to have taken only minimal interest in Gateshead as a port, preferring Stockton on the River Tees and the accessible natural harbour of Hartlepool.

Nevertheless they had certain rights to allow ships to trade from the south side of the River Tyne and were determined to protect these rights despite strong opposition from the merchants of Newcastle who wished to control the trade on both sides of the Tyne.

The Great Fire of Gateshead

Despite the early development of coal mining in the Gateshead area, Gateshead seems to have remained a rather small place which in the eighteenth century was still little more than a large village, noted for 'oak trees and windmills'.

As late as 1834, 'Mckenzies History of Durham' records that the Windmill Hills near the town were 'studded with corn mills which seen at a distance, impart a lively and picturesque effect to the landscape'. A Tyneside song further proclaims:

> *"The Quayside for sailors,*
> *The Castle Garth for Tailors,*
> *The Gateshead Hills for Millers,*
> *The North shore for Keelers."*

This idyllic rural situation was however beginning to change as industrialisation brought about a continuous increase in Gateshead's population with an increase from 8,597 to 108,024 between 1801 and 1901. As a result, the riverside area of the town became increasingly overcrowded and this contributed to a great disaster in the nineteenth century which affected the neighbouring town of Newcastle as well.

Old view of Newcastle from Gateshead.

At one o' clock on the morning of 6th October, 1854 a fire was discovered close to the River Tyne in a worsted factory in Hillgate, Gateshead. The fire quickly got out of control and spread to an adjacent warehouse containing huge stores of salt, iron, lead, manganese, nitrate of soda, guano, arsenic, copperas, naptha, and 3,000 tons of Brimstone.

Enormous blue flames began emitting from the building as it caught fire and large crowds began to gather in both Gateshead and Newcastle, to see the spectacle. Boats on the River Tyne were said to be alive with spectators.

At around quarter past three that morning, disaster struck; the whole building suddenly exploded, sending off flaming debris in all directions, the sight of which was described by onlookers as

'like flying fish'. It is said that the explosion was heard far off in Berwick upon Tweed and that houses were damaged as far up the Tyne as South Shields. The glow from the fire could be seen in northern Yorkshire, many miles to the south.

The flying debris caused ships and boats in the centre of the River Tyne to catch alight, but worse still, caused a second huge fire to break out on the northern bank of the river, which ultimately destroyed many of the medieval buildings on the Newcastle quayside. Hundreds of people were made homeless by the event which was known for many years after as 'The Great fire of Newcastle and Gateshead'.

The Great fire destroyed nearly all of the few historical buildings that existed in Gateshead and this is possibly one of the reasons why Gateshead has its greater share of the less attractive modern concrete buildings, than its famous city neighbour across the Tyne.

Jarrow - The Home of Bede

Despite its modern industrial appearance, Jarrow, on the south bank of the River Tyne to the east of Gateshead is one of the most historic towns in the North East of England. Its early history is centred around a humble Anglo-Saxon church dedicated to St. Paul, which overlooks the Don, a small river that joins the Tyne in the industrial surroundings of the mud flats called Jarrow slake.

St. Pauls was founded by a Northumbrian noble called Benedict Biscop, in the seventh century AD as a twin monastery for that at St. Peters Monkwearmouth. The dedication stone for the church is the oldest in the country, dating the building to the 23rd April of the year 681 AD. There are however two older churches in the North East of England at Monkwearmouth, Sunderland and Escomb, County Durham.

Biscop's Saxon monastery at Jarrow was a great centre of English learning and is famed the world over as the historic home of the Venerable Bede, (673-735 AD). Bede came to Jarrow at the age of twelve, where he was later the author of over forty scholarly works, including the 'Historia Ecclesiastica Gentis Anglorum' of AD 731.

This translates to 'The History of the English Church and People' and is a major source for the greater part of our knowledge of Anglo-Saxon England. Bede was without doubt the first historian of England and is widely regarded as the 'candle' of the period of history we call the 'Dark Ages'. The tomb of Bede can be seen in Durham Cathedral.

St. Pauls Jarrow.

South Shields

South Shields grew most rapidly in the Victorian era but its origins can be traced

back to Roman times, when it was the site of the important Roman fort called Arbeia.

Arbeia, built about AD 128 served as the sea port and supply base for Hadrian's Wall and in Roman times it was an important commercial centre with a large civilian settlement. Its Roman occupants included a small unit of barge men from the Tigris river valley (now in Iraq), who ferried troops and stores up and down the River Tyne.

The remains of the Roman fort at South Shields, can be seen today near the area of high ground called the Lawe overlooking the sea at the mouth of the Tyne. It is one of the best preserved and most extensively excavated Roman forts in Britain.

Little is known of South Shields' history in Anglo-Saxon times though evidence suggests it may have been the site of a monastery belonging to St. Hilda before she moved to Hartlepool and later Whitby.

The monastery may have stood on the site of South Shields parish church which is dedicated to St. Hilda. The name of South Shields originates from Anglo-Saxon times. Shields derives from 'Shieling' signifying a fisherman's hut.

South Shields.

Jack the Blaster and Marsden Rock

The limestone cliff formations that dominate much of the coast between Hartlepool and the River Tyne are much in evidence at Marsden to the north of Whitburn. Most notable of the limestone features is the massive Marsden Rock. This was once within jumping distance of the coast, but is now an isolated limestone stack providing a natural refuge for Kittiwakes, Cormorants and Fulmars.

Set within the coastal caves overlooking the Marsden Rock is the famous Marsden Grotto Public House. Its history begins in 1782, when an Allendale lead miner nicknamed 'Jack the Blaster' came to work in the limestone quarries at Marsden and blasted a home for himself and family out of one of the caves of Marsden Bay. Jack became known for his hospitality and his home developed into the Grotto Inn.

A Smuggler's Coast

Marsden Bay was once a frequent haunt of local smugglers, who numbered among Jack's best customers and suppliers. On one occasion the smugglers were nearly caught in the act at Marsden after one of their fraternity turned informer and passed information to the South Shields excise men regarding the landing of illegal cargo at Marsden Bay. The smugglers learned of the imminent danger of being caught and managed to warn off the vessel that was carrying the illegal merchandise. It dumped its cargo further down the coast at Souter Point near Whitburn.

When the identity of the informer was discovered by the smugglers he was hung from a bucket, inside a shaft called the Smuggler's Hole which had been bored into a cave near the Marsden Grotto. Here the poor man had to suffer the jibes of his former comrades who gluttonously feasted in front of his eyes and used him as a target for their refuse.

It is said that on cold dark stormy nights his ghostly wails can be heard above the sound of the howling winds. Smuggling took place in the vicinity of Marsden well into the nineteenth century and as late as 1851 there is a record of the capture of a cargo of 8,000 lb of contraband tobacco in the area with an estimated value of £4,000.

South Shields Salt Making

Like many other towns in the North East, coal was a major factor influencing the growth of South Shields. For over two hundred years it was used in the process of making salt and in 1768 the town was the site of 200 salt pans.

In fact South Shields was once the most important salt making town in Britain, having taken over this status from the town of Greatham near Hartlepool, which had been the 'salt making capital' in the fifteenth and sixteenth centuries - indeed salt making was the early chemical industry of Teesside and Tyneside.

For centuries the salt making gave South Shields a horrible, dense eye watering environment and the fumes from the huge salt pans could be seen clearly from Durham, and according to Daniel Defoe from the summit of the Cheviot many miles to the north.

So bad was the local atmosphere, that the wife of a local parson compared South Shields to 'Sodom and Gomorrah'. Fortunately South Shields is a much healthier place to live today.

Dance ti 'thy Daddy

"Come here me little Jacky
Now I've smok'd me backy
Let's hev a bit o' cracky
Till the boat comes in.

Dance ti' thy daddy,
My bonny laddie
Dance ti' thy daddy,
Ti' thy mammy sing;

Thou shell hev a fishy
On a little dishy
Thou shell hev a mackerel
When the boat comes in."

A Tyneside coastal song.

Press Gangs

South Shields is linked to North Shields on the north side of the Tyne by means of a ferry. North Shields is the site of a famous fish quay and the terminus of sea ferries to Norway and Holland. During the French Wars at the end of the eighteenth century North and South Shields were regular victims of Press Gang raids that were once a common occurrence on the North Eastern coast.

Tyneside suffered particularly badly from the Press Gangs, because of its large community of seamen and its reputation for skilled boatmen, like the keelmen of Newcastle upon Tyne. North Shields was particularly prone to Press Gang raids and in 1796, 250 mechanics and seamen

were pressed into service here during a raid in which the town was cordoned off by troops.

One of the naval vessels involved in the Press Gang raids was 'The Peggy' which is remembered in the name of Peggy's Hole, by the River Tyne near North Shields Fish Quay.

"Here's the Tender comin',
Pressing all the men;
Oh dear hinny,
what shall we dee then:

Here's the tender comin',
Off at Shields Bar
Here's the tender comin',
Full of men o' war.

They will ship yer foreign,
that is what it means
Here's the tender comin',
full of Red Marines.

So hide me canny Geordie,
hide yorsel' away,
Wait until the frigate
makes for Druridge Bay.

If they tyek yer Geordie,
whes te' win wor breed?
Me and little Jacky
would better off be deed."

A Tyneside press gang song.

Press Gangs were greatly feared on Tyneside as once a man had been unwillingly pressed into naval service his wife and family would have to rely on the local parish for support. Indeed the Poor Rate in those districts of Tyneside with large communities of seamen and boatmen rapidly increased following Press Gang raids.

Because of their importance to the national coal industry the keelmen of Newcastle were supposed to be exempt from the Press Gangs but even they did not escape the naval raids. The residents of Sandgate, Newcastle, home of the keelmen community, lived in constant fear of the Press Gangs of a certain Captain Bover whose men operated on the Newcastle quayside:

"Where has't the been
me canny hinny?,
Where has't the been
me winsome man?,

Aa've been te' the norrard,
Cruising back and forrard
Aa've been te' the norrard,
cruising sair and lang;

Aa've been te' the norrard,
cruising back and forrard,
But daren't come ashore
for fear of Bover and his gang."

Tynemouth

A large monument to Admiral Lord Collingwood (1750-1810) dominates the coastal scene to the east of North Shields at Tynemouth. Tyneside's most famous man of the sea, he was the second in command to Nelson at the Battle of Trafalgar in 1805.

The Admiral was opposed to the activities of the Press Gangs. Collingwood's monument overlooks the imposing Black Middens rocks at the entrance to the Tyne, which according to local folklore were thrown there by the devil in an attempt to curb the wealthy sea trade of Newcastle. Although this was never achieved, over the centuries the rocks have certainly claimed a victim of many a ship entering the mouth of the Tyne.

These dangerous rocks may have played an important part in bringing about the formation of the first ever volunteer life brigade service which was established at Tynemouth in 1869.

Tynemouth is one of the most historic and picturesque towns of Tyneside. Its two most notable buildings are a fourteenth century ruined castle and a ruined Norman priory both situated on the lofty Benebal crag, overlooking the sea.

History revolves around this part of the town where in Anglo-Saxon times there stood one of Northumbria's many coastal monasteries.

Tynemouth priory was originally built in stone by Oswald, King and saint of Northumbria in 637 AD. The site was the burial place of three notable kings, namely Osred and Oswy of Northumbria and Malcolm Canmore, King of the Scots whose body was interred here in 1094.

Tynemouth Castle.

148

Whitley Bay

Up the coast from Tynemouth, is Cullercoats, once famous as the home of Tyneside's famous fishwife fraternity. The fishwives could still be seen at the time of William Tomlinson's Guide to Northumberland of 1888 which records;

> *"Very familiar indeed is the figure of the Cullercoats fish-wife, as, clad in blue serge jacket, short petticoats with ample skirts, large apron and black straw bonnet she trudges along with a heavy creel of fish on her shoulders calling in, shrill and not unmusical tones of voice, 'Buy fee-s-ch'"*

Further to the north of Cullercoats is the town of Whitley Bay, the main seaside resort for Tyneside. The main coastal feature at Whitley Bay, is St. Mary's Isle which like a miniature version of Lindisfarne further north, is linked to the mainland by a short causeway at low tide.

St. Mary's Isle is also known as 'Bait Island' after an inhabitant of Tudor times called Thomas Bates. The island with its lighthouse is a popular picture postcard view.

Part Ten
North Tyne, Rede and Wansbeck

Morpeth

Part Ten
North Tyne, Rede and Wansbeck

The Battle of Heavenfield

Hadrian's Wall crosses the North Tyne a few miles to the north of Hexham, near the Roman fort of Chesters (Cilurnum). Most of the North Tyne valley lies entirely to the north of Hadrian's Wall.

One of Northumbria's first recorded battles, 'the Battle of Heavenfield' (635 AD), took place in the vicinity of the North Tyne, not far from where Hadrian's Wall crossed the river. Surprisingly, unlike most Northumbrian battles this was fought not between the English and the Scots, but between the Northumbrians and the Welsh, who were the great enemy of the Kingdom of Northumbria in early times.

Site of the Battle of Heavenfield.

The Welsh had formed an alliance with the Midland Kingdom of Mercia to defeat the Northumbrians. The Welsh, were led by King Cadwallon and the Mercians were led by a Pagan king called Penda.

In 635 AD the Welsh under Cadwallon, brought north a huge army into Northumbria to fight Oswald, the Northumbrian king. Oswald assembled his men for battle to the north of Hexham on high ground in the vicinity of the North Tyne, close to Hadrian's Wall. This area became known as Heavenfield.

Here they were well situated to meet the Welsh who were advancing up the old Roman road called Dere Street, which crossed the Tyne at Corbridge. Oswald placed a cross in the centre of what would become the battlefield and led his men into prayer for victory.

When the Welsh arrived in the north they were heavily exhausted from their long journey while the Northumbrians were alert and ready for the fight. Oswald's men chased the Welsh southwards into what is now called 'Hexhamshire', and their King, Cadwallon was slain on the banks of the Rowley Burn, near the valley of a stream called the Devil's Water.

Oswald believed that the victory over the Welsh confirmed his Christian faith and decided to set about converting the whole of his largely Pagan kingdom to Christianity. He employed St. Aidan, a Scottish monk from Iona, as the first Bishop of Lindisfarne and with Aidan he travelled throughout the Northumbrian kingdom preaching to the people. St. Aidan was later succeeded by many great Northumbrian saints like Cuthbert. It is therefore to Oswald that we owe the early development of Christianity in the northern part of England.

The reign of King Oswald, Northumbria's greatest king, continued until the year 642 AD when he was defeated in battle by King Penda of Mercia during an attempt to expand his Kingdom southwards. Oswestry in the midlands is said to be the place where Oswald met his death. Oswald was succeeded to the Northumbrian throne, by his brother Oswy, who later defeated the Mercians at the Battle of Winwaed in Yorkshire, where the Mercian King Penda lost his life.

Archie Armstrong's Ghost

Haughton Castle by the North Tyne, to the north of Hadrian's Wall, dates from the fourteenth century and is reputed to be haunted by Archie, a notorious clan chief of the Armstrong family who was imprisoned here during the reign of Henry VIII.

Many centuries ago a lord of Haughton castle, called Thomas Swinburne captured Armstrong and imprisoned him in the dungeon, but unfortunately, forgot to leave instruction for the provision of food and water for his prisoner.

A few days later, while attending a meeting in York, Swinburne suddenly remembered his ill-fated captive after discovering the keys to Armstrong's cell in his pocket. In panic Swinburne quickly stormed out of the meeting and mounted his horse to gallop home to Northumberland.

Swinburne was too late. When he opened the cell there Armstrong lay dead on the floor and what a horrifying sight it was, as it seemed that in desperation Armstrong had gnawed the flesh from his own arm.

For many years the ghost of Armstrong haunted the castle until it was exorcised by a local vicar, using a black lettered bible. The ghost returned to Haughton for a short time, while the bible was taken to London for binding, but when the book was returned to Northumberland, Armstrong's ghost was rarely seen again.

On the opposite bank of the North Tyne from Haughton Castle, is the village of Barrasford and a stream called the 'Swin Burn', which gave its name to the Northumbrian family called the Swinburnes. The Swinburnes lived at Great Swinburne Castle, which stood nearby. Members of this family included Algernon Charles Swinburne (1837-1909), the famous Northumbrian poet.

Not far to the north of Swinburne Castle is a farmstead with the curious name of 'Pity Me'. There are at least two places with this name in the region the other is a place near Durham City. The name of the Northumbrian Pity Me is said to derive from a corruption of Celtic words meaning 'Field of Grave's'. The Durham version is usually said to derive from the French 'Petit Mere' meaning 'small lake'. However both may simply be a reference to difficult farmland in times gone by.

Wark on Tyne

Wark on Tyne, a small North Tyne village up the valley from Haughton was once the capital of North Tynedale. Sessions of Scottish courts were at one time held here, because in the twelfth and thirteenth centuries it was the centre of the Liberty of Tynedale, which for a time belonged to the Scots. Wark and its district were in fact technically part of Scotland until 1296, when it was retaken for England by King Edward I.

Wark was once the site of a Norman motte and bailey castle, but the only remains of this today, are a large green mound. A castle probably stood here in earlier times as the Anglo-Saxon name of Wark, signifies an earthwork. In local dialect the word 'work' is still sometimes pronounced 'wark'.

Chipchase, one of the most picturesque castles in Northumberland, lies on the eastern bank of the Tyne not far from Wark. It was built around a fourteenth century pele tower in the 1700s and is one of the finest Jacobean period buildings in the County. For many years the castle was the home to a border family called the Herons, who were the Keepers of Tynedale.

Bellingham - Reiver Country

Bellingham (pronounced Bell-ing-jum), a village on the North Tyne, four miles north of Wark is regarded as the modern capital of North Tynedale. It is situated right at the heart of what was once Northumberland's Border Reiving country.

The nearby Hesleyside Hall was the home to one famous Border Reiving clan called the Charltons who derived their name from the hamlet of Charlton, to the west of Bellingham. The Charltons were one of the four main Border Reiving clans or 'Graynes' of North Tynedale. The others were the Milburns, Robsons and Dodds.

Bellingham.

The Dodd family were associated with Burnbank pele tower, which is situated in the valley of the Tarset Burn not far to the west of Bellingham. Dodds are said to be descended from Eilaf, an Anglo-Saxon monk who was one of the carriers of St. Cuthbert's Coffin at the time of the Viking raids in the 9th century.

Legend has it that Eilaf pinched some cheese from his fellow brethren, who prayed that the culprit be turned into a Dodd the Anglo-Saxon word for a fox. When the identity of the thief was revealed the monks had Eilaf turned back, but it is said that from that day on Eilaf and his descendants were known by the name of Dodd.

An old border cry regarding the Tarset Burn and the adjoining Tarret Burn was once heard in many a border fray involving North Tynedale reivers like the Dodds and Charltons:

> *"Tarset and Tarret Burn*
> *Hard and Heather Bred*
> *GYet! GYet! GYet!"*

The Legend of the 'Lang Pack'

The church at Bellingham is dedicated to St. Cuthbert and is said to have been one of the places where St. Cuthbert's body was brought to following the Viking raids on Lindisfarne in the ninth century AD.

In the churchyard of St. Cuthbert's is a long stone which marks a grave closely associated with a well known piece of North Tynedale folklore; 'the Legend of the Lang Pack'.

The story is set around Lee Hall on the banks of the North Tyne to the south of Bellingham, near to where the River Rede joins the North Tyne at Redesmouth. The hall was historically the home of the Ridley family who left their country residence each winter to reside in London. In the winter of 1723 the house was left in the care of three servants, who looked after the hall under strict instructions not to allow any guest or lodger into the house.

One afternoon that winter, a pedlar called at the hall carrying with him an unusually long package and asked if he could have shelter for the night. Remembering their master's orders the servants refused the pedlar, but when he asked if he could leave the package, while he sought shelter elsewhere, permission was granted.

As the night grew dark one of the servants, a young maid called Alice, became increasingly suspicious of the pedlar's long pack which had been left in the kitchen of the house. While lighting a candle the maid swore she saw the package move.

She quickly alerted the other two servants one called Richard and the other, a younger man called Edward. The older man scorned young Alice's suspicion, but young Edward not wishing to take any chances fetched his gun (which he called Copenhagen), and shot at the pack. To his astonishment a cry was heard and blood began to ooze from the mysterious package.

When the 'Lang Pack' was opened, the body of a dead man was found inside wearing a silver whistle around his neck.

It soon became apparent that the man had been brought to the hall as part of a plot. The plan was obvious, this man was going to break free from his package and open the door for fellow accomplices to burgle the household.

The servants realising that they were likely to be visited by the rest of the gang that night, summoned help from the neighbourhood and many locals came to Lee Hall, bringing with them their guns ready to deal with the gang.

Later that night the gang arrived and were given the signal on the whistle, but were astonished to be greeted with gunshot from the servants and locals waiting at the hall. Four of the gang immediately fell dead from their horses, the rest quickly fled.

At daylight the following morning the bodies of the four dead men had mysteriously disappeared and the Lee Hall servants were only left with the body of the unfortunate man from the 'Lang Pack'. The rest of the gang were never caught and the identity of the man from the pack remained a mystery for all time. The body was finally buried at Bellingham churchyard, where it is said to lie beneath the long stone cut in the shape of a Pedlar's pack.

Kielder

In the uppermost reaches of the River North Tyne to the east of Bellingham, we find the huge dam of Kielder Water, the largest man-made lake in Europe. The construction of the dam which is 170 feet high and three quarters of a mile wide was begun in 1976.

The lake opened in 1982 and was built to supply heavy industry and domestic users on Tyneside, Wearside and Teesside and can hold up to 44 billion gallons of water. Kielder stretches along the North Tyne Valley for about seven miles, has 27 miles of shoreline and a surface area of 2,684 acres.

Kielder Reservoir.

Water from Kielder can be released into the North Tyne, where after a journey of two days, it reaches the pumping station at Riding Mill on the River Tyne near Corbridge. From here it can be pumped through pipelines under the Durham hills and fed into the River Wear or River Tees.

Like many reservoirs in North East England it is hard to believe that Kielder Water is man-made, especially when it is viewed with your back to the dam.

The landscape of Kielder is in fact rich in natural beauty, despite the fact that it is almost entirely man made. For not only is the lake man made, but so is the countryside around it, because Kielder Water is surrounded on three sides by the huge Kielder Forest, the largest man made forest in Europe.

Kielder is naturally an important area for recreation, tourism and leisure, with water sport facilities on the reservoir for wind surfers, canoeists, water skiers, anglers and yachtsmen in addition to the visitor facilities provided by the Forestry Commission. Kielder Castle, a former hunting lodge for the Earls of Nothumberland lies to the north of the reservoir and is the main visitor centre for the Kielder area.

The England-Scotland border is only about a mile from Kielder Castle although the road north across the border does not enter Scotland for another three miles where it crosses from Tynedale into Liddesdale to the east of Deadwater Fell.

A 12 mile forest drive road begins at Kielder Castle, which runs west up the valley of the Kielder Burn towards Redesdale. The Kielder Burn is the main tributary source for the River North Tyne:

> "On Kielder side, the wind blaws wide,
> There sounds nae hunting horn,
> That rings sae sweet, as the winds that beat,
> Round banks where Tyne is born."

C.A. Swinburne, 'D.A Jacobite's Exile'.

The forest drive takes us into Redesdale, through forested and unforested sections of the southern Cheviot Hills. On its way it passes a hill called Oh Me Edge - perhaps a reminder of an old border feud.

A Very Long Place-Name

Leaving the valleys of North Tynedale and the Kielder Burn, the forest road from Kielder crosses the watershed between Tyne and Rede and follows the valley of the Blake Hope Burn into Redesdale where it crosses the River Rede, near the hamlet of Blakehopeburnhaugh.

This is said to be the longest place name in England, with eighteen letters. The name is of a an Anglo-Saxon, 'old Northumbrian' nature and means 'black valley stream, with flat riverside land'.

Blakehopeburnhaugh's status is challenged by a hamlet called Cottonshopeburnfoot (19 letters), which lies less than half a mile up the valley, but this does not qualify because the Ordnance Survey writes the name in two parts as Cottonshopeburn Foot.

Carter Bar

The valley of Redesdale has for many centuries provided an important through-route into Scotland and today it is followed by the A68 Jedburgh road into Scotland, which crosses the border six miles to the north west at Carter Bar in upper Redesdale.

Carter Bar was the scene in 1575 of the Redeswire Fray, one of the last major battles fought between the English and the Scots. The fray occurred when a violent battle broke out, following an argument between a Warden of the English Marches and the Keeper of Liddesdale, who ironically, were both employed to keep the peace on their respective sides of the border.

The meeting between these two men was meant to be a day of truce, but the arrogance of the English Warden, John Forster, aggravated the Scottish representatives and a battle ensued - the Forsters were a family with reiving traditions.

Among the Scottish contingent were members of the Crozier family and among the English, the Fenwicks of Wallington, arch-enemies of the Croziers.

This obviously gave added venom to the battle. At the end of the fray the English, who were largely unarmed, came off worst and among those killed was George Heron of Chipchase, the Keeper of Tynedale and Redesdale.

Elsdon

Although Otterburn is now regarded as the 'capital' of Redesdale, in more historic times Elsdon held that distinction, when it was an important gathering place and market town for the clans of the valley who included the Storeys, Hedleys, Dunnes, Potts, Millburns and Halls.

Elsdon and the Vicar's Pele.

The village, though pleasant and peaceful today, saw its share of rough border life in days gone by and was evidently not a great place for hospitality, as an old Northumbrian ballad records;

"Hae ye ivver been at Elsdon?
The world's unfinished neuk
It stands amang the hungry hills,
An' wears a frozen leuk.

The Elsdon folk like diein' stegs
At ivvery stranger stare;
An' hather broth an' curlew eggs,
Ye'll get for supper there.

Yen neet aw cam tiv Elsdon;
Sair tired efter dark
Aw'd trovell'd mony a lyensome meyle
Wet through the varra sark.

Maw legs were warkin' fit ta brik,
An' empty was me kite,
But nowther love nor money could
Get owther bed or bite.

At ivvery hoose iv Elsdon
Aw teld me desperate need,
But nivver a corner had the churls
Where aw might lay me heed.

Sae at the public hoose aw boos'd
Till aw was sent away;
Then tiv a steyble- loft aw crept
An' coil'd amang the hay.

Should the Frenchers land iv England
Just gie them Elsdon fare;
By George! they'll sharply hook it back,
An' nivver cum ne mair.

For a hungry hole like Elsdon
Aw nivver yit did see;
An' if aw gan back tiv Elsdon,
The De'il may carry me."

Vicar's Pele

Despite the poor image that the old rhyme creates of Elsdon in past times, it is quite an attractive village today. The most noticeable reminder of Elsdon's border history is the village Pele tower, which is one of the best examples of its kind in Northumberland. Dating from around 1400, the tower was a fortified rectory with walls 9 feet thick.

Its occupants once included the Reverend Charles Dodgson, a tutor of the Duke of Northumberland's son. He was also the Great Grandfather of Lewis Carroll. Dodgson was rector here between 1762 and 1765.

St. Cuthbert's church to the south of the vicar's pele, was the nearest graveyard to the Battle of Otterburn (1388). During church restoration in the early nineteenth century a mass grave containing the skeletons of hundreds of men and boys who died in the battle was uncovered.

Another notable feature of Elsdon are the two curious hills at the northern end of the village which mark the site of an old Motte and Bailey castle. Tomlinson's 'Guide to Northumberland' (1888) suggested that the earthworks were some kind of Celtic tribal capital at the time of the Roman occupation. There are certainly a number of ancient British camps and settlements near Elsdon.

In later times a Norman castle was built on top of these earthworks which became the home of the Umfravilles, Norman Lords of Redesdale. This family were heavily involved in many a border raid into Scotland and had a reputation which earned members of the family names like

Robin 'Mend the Market' - a reference to the destruction of Scottish towns.

Winter's Gibbet

An unclassified road from Elsdon to Wallington and Morpeth follows the course of an old drove road south eastwards, where it passes the site of Steng cross, an old medieval guiding post. Some good views of the Northumbrian border country can be obtained from this area looking north towards Harwood Forest, the Simonside Hills and the Cheviots, and south towards the Wild Hills of Wannie where the River Wansbeck rises.

Winter's Gibbet.

In the vicinity of Steng Cross, near to the roadside is the eerie site of a gibbet or 'stob', as the Northumbrians call them. Known as Winter's Gibbet it was from this that the body of a certain William Winter was hung, following his execution at Westgate, Newcastle in 1791. Winter, a gypsy had been executed for the murder of an old woman called

Margaret Crozier who lived in the vicinity of Elsdon.

The old woman ran a small drapery store in the neighbourhood which led Winter to believe she was wealthy. He murdered her after breaking into her home to find that she had little worth stealing. He seems to have been a rather desperate character as he had not long returned from transportation. His family did have a history of crime as both his father and brother also died by execution.

Winter's body was returned to the Elsdon area following his execution in accordance with an old custom that murderer's corpses should be displayed near the scene of their crime.

The site of the body hanging from the gibbet is said to have haunted a young shepherd boy by the name of Robert Hindmarch, who at the age of eleven, had given the evidence which largely convicted Winter. Hindmarch's life was dominated by a constant fear of reprisals from Winter's friends and this probably led to his early death at the age of twenty two.

For a time the morbid site of Winter's body drew sightseers from all around until the stench from the corpse became so bad that people began to avoid using the road that passed that way.

Eventually the corpse was taken down and buried, but was replaced with a carved wooden effigy of Winter, of which only the head now remains. This gives the gibbet the curious appearance of an incomplete game of hangman.

In the last century the gibbet was viewed with considerable superstition, with one of the strangest claims being that chips taken from it had the magical ability to cure toothache.

The Battle of Otterburn

Otterburn, the main village in the Rede valley, is famous the world over as the site of the Battle of Otterburn, which was fought to the north west of the village on the 19th August 1388. This battle was the bloodiest and best known encounter between those great arch enemies of the Borders, the Percys of Northumberland and the Douglases of Scotland.

The Scots, under the leadership of Earl James Douglas, invaded northern England with an army of some 4,000 men and ravaged the Northumberland and Durham countryside as far south as Brancepeth in Durham. Hamlets and villages were left burning and many of the local inhabitants were slain, though some fled to safety, taking refuge behind the walled defences of Durham City and Newcastle.

The region had been largely unprepared for this Scottish attack, though Harry 'Hotspur' Percy, the Earl of Northumberland's son, was at Newcastle ready to repel any Scottish attack upon that town.

The Scottish raid led by Douglas is commemorated in a lengthy Border Ballad recorded by Sir Walter Scott:

"It fell about the Lammas tide,
When the muir-men win their hay,
The doughty Douglas bound him to ride
Into England to drive a prey.

He chose the Gordons and the Grahams,
With the Lindsays, light and gay;
But the Jardines wald not with him ride,
And they rue it to this day.

And he has burn'd the dales of Tyne,
And part of Bamburgh Shire;
And three good towers on Redeswire fells,
He left them all on fire."

As the 'auld enemy' were returning from County Durham there was only a minor skirmish at Newcastle although Douglas is said to have challenged the Percys to battle. Hotspur responded to the challenge and warned Douglas he would not leave England alive.

The ballad of Otterburn records the visit of Douglas to Newcastle;

"And he march'd up to Newcastle,
And rode it round about;
'O wha's the lord of this castle,
And wha's the lady o't?'

But up spake proud Lord Percy, then,
And O but he spake hie!
'I am the lord of this castle,
My wife's the lady gay'

'If thou'rt the lord of this castle,
Sae well it pleases me!
For, ere I cross the Border fells,
The ane of us shall die'."

Crossing the Tyne near Newcastle, the Scots continued northwards burning the castle of Ponteland on their way, as they headed for Redesdale. Here they took up camp on the site of an ancient British hill-fort near Otterburn. Meanwhile Hotspur's army had increased in size and he marched north into Redesdale, arriving at Otterburn in the late evening of 19th August 1388.

With chants of A Percy! A Percy! Hotspur's contingent made their onslaught on the Scottish camp, but their shock and horror can be imagined when they discovered that in the confusion of darkness, they were not raiding the main camp, but instead a small encampment of Scottish servants and camp followers, who nevertheless still fought back.

Hotspur's mistake alerted Douglas and for a time the Scots were easily winning the battle but in his excitement Douglas pushed too hard and three spears pierced his body bringing wounds to his head and thigh. He fell from his horse and lay dying as the battle continued all around him. According to the Otterburn ballad, he told his men he had foreseen his fate:

"But I hae dream'd a dreary dream
Beyond the isle of Skye
I saw a dead man win a fight
And I think that man was I."

And so it was that the Scots gradually regained control of the battle. Many Englishmen were captured or slain and many of Percy's men fled. Douglas was by this time dead.

Despite the loss of their leader, the outcome of the Battle of Otterburn was a decisive victory for the Scots, who lost only two hundred men compared to English losses of over a thousand.

Hotspur was taken prisoner but later released for a ransom.

Sweethope Loughs and the Wild Hills O' Wannie

The road south from Elsdon and Steng cross in Redesdale, takes us to Kirkwhelpington, Wallington Hall and the upper reaches of the River Wansbeck, 20 miles north west of Newcastle upon Tyne.

Kirkwhelpington lies by the Wansbeck river, close to the A696, Newcastle to Jedburgh road in the vicinity of the Wild Hills O' Wannie. These hills take their name from the River Wansbeck and are the subject of a haunting Northumbrian pipe tune. The 'Beck' in Wansbeck has nothing to do with the Viking word for a stream as the name Wansbeck derives from the Anglo-Saxon 'Waeganspick' possibly meaning 'wagon bridge'.

Up the Wansbeck valley to the west is the Great Wanny Crag, site of one of Northumberland's many ancient forts to the north of the Sweeethope Loughs. These lakes form the source of the River Wansbeck.

St. Bartholemew's church at Kirkwhelpington, was the place where the Reverend John Hodgson wrote the greater part of his classic seven volume History of Northumberland between 1823 and 1832. The village is also noted as the burial place of Charles Algernon Parsons, (1854 - 1931), inventor of the steam turbine engine.

Capability Brown Country

To the south of Kirkwhelpington, is Kirkharle, birthplace of Lancelot Brown the landscape gardener, (1716 - 1783), famously known as 'Capability' Brown. He acquired this name from his usual saying when presented with a new plot of land that 'it has capabilities'.

Brown began his career as a gardener on the Kirkharle estates, where he learnt his trade before leaving Northumberland in 1739. He went on to become the head gardener at Windsor and at Hampton Court and played a major part in laying out the famous gardens at Kew and Blenheim Palace.

Wallington Hall

Along the Wansbeck valley to the east of Kirkwhelpington we find Wallington Hall one of the finest old houses in Northumberland. It was built in 1688, around the foundations of an old Pele Tower belonging to the Fenwicks, who were the principal Border clan of south east Northumberland. When the Hall was built in 1688 for Sir William Blackett, a man with coal mining and shipbuilding interests, the old pele tower was incorporated into the new building.

In 1777 Wallington Hall passed into the hands of the Trevelyan family and through them it became associated with three of the greatest British historians: G. M Trevelyan, George Otto Trevelyan and George Macaulay. The desk at which Macaulay wrote his 'History of England' is in the Wallington study.

Wallington Hall.

Wallington Hall has been in the care of the National Trust since 1942 and is most notable for its interesting furniture, pictures and fine plaster work.

For many the biggest attraction at Wallington are the eight large wall paintings by Sir William Bell Scott, which depict scenes from Northumbrian history. Beautifully painted with fascinating details, the subjects are: The building of Hadrian's Wall, St. Cuthbert on Farne Island, The Viking invasion of Tynemouth, The death of the Venerable Bede, The Spur in the Dish, Bernard Gilpin at Rothbury church, Grace Darling's Sea Rescue and a Tyneside industrial scene.

The subject of the 'Spur in the Dish' depicts the Charlton Border Reiving clan assembled for lunch in their home at Hesleyside Hall, in North Tynedale. The lady of the house has brought in a salver and dish for her hungry husband and his

retainers, but the salver has been lifted to reveal not the expected Sunday joint, but instead the dish contains a riding spur.

This is an illustration of an old border custom, most strongly associated with the Charltons. The lady is giving a subtle hint to the men of the household that the larder is almost empty and that they must ride and steal some cattle or sheep if they want to be fed.

The estate grounds of Wallington Hall, which were partly laid out by Capability Brown, are the site of four curious stone gargoyle or griffin heads. Originating from Old Aldersgate in London, they were brought to the North East as ballast in one of Sir Wiliam Blackett's ships, which worked between London and Newcastle.

A mile to the north of Wallington Hall is the village of Cambo, built in 1740 as a model village for Wallington Estate workers. Capability Brown went to school here.

Morpeth - The County Town

The Wansbeck valley leads us to Morpeth, the County town of Northumberland, which lies fifteen miles to the north of Newcastle upon Tyne.

Situated within a U-shaped bend of the River Wansbeck, Morpeth grew in importance as a coaching stop and market town on the Great North Road between London and Edinburgh. The name of the town could in fact take its name from this road, which leads north across the moors, as the name is said to derive from 'moor path'. An alternative suggestion is that it derives from 'Murder Path', which is not unlikely when we consider the bloody border history of Northumberland.

Like many Northumbrian towns Morpeth suffered regularly at the hands of Scottish attacks, although when the town was sacked and burned in 1216 it was King John of England and not the Scots who were responsible. This raid on the town followed disagreements between the king and local barons.

Morpeth.

Morpeth was never a walled town like Newcastle or Berwick, but it did once have a castle, of which only the mound remains at the Ha' Hill overlooking the town's park. The castle was occupied by the Scots under General Lesley during the Civil War, when a garrison of 500 Scots held out against the Royalists for twenty days.

In 1715 Morpeth was involved in the first Jacobite Rising, in which most Northumbrians supported the attempt to put James Stuart, the 'Old Pretender' on the throne. Supporters of the Jacobites did not include the 'Geordies' of Newcastle who supported the claim of King George.

The centre of Morpeth is dominated by the town hall and the fifteenth century clock tower, which stands in the centre of the street called Oldgate. This street is the site of Collingwood House, where the famous Northumbrian sailor, Admiral Lord Collingwood (1750-1810) once lived.

For a county town Morpeth is fairly small, with a population of around 20,000, but perhaps its size is not surprising, for the most thinly populated county in England. Most of Northumberland's population is concentrated in a number of small towns between Morpeth and Newcastle upon Tyne, that is within that south eastern portion of the county which once formed part of the Great Northern Coalfield. Many of the towns in this part of Northumberland, have coal mining origins such as Blyth, Bedlington and Ashington, while others such as Ponteland, Darras Hall and Cramlington have grown mainly as modern dormitory suburbs of Newcastle upon Tyne.

A Suicidal Suffragette

St, Mary's, the parish church of Morpeth, is unusual in that the churchyard has a watchtower, built in the 1830s to guard against bodysnatchers. The churchyard is also notable in that it contains the grave of Emily Wilding Davison (born 1872), the suffragette who threw herself in front of the King's horse at Epsom on Derby Day, 1913.

Miss Davison, who was from Longhorsley, to the north of Morpeth, died four days after her suicidal feat. Her body was brought to Morpeth for burial, where her funeral was treated as quite an event, with many suffragettes attending.

During her campaigns as a suffragette Emily Davison had been imprisoned several times, had been force fed and once locked herself in her cell only to be flooded out by a magistrate using a hose pipe. On one occasion she had attempted to disrupt the House of Commons and once even managed to brutally whip an unfortunate church minister, whom she had mistaken for Lloyd George.

Part Eleven
Rothbury, Alnwick and Wooler

Rothbury

Part Eleven
Rothbury, Alnwick and Wooler

Ancient Sites and Stones

The A697 road from Morpeth takes us 8 miles north to Weldon Bridge, where it crosses Northumberland's longest river, the River Coquet, to the east of Rothbury:

"At Weldon Bridge ther's wale o' wine
If ye hae coin in pocket
If ye can thraw a heckle fine
Ther's wale o' trout in coquet."

Rothbury, the capital of Coquetdale derives its name from Anglo-Saxon, times when it was called Routh Biria meaning 'Routha's Place, but the history of the surrounding district goes back into even earlier times, as proved by the evidence of numerous ancient camps, cairns and stones, in the neighbouring countryside.

Most notable of the ancient sites, is the prehistoric fort of Lordenshaws, which is situated at the junction of four ancient trackways. It was probably an important cult centre, judging by the number of mysterious unexplained cup and ring markings in the area (these can also be seen at Doddington Moor near Wooler and in Teesdale, County Durham).

Other ancient sites in the Rothbury area include 'Old Rothbury', a notable promontory fort on Tosson Hill, to the north west, and the nearby Westhill

Camp. There are also a number of ancient hut circles and barrows on Debdon and Whitfield Moors to the north of the town.

Bernard Gilpin at Rothbury

Though an attractive and peaceful little place today, Rothbury was in times gone by a typically rough border town, as William Tomlinson records in his Guide to Northumberland (1888);

"The people of Rothbury in former times were among the wildest and most uncivilised in the county. For fighting, gaming and drinking they had a worse reputation than the inhabitants of Tynedale and Redesdale. Very little regard had the good folk of Rothbury for the laws and their love of venison frequently led them into trouble."

Religion did not have a particularly strong influence in Rothbury and other parts of the Border country, in days gone by and preachers tended to avoid the area, particularly in winter when the Northumbrian weather was regarded as almost as inhospitable as the rough border folk themselves.

Rothbury.

It was avoided by all that is, except one Bernard Gilpin, the sixteenth century rector of Houghton-le-Spring in County Durham, who deliberately set out for Northumberland each winter, to evangelize among the border peoples earning himself the unofficial title 'Apostle of the North'.

Gilpin was respected and somewhat feared by the dalesmen of Tyne, Rede and Coquet, so much so that on one occasion a mosstrooper stole Gilpin's horses, but immediately returned them when he discovered the identity of the owner, for fear that the devil would seize him.

Rothbury church was one of the places in which Gilpin would frequently preach and it was here on one occasion that two rival gangs began threatening each other, with clashing weapons while Gilpin was giving a sermon. It seemed as though they were about to embark on a pitched battle inside the church. Gilpin reacted quickly, and bravely stepping between them, asked the gangs to reconcile. The two surprised factions agreed to refrain from violence, so long as Gilpin remained in their presence.

Another famous story regarding Bernard Gilpin at Rothbury church, is the subject of one of William Bell Scott's paintings at Wallington Hall, near Morpeth.

While preaching one Sunday morning, Gilpin observed a glove hanging up in the church and asked the Sexton what it was for. The Sexton told Gilpin that it was meant as a challenge to anyone who removed it. Gilpin asked the Sexton to take the glove down, but he not surprisingly refused, fearing for his life.

Gilpin therefore removed it himself, placed it in his breast pocket and continued with his sermon against the evil ways of his congregation. For some reason no one had the courage to challenge Bernard Gilpin.

Cragside

The most popular attraction of the Rothbury area is undoubtedly Cragside House and its 1200 acre parkland estate to the north, which is owned by the National Trust. Cragside was largely the creation of William, the First Lord Armstrong (1810-1900), the famous Victorian Engineer, gun maker and inventor.

A scientific 'magician' and also a powerful industrialist, Armstrong's life and lifestyle are almost like a history of the Victorian age. It is not surprising that his house at Cragside is often described as a shrine to Victoriana.

Cragside was first built between 1864 and 1866 as a small modest hunting lodge located on the craggy moors overlooking Rothbury,

In 1869 Armstrong employed the Scottish architect Richard Norman Shaw, to transfer this building into the magnificent 'fairytale' house we see today, its appearance earning it a comparison to a wizard's palace.

Cragside.

Armstrong also transformed the land around the house into a beautiful wooded park with lakes and pleasant walks. The lakes served a functional, as well as an aesthetic purpose as Armstrong used some of them to create hydro-electricity. Indeed Cragside, was the first house in the world to be lit by electricity derived from water power. Cragside also had a kitchen spit and two elevators operated hydraulically. Armstrong was a man before his time.

The Druid's Stone

The River Coquet rises in the Cheviot Hills, many miles to the west of Rothbury, on the England Scotland border, near the remote Roman camp at Chew Green to the north of Redesdale. From here it winds its way eastwards through some of the remotest scenery in the region and is joined by a number of side valley streams called 'Hope Burns' and by the River Alwin at Alwinton (pronounced Alenton), nine miles to the west of Rothbury.

Near to Alwinton we find the Village of Harbottle, the site of a ruined castle, once owned by the Umfraville family.

The castle was an important part of the defences of the English border and was for many years the headquarters for the Wardens of the English Middle March. These men were responsible for maintaining peace, law and order in the turbulent days of Border warfare.

On the Harbottle Hills overlooking Harbottle village to the south, is the tiny Harbottle Lough and nearby a thirty feet high sandstone rock called the Dragon stone or Draag stone. This was once associated with Black Magic and ancient Druidic rites. Even in relatively recent times children were passed over the rock to cure them from sickness.

The Harbottle Hills do seem to be steeped in legend and superstition, for it is said there was once a plan to drain the Harbottle Lough, but the idea was abandoned after the workmen fled, upon hearing some mysterious, unseen person speak out against their actions:

> *"Let alone, let alone*
> *Or a'll droon Harbottle*
> *And the Peels*
> *And the Bonny Holystone."*

The Holy Well of Holystone

The village of Holystone (sometimes pronounced Halystane in the local dialect), is on the south side of the Coquet, to the east of Harbotttle.

It is said to be the place where in the Easter of 627 AD, the Roman missionary, Paulinus baptised 3000 Anglo-Saxons, including the Northumbrian King, Edwin.

The site of the baptism is said to be marked by the ancient Lady's Well, now looked after by the National Trust.

The well consists of a spring fed pool, at the centre of which stands a Celtic style cross dedicated to St. Paulinus.

The Holy Well, Holystone.

Like many parts of Coquetdale, Holystone has its share of ancient remains, such as a Roman road linking Dere Street and the Devil's Causeway, to the north of the village, and five standing stones to the south called the 'Five Kings', which form a line forty six feet in length.

Alnwick Seat of the Percys

Ten miles north of Rothbury is Alnwick, one of Northumberland's most attractive towns. Pronounced 'Annick', the town grew as a crossing point on the River Aln. Its Anglo-Saxon name Aln-Wick simply means farm on the Aln.

Throughout its history Alnwick was very much a border town, with an important castle and town walls. The main reminder of the old town walls today is the Hotspur tower gate, the narrow arch of which straddles Alnwick's main

thoroughfare called Bondgate, causing a historic inconvenience for modern traffic.

Hotspur Gate, Alnwick.

The street changes its name from 'Bondgate Without' to 'Bondgate Within', as it passes through the arch. The Hotspur tower dates from the fifteenth century and commemorates the name of that famous warlike member of the Percy family, nicknamed Harry 'Hotspur'.

It was one of four gateways to Alnwick, the others were the Clayport Gate, Pottergate and Narrowgate.

Alnwick Castle from the River Aln.

The Farmer's Folly

One of the most imposing reminders of the Percy family in Alnwick is an eighty three feet high Percy Tenantry Column which is known locally as the Farmers Folly. The column designed by the Newcastle architect David Stephenson was constructed in 1816 and lies close to the southern end of the street called Bondgate - Without. It is one of the first sights to greet the visitor to Alnwick from the south.

Legend is that the second Duke of Northumberland (a Percy) lowered the rents of his agricultural tenants by twenty-five per cent to help them through the period of agricultural depression which followed the Napoleonic Wars.

It is said that the tenants were so grateful to the Duke that they erected the great column in his honour - topped of course by a stone statue of the famous Percy Lion which had been the emblem of the Percy family for centuries.

But the story is that the Duke, far from showing gratitude for the monument to his honour was more interested in the fact that his tenants had been able to raise the money for the monument. His apparent reaction was to raise the rents once more. The story is only a legend.

The Dread of Scottish Kings

Not far to the north west of Alnwick castle are the extensive grounds of Hulne Park, where there are the remains of both a priory and an abbey. The grounds were mainly landscaped by Capability Brown and feature some of his finest work in his home county.

At the entrance to the park is the William the Lion stone, which marks the point where that king of Scotland, was captured while besieging Alnwick in 1174. He was not the first Scottish king to fall unlucky at Alnwick, for less than a mile to the north of the town near Alnwick's Lion bridge is Malcolm's Cross, marking the place where King Malcolm Canmore, (1057-1093) was killed during an invasion of England.

Till or Breamish?

From Alnwick and Hulne Park, a road leads north west, across Eglingham Moor, towards Chillingham and Wooler. The road passes through the village of Eglingham, which in typical Northumbrian fashion is pronounced 'Egling jum'.

There are also villages called Ellingham and Edlingham to the north and south of here, which are both pronounced in the same manner. Chillingham is pronounced in the normal English way.

Chillingham, is the small estate village for Chillingham Castle, which lies to the east of the River Till. This river is unique to North East England in having two names, for in its upper stretches it is called the River Breamish (not to be confused with Beamish). The name change, takes place a few miles to the

south of Chillingham, near a place called Bewick (not to be confused with Berwick), where according to tradition:

*"Foot of Breamish and head of Till,
Meet together at Bewick mill."*

Chillingham Castle and Cattle

Chillingham Castle is a fourteenth century four corner towered building, constructed around an old pele tower. The castle is noted for its dungeon which lies below the north eastern tower of the building. It now displays some rather gruesome (no longer used) implements of punishment including a stretching rack, a bed of nails, a nailed barrel and a spiked chair labelled with a warning not to sit on it because 'it is very old and easily damaged'.

Perhaps Chillingham's resident ghost known as the 'Radiant Boy' was a victim of dungeon punishment. He was regularly seen at the castle until the bones of a child were discovered buried within the walls of one of the bed-rooms in an earlier century. The bones were removed and buried in a nearby churchyard.

Chillingham is certainly one of Northumberland's most impressive buildings but perhaps the castle is best known for the herd of wild cattle, which have inhabited its grounds for seven hundred years.

The Chillingham Cattle are the purest surviving native wild white cattle in Britain and are descended from the British wild ox, which roamed the forested hills of northern Britain as early as the Bronze Age.

When Chillingham Castle's parkland estate was enclosed in 1220, a wandering herd of the wild cattle are said to have been trapped within the grounds, where they were left without any interference from livestock breeders. Another explanation for their existence at Chillingham is that the beasts were deliberately kept there as a food supply for the castle.

They had an advantage over domesticated beasts in that because of their wild nature, they could not be easily stolen by the cattle thieving Border Reivers and mosstroopers, who inhabited Northumberland in days gone by.

Today the cattle can still be seen roaming the 365 acre walled parkland of the Chillingham estate. They may however only be viewed at certain times in the accompaniment of the keeper, and then only from a safe distance. They are creamy white in colour with curved horns, are quite shy, potentially dangerous and are ruled over by a king bull, in the same way as wild deer. The king bull keeps his status until challenged and defeated by a younger male.

The Chillingham Cattle were studied by Thomas Bewick (1753-1828), the famous Northumbrian born, naturalist and engraver, who on one occasion while painting a portrait of a Chillingham bull, was chased by the beast and forced to climb a tree for refuge. Here he gained a perfect close up view of his furious subject down below.

On the 17th October 1872, Chillingham was visited by Edward the Prince of Wales, who looking for a bit of 'sport' decided to take a chance at shooting the king bull of the Chillingham herd.

Concealing himself in a hay cart the prince shot dead the bull, from a distance of seventy yards. His exploits do not seem to have impressed the locals, including one local poet called Robert Elliott, who wrote:

> "He's a warrior ye knaa
> and the papers are full
> Iv a terrible encoonter
> he had wiv a bull!
> He slowtered the bull,
> but his critics will say
> That the prince was concealed
> in a bundle iv hay;
> An' thit it was ne
> feat at a' te lie hid;
> An' slowter the bull
> in the way that he did;
> But some folks are selfish,
> an' winna hear tell
> Iv ony greet feats
> unless done by thorsel."

Overlooking the grounds of Chillingham Castle, on a hill-top, not far to the south, are the remains of a much older fortress called Ross Castle, a promontory dating from Iron Age times.

Good views of the Northumbrian countryside can be obtained from Ross Castle encompassing Alnwick, Lindisfarne, the Farne Islands, Bamburgh Castle, Dunstanburgh Castle and the Cheviot Hills, including views of Hedgehope Hill (2,348 feet) and The Cheviot itself (2,676 ft).

Wooler - Gateway to the Cheviots

Wooler in Glendale, a small market town and popular centre for touring the Cheviots is situated by a large stream called the Wooler Water and lies at the junction of a number of major roads into north Northumberland and Scotland. The Wooler Water, (part of which is also known as 'Happy Valley'), is a tributary of the River Till and is formed by a confluence of the Harthope and Carey Burns which rise in the Cheviot Hills, to the south of Wooler. The Harthope valley, formed by a geological fault, cuts its way between the Cheviot and Hedgehope Hill and is the site of the remote Harthope Linn waterfall. Good views can be obtained from this remote and beautiful Cheviot valley.

Mysterious Markings

Milfield Plain is enclosed on all sides, by the high ground of Doddington Moor in the east and by the Cheviot foothills to the west. This higher ground, surrounding the plain, is littered with the remains of many ancient sites, associated with the Welsh speaking ancient Britons and other earlier peoples.

Doddington Moor is particularly rich in ancient sites, especially in the vicinity of the hill called Dod Law, and also near the waterfall called Roughting Linn, further to the north. Most notable of the ancient sites is the 'Ringses Camp', on the hills less than a mile to the east of the village of Doddington.

Mysterious markings.

The Ringses camp seems to be a focal point for the mysterious Cup and Ring Markings, which are in abundance hereabouts.

The markings, which are found on rocks and stones, consist of dug out cup shapes and concentric rings. Northumberland seems to have the highest concentration of these in the country. Their ancient purpose is unknown.

Battle of Humbleton Hill

North west of Wooler, a road leads us into the valley of Glendale, passing the site of the Battle of Humbleton Hill. Here on the 13th August 1402, Harry 'Hotspur' Percy defeated and captured Earl Archibold Douglas, who was returning to Scotland with an army of ten thousand men, following a raid on Northumberland. The Scots had taken up position on the slopes of the hill, but were heavily defeated by the superior skills of the English archers.

Hotspur was not given much credit for his victory by King Henry IV, who arrogantly claimed the ransom money for the release of the Scottish prisoners. This snub infuriated Percy and it was probably this that eventually led the great Northumbrian warrior into rebellion against the King. A rebellion that ultimately resulted in Hotspur's death at the Battle of Shrewsbury in 1403.

Yeavering Bell

The best known feature of Glendale, to the west of Wooler (the Glen is a tributary of the Till), is the distinctive outline of the hill called Yeavering Bell (1,182 ft). Its summit, is the site of a large Iron Age Fort. Here there are the remains of 130 ancient huts. Good views of the Northumbrian countryside can be obtained from the top of Yeavering Bell,

as described in Tomlinson's 'Guide to Northumberland':

"Famous hills plains, rivers, castles, villages, pele towers and battlefields lie stretched like a beautiful picture before the delighted gaze".

At the foot of Yeavering Bell once stood the Royal Anglo-Saxon Palace called Ad Gefrin. Excavated in 1955, the building consisted of timber halls and defensive works. It is most closely associated with Edwin, the 6th century King of Northumbria. Ad Gefrin was later replaced by another Royal palace called Melmin, which was situated in Milfield Plain nearby.

Site of Yeavering Palace.

A Christian Debate

King Edwin's Palace at Yeavering, is sometimes associated with the debate in which the King and his senior followers, made the decision to convert from Paganism to Christianity.

In the 'History of the English Church and People' written only a century later by the Venerable Bede, details of a speech are recorded in which one of Edwin's heathen followers speaks out in favour of converting to Christianity.

The speech seems to give us an insight into the Anglo-Saxon mind:

> *"Your majesty, when we compare the present life of man on earth with that time of which we have no knowledge, it seems to me like the swift flight of a single sparrow through the banqueting-hall where you are sitting at dinner on a winter's day with your thanes and counsellors. In the midst there is a comforting fire to warm the hall; outside, the storms of winter rain or snow are raging. This sparrow flies swiftly in through one door of the hall, and out through another. While he is inside, he is safe from the winter's storms; but after a few moments of comfort, he vanishes from sight into the wintry world from which he came. Even so, man appears on earth for a little while; but of what went before this life or of what follows, we know nothing. Therefore, if this new teaching has brought any more certain knowledge, it seems only right that we should follow it."*

Not a great deal is known of Yeavering's history following Anglo-Saxon times, though in 1415 it was the site of a little known battle in which an army led by Robin 'Mend the Market' Umfraville, defeated 4,000 Scots.

Further up the Glendale valley is the village of Kirknewton to the north west of Yeavering Bell. Kirknewton's church is famous as the home of a strange Anglo-

Saxon carving depicting three wise men wearing kilts. They are known as the 'Kilted Magi'.

Kirknewton lies at the head of the River Glen, which is formed by the confluence of the wild valleys of the College Burn and Bowmont Water. Most of the latter stream lies on the northern side of the border and passes through the Scottish town of Kirk Yetholm, at the northern terminus of the long distance footpath called the Pennine Way. In days gone by Yetholm was associated with a family called the Faas, who were the principal Gypsy clan of the Border Country.

Till Meets Tweed

The River Glen is a tributary of the River Till which in turn is the only English tributary of the Scottish River Tweed. The meeting of the waters of the Northumbrian Till and Scottish Tweed is commemorated by a delightful piece of local folklore:

> *"Tweed said to Till*
> *'What gars ye rin sae stil?'*
>
> *Says Till to Tweed,*
> *Though ye rin wi' speed*
> *And I rin slaw*
> *Whar ye droon yin man*
> *I droon twa."*

Norham and the Shire

Norham on Tweed to the north of Tillmouth, is on the English side of the River Tweed near Berwick and the site of the northernmost castle in England. The ruins of the keep and its surrounding walls, are all that remain of this fortress, which

178

was once the chief border stronghold of the Prince Bishops of Durham.

Norham Castle.

First built by Bishop Ranulf Flambard in 1160, for many years it was thought virtually impregnable. It withstood many a siege by Scottish kings, including Robert the Bruce, but in 1513 the castle was partly wrecked by James IV prior to the Battle of Flodden. From then on it fell into disrepair.

The castle has seen much history, for here Anthony Bek, Bishop of Durham (1284-1311), entertained Edward I King of England while Edward decided who should become the next king of Scotland. It was here that the chosen John De Balliol paid homage to Edward, to the fury of Robert the Bruce.

Norham Castle has a close association with Sir William Marmion, who later became one of the many heroes of Flodden. Sir Walter Scott's poem 'Marmion' is named after this knight, its opening lines feature Norham:

> *"Day set on Norham's castled steep,*
> *And Tweed's fair river, broad and deep,*
> *And Cheviot's mountain lone;*
> *The loophole grates where captives weep,*
> *The flanking walls that round it sweep,*
> *In yellow lustre shone."*

The attractive village of Norham, was until 1836, the capital of a district called 'Norhamshire', an outlying part of the County Palatinate of Durham belonging to the 'Prince Bishops'. The district was included in Bishop Pudsey's Boldon Buke of 1183 - County Durham's equivalent of the Domesday Book.

Norham's church of St. Cuthbert, though now a largely nineteenth century structure was originally founded in 830 AD by Eadfrith, Bishop of Lindisfarne. It had been built to house the remains of a converted Christian Northumbrian King called Ceolwulph, to whom the Venerable Bede dedicated his history of England. The church was rebuilt in Norman times, by Bishop Flambard of Durham.

Norham Church.

The Legend of the Garter

In the turbulent days of Border history, the village of Wark on Tweed on the English side of the river seven miles south west of Norham was regularly a front line victim of Scottish attacks:

> *"Auld Wark on Tweed.*
> *Has been many a man's dede."*

Today we are reminded of this village's violent past by the scant remains of a 12th century motte and bailey castle, which was besieged no fewer than eleven times between 1136 and 1523. The castle is associated with a notable legend.

In 1346 it was defended by the attractive Countess of Salisbury against a party of raiding Scots, when King Edward III came north to her rescue and drove the raiders home. To celebrate the English success the Countess held a hearty victory celebration during which it is said she accidentally dropped her garter. The King immediately responded by retrieving the garter with his sword placing it around his leg and shouting the words:

'Honi Soit Qui Mal Y Pense'

Meaning 'evil be to him who evil thinks', the phrase subsequently became the motto of a great British tradition - the Order of the Garter.

The Battle of Carham

To the west of Wark the England-Scotland border leaves the course of the Tweed, near the village of Carham from where it heads south west through the imposing natural boundary of the Cheviots. At Carham the border is not naturally defined and historically Carham was at a highly exposed part of the border. It is perhaps not surprising that Carham gives its name to a very important battle.

The Battle of Carham occurred in the year 1018, and was fought by Malcolm II King of Scotland against the Northumbrians under the leadership of

their Earl Uchted, who levied all Northumbrian men north of the Tees. Northumbria was easily defeated as it was no longer the huge northern kingdom it had been.

The outcome of the battle had an important result as it established the River Tweed as the Anglo-Scottish boundary. Until this time Northumbria's boundaries had extended beyond the River Tweed towards Edinburgh and the Lothians. We are still reminded of this fact by a predominance of Anglo-Saxon place names in Scotland between the Tweed and the Forth.

The Battle of Flodden Field

The Battle of Flodden Field took place eight miles north west of Wooler near Branxton on the 9th September 1513 during the reign of Henry VIII. In 1513 England was at war with France and the Queen of that country persuaded James IV of Scotland to assist.

On the 22nd August James crossed the Tweed at Coldstream entering England with 60,000 to 100,000 men who burned the fortress of Norham and the castles of Ford and Etal. James made Ford Castle his headquarters.

Thomas Howard, Earl of Surrey, was in charge of England's defence, while Henry VIII was fighting in France. Surrey marched to Durham and prayed at the shrine of St. Cuthbert before continuing north to Newcastle where he was joined by the men of Northumberland and Durham.

Other additions to the English army included a regiment of archers under Sir Edward Stanley and the men of the Lord Admiral, Thomas Howard, Surrey's eldest son. Marching north Surrey's men continued north to Wooler.

James moved his headquarters to the western side of the River Till where he set up camp on Flodden Hill. Here the English sent a messenger challenging the Scots to a battle on Milfield Plain but the Scots refused to vacate their advantageous position.

On the drizzly morning of Friday 9th September, 1513 the English assembled for battle and in two parties made their way north, along the eastern flank of the Till. The rearguard crossed the river by a ford while the vanguard crossed further north at Twizell Bridge.

James could see the English but decided against attacking them at this vulnerable stage. Instead he ordered the burning of camp refuse, creating a dense wall of smoke that temporarily blocked out the English view of his movements.

When the smoke cleared the Scots had moved their position north to Branxton Hill. It is worth noting that the Battle of Flodden, was known for many centuries as the 'Battle of Branxton'.

It was an important move since the English could well have planned to occupy Branxton Hill. Now all that lay between them and the Scots was flat land. This meant that when the English attacked they had to fight up hill. The Scots could charge down the slope against their enemy.

Before the English could contemplate battle they had to cross a large marshy area formed by a tributary of the Till. James thought this would tire the English but the English crossed the marsh by means of Branxton Bridge, a feature unknown to James. The English assembled in a field at the foot of Branxton Hill with the Scots looking down upon them.

Battle at the Bottom of Branxton Hill

When the Scots opened fire, the inexperience of their gunmen was apparent. Unable to handle their cumbersome artillery the Scots missed their targets while the English fired back with great precision. The Scottish guns and gunmen were blown to pieces.

James noticed a weakness in the right wing of the English army and ordered the Scottish left wing, composed mainly of Scottish borderers, under the leadership of Lord Home, to attack.

Home's men went charging down the hill towards the English right wing, causing most of the English wing to flee. Fortunately for the English, Lord Dacre and the English borderers appeared on the scene and engaged themselves in a battle with their Scottish counterparts.

James was excited by the scene and was impatient to get involved with the action. He impulsively led his Scottish centre charging down the hill towards the English centre. The English stood their ground and greeted the charge with an onslaught of arrows.

At the base of the hill the Scottish charge was considerably slowed down and almost brought to a halt by an unexpected ridge and boggy area at the foot of the hill. This was a stroke of luck for the English, for it meant that the Scottish charge had lost is momentum. A fierce battle now began at the base of the hill.

Battle at Branxton Hill Top

Now only the Scottish right wing and English left wings were not engaged in battle. This time the English took the initiative with Edward Stanley marching his men up Branxton Hill towards the Scots at the top.

Here the Scots army was comprised of fierce looking highland clansmen under the leadership of the Earls Lennox and Argyle, but Stanley's skilled fighting men were too much for the highlanders. Some fled for their lives, while others including the chiefs of the Campbells and the McCleans, who remained, were slain.

A Victory for the English

Defeat was occurring all around for the unfortunate Scots so the king desperately began charging towards the English banners held high where the English leaders were located. His actions proved fatal, he was felled from his horse almost unrecognised by his enemies. The following morning he was to become one of ten thousand Scottish victims who lay dead on the battle field.

The Battle of Flodden was a decisive victory for the English. For the Scots it had been a disaster, with many of the most important members of Scottish society killed in the conflict.

The Scottish dead included twelve earls, fifteen lords, many clan chiefs an archbishop and above all King James himself. It is said that every great family in Scotland mourned the loss of someone at the Battle of Flodden.

The dead were remembered in the famous Scottish pipe tune 'The Flowers of the Forest':

"We'll here nae mair lilting at our ewe milking,
Women and bairns are heartless and wae,
Sighing and moaning on a ilka green loaning,
The flowers of the forest are a wede away."

Today a large granite cross marks the site of the Battle of Flodden. It is touchingly inscribed:

"To the Brave of Both Nations"
Flodden Field

Part Twelve
The Northumberland Coast

Bamburgh Castle

Part Twelve
Northumberland Coast

Seaton and the Delavals

At Seaton Sluice, just up the coast from Whitley Bay and Tyneside the coast of Northumberland officially begins. Seaton Sluice is notable for its small harbour, drained by means of a 900 feet long cut. Fifty two feet deep and thirty feet wide, the cut was made in the 1770s by a member of the Delaval family.

Seaton Sluice.

Not far inland, to the east of Seaton Sluice, is Seaton Delaval Hall which was built by Vanbrugh in 1720. It is recognised as one of the finest old houses in North East England. The hall is strongly associated with the Delaval family who can trace their origins back to Norman times when a certain Guy De La Val came over to Britain with William the Conqueror.

The most notorious members of this family were the practical joking brothers Lord Delaval and Sir Francis Blake Delaval, who lived here in the eighteenth century. Their pranks included placing trapdoors under the beds of house guests who haplessly dropped through the floor into huge tanks of water in the middle of the night.

Seaton Delaval Hall.

On one other occasion after retiring for the evening, unfortunate guests found themselves exposed to each other after undressing and de-wigging in their bedrooms. The Delavals had fitted sliding walls to the rooms, which were pulled up into the ceiling by means of a pulley.

Where Little Rivers Meet the Coast

The most south easterly portion of Nothumberland's coast encompasses the county's coalfield and most of the towns in the area are former coal mining settlements. Today Northumberland's only colliery is at Ellington near the mouth of the River Lyne.

Blyth, a coal port on the River Blyth, is the site of a large imposing power station which is located at Cambois on the northern side of the river. Cambois (pronounced Cammus) seems a rather exotic name for the site of a power station. Its name derives from an old Celtic word meaning 'bay'.

The River Blyth separates the Northumberland County district of Blyth valley from Wansbeck district, which takes its name from another local river. Wansbeck has been described as the only beck in Northumberland, but is in fact not a beck at all as the 'Oxford Dictionary of English Place Names' says Wansbeck derives from the Anglo-Saxon 'Waeganspick'. A 'spick' was a bridge made from tree trunks and a Waegan was a wagon so Wansbeck literally means 'Wagon Bridge' - a reference to a river crossing.

Bedlington and Bedlingtonshire

Much of the area on the coast between the Wansbeck and the Blyth once formed a district called Bedlingtonshire which until 1844 formed part of the County Palatinate of Durham, belonging to the Prince Bishops. Bedlington town was the capital of the shire which had been created because of an association with St. Cuthbert. The saint's coffin had been brought here for a short period, at the time of the Norman Conquest. For centuries Bedlingtonshire was administered separately from the rest of Northumberland and had its own justices, sheriffs and coroner.

The larger districts of Islandshire and Norhamshire, in North Northumberland, also belonged to the Prince Bishops and collectively, the three areas, were long known as 'North Durham'. In 1183 Bedlingtonshire was surveyed in Bishop Pudsey's 'Boldon Buke' the Domesday Book of County Durham.

Ashington Coal Mining Origins

Ashington, situated on the northern bank of the River Wansbeck was once described as the world's largest pit village, but no longer has a colliery.

The town is mainly a product of the nineteenth and twentieth centuries. Followers of English football, know Ashington as the place that produced three famous footballing sons, namely the legendary Jackie Milburn, known to fans of Newcastle United as 'Wor Jackie' and his relations, the footballing brothers Bob and Jack Charlton who represented England in the World Cup winning team of 1966.

A mile north of Ashington near Newbiggin by the Sea, is the Anglo-Saxon church of St. Mary the Virgin. It is reputedly the oldest in Northumberland.

Bedlington is of course noted for giving its name to a famous breed of dog, the Bedlington Terrier, which was originally bred by the miners of the area.

Druridge Bay and Coquet Island

To the north of Newbiggin and Ashington are Lynemouth, Ellington and the village of Cresswell at the southern edge of the seven mile long Druridge Bay. This is undoubtedly the best known strand of the North Eastern coast. Typical of Northumbrian beaches it is backed by long stretches of dunes but also by a number of small lakes and ponds which form nature reserves for wildfowl and sea birds.

At the northern edge of Druridge Bay, are the villages of Hauxley, Amble, Warkworth and a mile out at sea the historic Coquet Island.

The island was the site of a Benedictine monastery in Anglo-Saxon times and was the place where Elfleda the abbess of Whitby and sister of the King of Northumbria, persuaded St. Cuthbert to become a Bishop. Many centuries later during the Civil War, the island was the home of a Royalist garrison which surrendered to the Scots in 1643.

Today there is no public access to Coquet Island, which is protected as a nature reserve for sea birds. Its main residents are rabbits, gulls, puffins and eider duck which are known in the North East as 'Cuddy's Ducks' because of their association with St. Cuthbert.

Coquet Island takes its name from the River Coquet which enters the sea on the shore opposite Amble by the Sea.

"The Coquet forever the Coquet for aye! The Coquet the king o' the stream and the brae; From his high mountain throne, to his bed in the sea, Oh! where shall we see such a river as he?

Then blessings be on him, and lang may he glide, The fisherman's home and the fishermen's pride; From Harden's green hill to old Warkworth sae grey, The Coquet forever the Coquet for aye!"

Warkworth and its Castle

Amble by the Sea, a former coal mining village at the mouth of the River Coquet, is the harbour for the tiny town of Warkworth which lies just inland. Warkworth, an old fortified village, is situated within a narrow loop of the River Coquet and as at Durham City, the exposed neck of the river meander is protected by a castle which adds to the natural defences of the site. The castle, now a deserted but picturesque ruin, under the protection of English Heritage, was built in the 12th century on the site of an Anglo-Saxon stronghold belonging to the Northumbrian King Ceolwulph.

The Anglo-Saxons are said to have used Warkworth as a natural harbour for their boats which were called keels (ceols). In 1332 Warkworth became the principal residence of that great northern family, the Percys, Earls of Northumberland. Alnwick Castle, further north was also associated with the Percy family.

Warkworth.

Warkworth was once the home of the war hungry Harry 'Hotspur' Percy, whose father was an Earl of Northumberland and mother a Neville, of Raby Castle in County Durham.

Warkworth is the setting for a number of scenes in William Shakespeare's 'Henry IV'. Hotspur is a principal character of 'Henry IV' and in one scene this most notorious of Northumbrians, is described by Henry, the Prince of Wales:

"I am not yet of Percy's mind, the Hotspur of the North; he that kills me some six or seven dozen of Scots at a breakfast washes his hands and says to his wife -

'Fie upon this quiet life! I want work' 'O my sweet Harry,' says she 'how many has thy killed today?'.... 'some fourteen,' an hour after; 'a trifle a trifle."

From Henry IV, Part1, Act 2, Scene 4
William Shakespeare.

187

Warkworth Castle.

Alnmouth

From north of the Coquet, a long stretch of sandy bay, leads three miles on to Alnmouth. In its pleasant situation at the mouth of the River Aln, it is hard to believe that John Wesley once described Alnmouth as "a small sea port town famous for all kinds of wickedness".

During the American War of Independence, Alnmouth was the surprised victim of an attack by the American privateer John Paul Jones. On September 23rd 1779, Jones fired a canon ball at the defenceless Alnmouth church from his boat offshore. Fortunately for the church it missed and landed in a field, bounced three times and hit a farmhouse roof. Jones also attacked the town of Skinningrove on the Cleveland coast further south.

Smuggling at Boulmer

The coast becomes increasingly rocky to the north of Alnmouth, near the village of Boulmer, which was once the smuggling 'capital' of Northumberland. Contrabanders came from all over Northumberland and the Scottish borders to Boulmer, to deal in illicit goods during the smuggling heyday of the eighteenth and early nineteenth centuries. The smuggling fraternity included Isaac 'the Smuggler' Addison, a landlord of Boulmer's Fishing Boat Inn and the Scottish smugglers Wull Faa, the gypsy king of Kirk Yetholm and Wull Balmer of Jedburgh;

"Blind Wull Bawmer o' Jethart
His grips are no guid to come in;
He felled all the gaugers i' Jethart
When comin' frae Boomer wi' gin."

Many of the smugglers would make their way to Boulmer, from the wilds of Coquetdale and other border valleys, where numerous camouflaged distilleries were hidden in the hillsides out of the sight of the excisemen.

Smuggling was a highly profitable business and many of the participants, became local folk heroes, but it should be remembered that the activity could be of a highly dangerous nature. Those caught in the act would almost certainly face a sentence of death. William Weaver Tomlinson's Guide to Northumberland of 1888 claims that smuggled goods such as silks and casks of spirit were still occasionally dug up on the coast at Boulmer in the late nineteenth century. Today Boulmer is best known as the site of an RAF station.

Craster

Continuing along the coast from Boulmer we pass Howick, once the seat of Earl Grey, a former Prime Minister of England (1830-1834).

Further on we find the village of Craster, near a rocky whin sill outcrop called Cullernose Point. Whin sill outcrops can be found across the entire length of North East England from Teesdale to the Farne Islands and are are formed of a hard black basaltic rock called Dolerite.

The outcrops were caused by a volcanic intrusion 280 million years ago. Craster may take its name from a local family called the Crasters, who have lived in this area since before Norman times. The village is known for its kippers which are smoked on oak chippings to give them the distinctive Northumbrian flavour.

Dunstanburgh Castle

At Craster a mile long footpath leads to the extensive coastal ruins of Dunstanburgh Castle, which are situated on a whin sill outcrop overlooking the sea. Said to be on the site of an ancient stronghold of the ancient Britons it was built in 1313, and though today a ruin it occupies the largest site of any castle in the region.

According to legend, there is a secret cavern hidden beneath the ruins of Dunstanburgh Castle in which a beautiful young maiden lies sleeping in a deep spell cast upon her by an evil wizard.

Dunstanburgh Castle.

The legend states that on a wild stormy night, many centuries ago, a young knight by the name of Sir Guy the Seeker was looking for shelter at Dunstanburgh when he was approached by the wizard. With a fierce expression and flaming hair, the wizard terrified Sir Guy, but he meant the knight no harm and instead presented him with a challenge:

"Sir Knight! Sir Knight!
If your heart be right,
And your nerves be firm and true,
Sir Knight! Sir Knight a beauty bright
In durance waits for you."

Sir Guy accepted the challenge and asked to be taken to the place where the young girl lay sleeping. The wizard escorted Sir Guy along a dark winding stairway. Sir Guy's heart started beating fast; Was he the victim of a trick? Could he trust the wizard to keep his promise that a young maiden lay sleeping awaiting a rescuer? He followed the wizard with fear:

"And now they go both high and low,
Above and undergound,
And in and out, and about and about,
And round, and round, and round."

Eventually after much walking the stairway finally terminated at a great door which was bolted shut with the aid of a hideous venomous snake.

Without fear the wizard removed the snake from the door which opened to reveal a huge but darkened hall. At the end of the hall lay the beautiful young maiden as the wizard had promised.

She was indeed beautiful as she lay sleeping in a tomb of crystal which was guided on either side by two ugly skeleton figures, the one on the right holding a falchion bright, the one on the left holding a horn.

The Wizard explained that the young maiden's fate depended on whether he chose the horn or the sword.

After considering for much time, Sir Guy finally chose to blow the horn, but his choice proved disastrous, he fell into an immediate sleep and awoke to find himself caught once more in the storms outside Dunstanburgh Castle.

As might be expected Sir Guy was to spend the rest of his life searching for the secret cave where the girl lay sleeping. Alas, it was to no avail, the unhappy knight was to die a remorseful man. The words of the old wizard haunted his mind to the very end:

> *"Shame on the coward*
> *who sounded a horn*
> *When he might have*
> *unsheathed a sword."*

The Farne Islands

Six miles along the coast from Dunstanburgh, to the north of Embleton and Beadnell Bays, is the village of Seahouses, (formerly North Sunderland Seahouses), where boat trips can be taken out to the famous Farne Islands. The Farnes consist of almost thirty islands, which are visible at high tide and many others visible at low tide.

The Farne Islands.

Some of the islands have wonderful names like Megstone, Elbow, Wideopens, Goldstone, The Bush, Glororum Shad, Gun Rock, Staple Island, Brownsman, Callers, Crumstone, Fang, North and South Wamses, Roddam and Green, Big and Little Harcar, Nameless Rock, Blue Caps, Longstone and furthest out at four and half miles from the shore, Knivestone.

The Farnes are formed by the most seaward outcrops of the Great Whin Sill volcanic intrusion, which can be traced from upper Teesdale to the north Northumberland coast. It gives the Farne island their distinctive blackened appearance.

Inner Farne and St. Cuthbert

Largest innermost and most historic of the Farne islands is Inner Farne, which is also known as House Island, or quite simply Farne Island. Only a mile and a half from the mainland, this island gives its name to the whole group. For many years Inner Farne was the home of St. Cuthbert who lived here in solitude.

St. Cuthbert's life here was not always one of peace and seclusion, as his reputed gift of healing brought pilgrims to the island from all over the Kingdom of Northumbria. Indeed one suggested meaning for the name of the Farne Islands is that it derives from 'Farena Ealande' - 'Island of the Pilgrims'.

St. Cuthbert left his favourite island, for some time when he was called upon to become a Bishop on Lindisfarne but the saint later returned to the island, where he died in the year 687 AD. He was eventually buried at Durham.

It may be hard to appreciate the often reclusive lifestyle of St. Cuthbert today, but it is clear that he was a well liked and respected man with a caring and peaceful nature, in what was often a violent period of history. Cuthbert, a healthy and athletic man was also known to have had a great love of nature and especially of birds and seals, who were often his only companions on the lonely island. Indeed he is claimed by some to be one of the first ever nature conservationists.

Today the Farne Islands are still an important reserve for wildlife and are the home to many species of sea bird, including Puffins, Eiders, Razorbills and Cormorants. There is also a large colony of Grey Seals. Many legends and miracles are associated with St. Cuthbert both before and after his death. Some of these legends are hard to believe and can be put down to the ignorance of the people of the time, while others such as the belief that St. Cuthbert disliked women have no foundation at all. This rumour was probably started by the Benedictine order of monks of later times, who would not let women join their order.

The Farne Devils

Before St. Cuthbert could come to live on Inner Farne, there is a record that he had to banish certain 'demons' or 'devils' from the island to the nearby isle of Wideopens. Later inhabitants of Inner Farne, long after Cuthbert's death occasionally caught sight of these strange 'demons' who were described as:

"..... clad in cowls, and riding upon goats, black in complexion, short in stature, their countenances most hideous, their heads long - the appearance of the whole group horrible. Like soldiers they brandished in their hands lances, which they darted after in the fashion of war. At first the sight of the cross was sufficient to repel their attacks, but the only protection in the end was the circumvaliation of straws, signed with the cross, and fixed in the sands, around which the devils galloped for a while, and then retired, leaving the brethren to enjoy victory and repose."

It is thought that these demons were in fact the descendants of early settlers or 'aborigines' who had been cut off from the mainland. Perhaps it was their ancestors who were responsible for the mysterious 'Cup and Ring Markings' that litter the remoter parts of the Northumberland countryside.

The wonderfully hideous looking sanctuary knocker, on the main doorway of Durham cathedral is said to have been modelled on these intriguing little 'Farne Demons'. In medieval times this bronze carving granted refuge to 'evil doers', seeking asylum at the great cathedral of St. Cuthbert.

The Grace Darling Rescue

The Farne Islands can be broken into two main groups, the first is dominated by Inner Farne, the second a mile away across the Staple Sound includes Staple Island, Brownsman, the Wamses and Longstone. The last of these will be forever associated with the story of Northumbria's greatest heroine; Grace Darling.

Born on the 24th November 1815, Grace was the daughter of the lighthouse keeper on the island of Brownsman, but at the age of eleven she and her family moved to Longstone, when her father was appointed the lighthouse keeper there. Grace was only 22 when in the early hours of the morning of 7th September 1838 a steamer named the 'Forfarshire' struck the Harcar Rock in view of the lighthouse while en route from Hull to Dundee.

The steamer was severely wrecked and most of its passengers were drowned, but from her bedroom window in the lighthouse, Grace caught sight of a number of survivors desperately clinging to a reef for their lives. Shortly after 7 o'clock that morning Grace and her father William Darling, bravely launched their small rowing boat (a coble) and in two trips succeeded in rescuing the nine survivors, who were taken to the lighthouse for shelter.

"Twas on the Longstone lighthouse,
There dwelt an English maid:
Pure as the air around her,
Of danger ne'er afraid
One morning just at day break,
A storm toss'd wreck she spied;
And tho' to try seemed madness
"I'll save the crew" she cried."

From the 'Grace Darling Song'.

Grace Darling became a heroine overnight. Poets like William Wordsworth were inspired to write of her courage, portraits were painted, proposals of marriage were made and Grace was even requested to appear nightly at the Adelphi Theatre, in London at a stage production of her story. This was an offer

that Grace declined. Grace was in fact a shy and modest girl and her newly found fame came as a great shock to her.

Sadly this most reluctant of celebrities died of consumption on the 20th October 1842, at the age of only twenty six. Grace Darling is buried in the churchyard of the village of Bamburgh, on the mainland, where there is an ornate memorial to her honour. Bamburgh village also has a Grace Darling Museum, dedicated to the life of the heroine. It includes the coble boat used by Grace in her famous rescue.

Bamburgh - Joyous Guard?

The village of Bamburgh is dominated by its great sandstone castle which stands on a massive whin sill outcrop, overlooking the Farne Islands. When viewed from the golf course near the Harkess Rocks to the north of the village, the castle in its lofty coastal location looks to good to be true. The building is well described in William Tomlinson's 'Guide to Northumberland':

"A more impregnable stronghold could not be imagined, for rugged strength and barbaric grandeur it is the king of Northumbrian castles. From nearly every point of the compass its majestic outlines are visible. To the mariner plying between the Tyne and the Elbe it is the most conspicuous landmark on the North East coast."

In pre Anglo-Saxon times Bamburgh was called Din Guyardi, and was a tribal stronghold of an ancient British tribe called the Votadini. The old name has lead some to believe that Bamburgh was in fact the legendary 'Joyous Guard', the castle of Sir Lancelot and Sir Gallahad in the time of King Arthur.

Bamburgh Castle.

Bamburgh and Northumbria

Bamburgh's recorded history begins in 547 AD when King Ida the Flamebearer established the royal city and capital of Bernicia at Bamburgh. Bernicia was an expanding kingdom centred upon the Rivers Tyne and Wear. King Ida's people were Angles, a fierce piratical race originating from a region now in southern Denmark near the border with Germany.

Bamburgh Castle by the sea.

As Bernicia expanded it conquered the ancient Celtic speaking tribes of the region including the kingdom of Catraeth (centred on the River Tees) and the kingdom of Rheged, in what is now Cumbria.

The rise of Bernicia reached a climax in AD 603 when King Aethelfrith of Bernicia (Grandson of Ida), seized control of the neighbouring Angle kingdom of Deira (now the Yorkshire wolds). This resulted in the formation of a new powerful kingdom called Northumbria, stretching from the River Humber northwards. Northumbria, occupying almost a third of the whole British mainland became, at the height of its influence, one of the strongest Anglo-Saxon kingdoms of Britain and was ruled from two capitals at York and Bamburgh.

Although for a time the supremacy of the Northumbrian kings, was challenged by the great midland kingdom of Mercia, and the later Viking kingdom of York, Northumbria remained a fiercely independent Anglo-Saxon province, right up until the time of the Norman Conquest.

Bebba's Burgh

The name Bamburgh originates from the time of Aethelfrith, the first King of Northumbria, who named the fortress or 'burgh' after his wife and queen called Bebba. Over the years the name Bebba's Burgh was simplified to Bamburgh. Before Aethelfrith's time Bamburgh had continued to be known by its Celtic-British name Din Guyardi.

Over the centuries Bamburgh Castle has been greatly restored, most notably by the Victorian industrialist William, Lord Armstrong (1810-1900) and the oldest remaining part of the building, is now the twelfth century keep.

Today the modern visitor to the castle is more likely to be reminded of the Victorian age of Armstrong than of Bamburgh's Celtic, Anglo-Saxon and medieval history. Nevertheless when viewed from afar, the castle still retains a romantic historical appearance.

Bamburgh Village.

Kingdom Within the Walls

One curious though little known event in Bamburgh's history took place long after Northumbria's 'Golden age', at the time of the Wars of the Roses, when the castle was a staunchly Lancastrian stronghold. It was to here in 1464, that King Henry VI and his wife, Queen Margaret of Anjou fled, following a defeat by the Yorkists in a Battle at Hexham.

For a short time the disheartened monarch held court at Bamburgh during which time, the great building encompassed the total extent of his kingdom.

Eventually Henry was defeated when Bamburgh came under siege from the artillery of Edward IV. It was the first castle in England to come under fire from canons.

Legend of the Laidley Worm

Bamburgh is the setting for one of the curious 'worm' legends, which seem to be a regular feature of North Eastern folklore. The story is that in ancient times the jealous step mother of a Bamburgh princess turned the young maiden into a laidley (or loathsome) 'worm', who began to terrorise the neighbourhood of Bamburgh and Budle Bay.

> *"For seven miles east and seven miles west,*
> *And seven miles north and south,*
> *No blade of grass or corn would grow,*
> *So deadly was her mouth.*
>
> *The milk of seven streakit cows,*
> *It was their cost to keep;*
> *They brought her daily which she drank*
> *Before she went to sleep.*
>
> *At this day might be seen the cave*
> *Where she lay faulded up,*
> *And the trough o' stone the very same*
> *Out of which she supped."*

The princess's brother hearing of the activities of this terrible beast, returned to England from business abroad (in the expected tradition) to deal with the serpent. The creature greeted the prince's ship at Budle Bay near Bamburgh with the following well chosen verses:

> *"O' quit thy sword, unbend thy brow,*
> *And give me kisses three;*
> *For though I am a poisonous worm,*
> *No hurt I'll do to thee.*
>
> *O' quit thy sword, unbend thy brow,*
> *And give me kisses three;*
> *If I'm not won here the sun goes down,*
> *Won shall I never be.*

So,

He quitted his sword
and smoothed his brow,
And gave her kisses three;
She crept into the hole a worm,
And came out a fayre lady."

When the prince confronted the stepmother, to whose magic powers he was immune, she desperately pleaded for his forgiveness. Showing no mercy the prince responded with revengeful anger and turned his stepmother into a loathsome toad. The ballad concludes:

"And on the land's near Ida's towers,
A loathsome toad she crawls;
And venom spits on everything
which cometh to the walls."

The Ballad of the 'Laidley Worm' has similarities with the Lambton and Sockburn Worm legends of County Durham, but is probably not of their antiquity. It is said to have been written by a Cheviot mountain bard in the thirteenth century, but evidence suggests that the true author was a vicar of Norham on Tweed, many centuries later.

Holy Island - Lindisfarne

Beyond Bamburgh and the tidal estuary-like mud flats of Budle Bay, is Holy Island, still often known by its more ancient name of Lindisfarne. It is only accessible from the mainland at low tide by means of a causeway, which can be reached from the village of Beal. To the south of the more modern road-surface causeway, a series of stakes mark the old route across to the island called the 'Pilgrims Way' which was used in ancient

times by visitors to the great Christian centre of Lindisfarne. Again this could be crossed only at low tide, a situation perfectly described by Sir Walter Scott:

"For with the flow and ebb, its style
Varies from continent to isle;
Dry shood o'er sands, twice every day,
The pilgrims to the shrine find way;
Twice every day the waves efface
Of staves and sandelled feet the trace."

The modern causeway reaches the island at a point called the snook, at the western tip of a long sandy peninsula, which leads the road to the attractive Holy Island village and the nearby ruins of a Norman priory.

A Cradle of Christianity

Lindisfarne's Norman priory stands on the site of an Anglo-Saxon monastery founded by St. Aidan in AD 635, on land granted by Oswald, King and Saint of Northumbria. Aidan is believed to have chosen the island site because of its isolation and proximity to the Northumbrian capital at Bamburgh.

Aidan the first Bishop of Lindisfarne, a Scots-Celtic monk from the isle of Iona, travelled widely throughout Northumbria and with the help of King Oswald as interpreter, began the conversion of the pagan Northumbrians to Christianity. The conversion of the Northumbrians to Christianity by Aidan and Oswald, cannot have been an easy task.

The Northumbrians were the descendants of a heathen race of people who were in many ways no more civilised than the Scandinavian Vikings, who invaded Britain centuries later.

St. Aidan's death in 651 AD, is said to have been related in a vision to a young shepherd boy called Cuthbert who lived in the hills somewhere near the River Tweed. The vision convinced Cuthbert that he should take up the life of a monk and at the age of sixteen, he entered the Northumbrian monastery of Melrose in Tweeddale (now in the southern borders of Scotland).

Lindisfarne Castle.

In 654 Cuthbert came to the monastery at Lindisfarne, where his reputed gift of healing and legendary ability to work miracles, achieved far reaching fame for the island. Cuthbert was elected Bishop of Hexham in 684 AD but exchanged the see for Lindisfarne, to become the fifth successor to Bishop Aidan.

When Cuthbert died in 687 AD, he was buried in accordance with his wishes on the island of Lindisfarne, but eleven years after his death, his body was found to be in an incorrupt state by the astonished monks of the island. The monks were now convinced that Cuthbert was a saint and pilgrims continued to flock to Lindisfarne in numbers as great as during Cuthbert's lifetime.

Viking Raids on Lindisfarne

In 793 AD Lindisfarne was to witness the first Viking raid on the coast of Britain, which was recorded with much drama by an informative history of the period called the 'Anglo-Saxon Chronicle':

"793. In this year terrible portents appeared over Northumbria, which sorely affrighted the inhabitants: there were exceptional flashes of lightning, and fiery dragons were seen flying through the air. A great famine followed hard upon these signs; and a little later in that same year, on the 8th June, the harrying of the heathen miserably destroyed God's church by rapine and slaughter."

The Anglo-Saxon chroniclers were largely responsible for giving the Vikings the 'bad press' they still have today. The chroniclers fail to mention that the Anglo-Saxons had invaded Britain in much the same way, two and a half centuries earlier. Nevertheless Viking raids on Lindisfarne's wealthy coastal monastery did continue throughout the following century and in 875 AD the monks of Lindisfarne fled their Holy Island with the body of Cuthbert, remembering the dying wishes of their saint:

".... if necessity compels you to chose between one of two evils, I would much rather you take my bones from their tomb and carry them away with you to whatever place of rest God may decree, rather than consent to iniquity and put your necks under the yokes of schismatics."

For many years the monks wandered the north of England, with the coffin of St. Cuthbert, until they eventually settled at Durham in 995 AD where St. Cuthbert's body lies to this day.

Hobthrush

Just offshore from Holy Island village, is the small Island of Hobthrush, or St. Cuthbert's Isle, where the saint was said to have crafted the legendary beads described by Sir Walter Scott in 'Marmion':

"But fain St. Hilda's nuns would learn
If on a rock by Lindisfarne
St. Cuthbert sits and toils to frame
The sea borne beads that bear his name.

Such tales had Whitby's fishers told,
And said they might his shape behold,
And here his anvil sound:
A deadened clang - a huge dim form
Seen but and heard when gathering storm
And night were closing round.

But this, a tale of idle fame,
The nuns of Lindisfarne disclaim."

Cuthbert's or 'Cuddy's Beads' can still sometimes be seen washed up on the shores of Holy Island. They are in fact the fossilised remains of tiny sea creatures of the Crinoid type, which inhabited the ocean depths in prehistoric times. Supposedly resembling the shape of the cross, they were once used as Rosary beads.

Less Civilised Times

Although in Norman times Holy Island priory became a cell of Durham Cathedral little is known of the island's history or people in the centuries following the Norman Conquest.

There is, however one account which gives us an amusing insight into the attitudes of the island people in later centuries. The account is an observation by Captain Robin Rugg, the seventeenth century governor of Holy Island:

"The common people there do pray
for ships which they see in danger.
They all sit down upon their knees
and hold up their hands and say
very devotedly, 'Lord send her to us,
God send her to us.' You seeing them
upon their knees, and their hands
joined, do think that they are
praying for your safety; but their
minds are far from that. They pray,
not to God to save you, or send you
to port, but to send you to them by
shipwreck, that they may get the
spoil of her. And to show that this is
their meaning if the ship come well
to port, they get up in anger crying
'the Devil stick her, she is away from
us'."

Not exactly what we would expect from a 'Holy' Island. It seems that the islanders had inherited the rough ways of the border folk, so typical of Northumberland in those days gone by.

Lindisfarne Castle

Today the only feature of Holy island, that suggests any involvement with the violent border history of Northumberland, is Lindisfarne Castle. First built in 1550, it sits romantically on the highest point of the island on a whin stone hill called Beblowe.

The Castle has never witnessed any major battle or Border siege although it was occupied by some Northumbrian Jacobites at the time of the 1715 Rising.

Lindisfarne Castle was converted into a private residence by the well known British architect Sir Edwin Lutyens in 1903. A small but superbly rugged looking building, it has been a National Trust property since 1944.

Berwick upon Tweed

"Berwick is an ancient town
A church without a steeple
A pretty girl at every door
And very generous people."

A bridge without a middle arch
A church without a steeple
A midden heap in every street
And damned conceited people."

The less complimentary verse is attributed to Robbie Burns.

On the mainland five miles north of Holy Island, is the mouth of the River Tweed and the historic town of Berwick upon Tweed. The most northerly town in England, perhaps no other town in North East England has had a more eventful history than Berwick.

Berwick Old Bridge.

There is no doubt that Berwick upon Tweed can claim the distinction of being *the* Border Town, as it has changed hands between England and Scotland thirteen times. Its history is inextricably tied up with the struggle for the Anglo Scottish frontier. An old legend is said to explain the fascinating history of Berwick:

> *"During the temptation while the*
> *Evil one was showing to the Holy*
> *one all the kingdoms of the earth he*
> *kept Berwick hidden beneath his*
> *thumb, wishing to reserve it as his*
> *own little nook."*

Berwick with an English name meaning 'Corn Farm' began as a small settlement in the Anglo-Saxon Kingdom of Northumbria, in which it remained until the Battle of Carham of 1018 when it was taken by the Scots. From then on Berwick became a hotly disputed territory.

In 1174 Berwick was retaken by England in a ransom following the failure of a raid into Northumberland by the Scottish king, William the Lion. The town returned to the northern side of the border in the reign of Richard I (1189-1199), who sold it to obtain money for the Crusades. At the beginning of the following century Berwick returned once more to England, after Richard's brother,

King John sacked the town, but Berwick continued to change hands until 1482 when the town finally became part of England within which it still (technically) remains.

English or Scottish?

Today the visitor to Berwick can be forgiven for believing it to be a Scottish town, as after all it stands on the northern bank of the River Tweed, an entirely Scottish river and it does seem to have a rather Scottish appearance.

Berwick is also the name of a large Scottish Burgh and the old county of Berwickshire of which Berwick was not part was in Scotland. Furthermore Berwick, is a little bit more closer to the Scottish capital of Edinburgh, than it is to the North East's regional centre of Newcastle upon Tyne.

The belief that Berwick is Scottish is also reinforced by the fact that most of the commercial banks in the town are Scottish and that the local football team plays in the Scottish league.

Dialect also leads to the belief that Berwick is Scottish as to most Englishmen the local 'Tweedside' accent spoken in Berwick sounds Scottish, although most Scots recognise the Northumbrian influence and regard the dialect as English.

The Scottish claim for Berwick is certainly strong but the English influence upon the area is also very significant. Berwick, as already stated began as an English or at least an Anglo-Saxon settlement, in the Kingdom of Northumbria and although for four hundred years it regularly changed hands between England and Scotland it has remained in the former part of the United Kingdom for the past five centuries.

Berwick's policeman and laws are therefore English, and its most senior councillor is an English mayor not a provost as in the Scottish system of local government. Berwick town also has an important status, as the administrative centre for the Northumberland County District of Berwick upon Tweed, which includes the Farne islands, Lindisfarne and the very Northumbrian villages of Wooler, Bamburgh and Belford.

Independent Town, Prosperous Past

It is hardly surprising that given Berwick's curious Anglo-Scotish location, the local residents tend to regard themselves as independent 'Tweedsiders' or 'Berwickers' rather than English or Scottish. In fact until the Reform Act of 1885 Berwick did have a considerable degree of independence with the status of a 'Free Burgh' meaning that it had to be mentioned separately in Acts of Parliament.

Berwick's status was such that even the Crimean War had to be declared in the name of Great Britain, Ireland and Berwick upon Tweed. Strangely after this war, when the peace treaty was signed Berwick's name was omitted and for many years the town was said to be technically still at war with the Russians.

It is hard to believe that a town with such a turbulent history as Berwick was once one of the most prosperous merchant towns in Britain and was worth to Scotland an annual customs value of £2,190, which was equivalent to about one quarter of the customs of the whole of England.

In the thirteenth century the wealthy town was described as, "so populous and of such commercial importance that it might rightly be called another Alexandria, whose riches were the sea and the water its walls".

Berwick upon Tweed.

Town Walls, Buildings and Bridges

In the fourteenth century Berwick became a real walled town when King Edward I fortified it against Scottish attack. His defensive walls supplemented the stronghold of Berwick Castle which stood on the site of the present railway station. Some of the town walls can still be seen today, dating mainly from the later Elizabethan period. They are among the finest of their kind in Europe.

Berwick is arguably one of the most picturesque towns on the region's coast, mainly because of its attractive red roofed houses, pinkish grey Georgian buildings

and the fine seventeenth century bridge, which spans the River Tweed.

Most notable of the town's buildings are the spired town hall of 1754 and the Berwick parish church, called Holy Trinity which is one of only a few built in England in Cromwellian times. For an historic parish church it is unusual, in that it has no steeple, tower or church bell. Instead a bell in the Town Hall is used to summon people to the church services at Holy Trinity. It is no wonder that many visitors to Berwick mistake the Town Hall for the parish church.

The River Tweed at Berwick is almost as well known as the Tyne at Newcastle for its bridges. There are three here namely - Old Bridge, the Royal Tweed Bridge, and the Royal Border Bridge. The Royal Tweed is the most recent, built in 1925 it carries the old A1 through the town, although the more modern road now bypasses the town to the west.

The Royal Border Bridge is an impressive nineteenth century railway viaduct. Opened by Queen Victoria in 1850, it was built by Robert Stephenson, creating an important rail link between London and Edinburgh.

The 'Old Bridge', also known as 'Berwick Bridge' dates from 1611. It is a fine red sandstone structure with fourteen arches. Until the nineteenth century it was the main crossing point of the Tweed at Berwick, but did not as might be expected link Northumberland to Scotland. It in fact linked the Norhamshire district of the County Palatine of Durham to the County Burgh of Berwick upon Tweed. County boundaries are a little more logical today.

Coldingham - St. Cuthbert and the Otters

Leaving Berwick, we can continue northwards along the coast for two miles, passing Marshall Meadows Bay before we reach a point near the east coast railway line, where a sign marks the England Scotland Border. Here we have reached the northernmost point in England.

The coast from here northwards, towards Edinburgh, was once part of Northumbria but was lost to Scotland many, many centuries ago. Of course Northumbria's history does not end at the Scottish border, as only seven miles to its north, near St. Abb's Head we find the village of Coldingham.

This was the site of a Northumbrian monastery founded in 655 AD by St. Ebbe (or St. Abbe), the sister of St. Oswald, King of Northumbria. Coldingham was a home to both nuns and monks and was frequently visited by St. Cuthbert, who was a friend of St. Ebbe. During his visits to Coldingham, St. Cuthbert would often wander the seashore during the night arousing the curiosity of a Coldingham monk who spied on him from a distance.

What the monk witnessed is remembered in the famous legend of 'St. Cuthbert and the Otters'. The monk saw Cuthbert walk into the sea until the freezing water came up to his neck, after a while Cuthbert left the water and on the shore he began to pray. The monk's delightful story is told by St. Bede:

"...immediately there followed in his footsteps two little sea animals, humbly stretching themselves on the earth; and, licking his feet, they rolled upon them, wiping them with their skins and warming them with their breath. After this service had been fulfilled and his blessing had been received they departed to their haunts in the waves of the sea"

Index

Publications by the same Author

Northern Roots: Who we are, Where we come from, Why we speak the way we do
by David Simpson
Size: 246mm x 173mm   Pages: 160   *Price: £7.95*

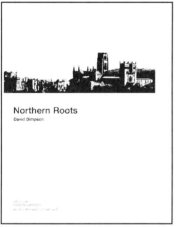

The people of Northern England are a breed apart.

Northerners speak with distinct local dialects and have their very own sense of history. In the guise of Yorkshiremen, Cumbrians, Geordies, Scousers, Lancastrians or Northumbrians, all have contributed to the rich culture of Britain.

But who are these Northerners and where did they come from?

What clues exist in history to the ancient and more recent origins of Northerners and their speech?

This book traces the languages and origins of various people who have settled in the North over two thousand years to give it the distinct character it has today.

The Millennium History of North East England by David Simpson
Size: 255mm x 255mm   Pages: 336   Full Colour   Hardback
~~RRP: £24.99~~ *Now £9.99*

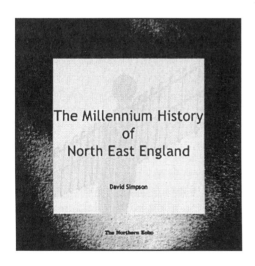

North East England has a strong sense of identity that sets it apart from other areas of England. The roots of this identity lie in two thousand years of distinct history that have made the region what it is today. From the Roman frontier zone of Hadrian's Wall, to the powerful Christian Kingdom of Northumbria, through the gloomy days of Border warfare up to the great age of coal mining and railways, each era has played its part. This unique, 336 page, beautifully illustrated hardback book explores the events, people and places that have shaped the region's history over the last two thousand years.

New local history publications

Britain and the Baltic
Studies in Commercial, Political and Cultural Relations 1500-2000
Edited by Patrick Salmon and Tony Barrow
Size: 225mm x 150mm   Pages: 384   *Price: £17.95*

Britain and the Baltic
East Coast Connections

Political, commercial and cultural connections between Britain and the Baltic are amongst the oldest and most enduring in the historical record. And yet, paradoxically, they are also amongst the least known and poorly understood. The essays contained within this volume demonstrate that scholarly study of Britain's historical relationship with the countries of Scandinavia and the Baltic region is both varied and dynamic. Merchants, trade, travel writing, diplomacy, war and international relations represent the central themes and the period 1500-2000 the chronological focus. The content of this volume of essays represents the cutting edge of modern historical scholarship and will not fail to fascinate, as well as inform, the reader.

Questions of Controversy: The Kennedy Brothers by Mel Ayton
Size: 216mm x 135mm   Pages: 416   *Price: £9.95*

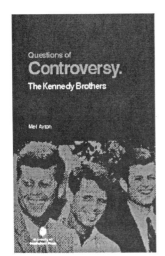

Intense controversy surrounds the lives of the Kennedy bothers: John, Robert and Edward Kennedy have all been the subject of close scrutiny for the latter part of the 20th century.

Based on his meticulous research, Mel Ayton attempts to sort fact from fiction and to establish the truth about the three Kennedy brothers.

The book provides an historical antidote to the popular revisionist biographies of the brothers. Many of these have sought to sensationalise and poison the Kennedy legacy through misinterpretation and distortion of the facts.

The Whaling Trade of North-East England 1750-1850 by Tony Barrow
Size: 246mm x 173mm   Pages: 192   *Price: £14.95*

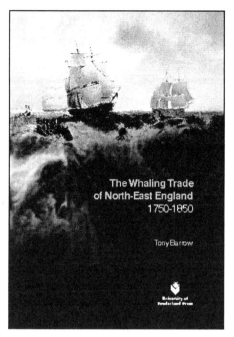

During the century 1750-1850, North East England was one of the most important centres of British whaling enterprise. From Berwick in the north to Whitby in the south, stoutly built whaling ships sailed annually to the Arctic grounds in search of the Greenland whale. Their voyages sustained a shore-based processing and distribution industry of considerable value. But hunting whales from open boats, with hand-held harpoons, in sub-zero temperatures was not a venture for the faint hearted. It called for the specialist skills of the 'Greenlanders' and North East England was renowned for them.

The Whaling Trade of North-East England 1750-1850, is the first comprehensive, academic account of this fascinating aspect of the maritime heritage of the region. It traces the origins and economic history of Arctic whaling as it was conducted from local ports, the ships it employed and the social history of the men who sailed in them.

Old Wives' Tales: Remedies Pills and Potions by Carol Cooke
Size: 165mm x 145mm   Pages: 80   *Price: £5.95*

There's nothing Northern folks like better than getting together for an evening's entertainment. And what better entertainment is there than a walk down memory lane, discussing ancient ailments and alarming cures?

Carol Cooke's book will make you laugh, teach you practical skills such as amateur dentistry, remind you of your granny and her home made remedies for chilblains, as well as giving you reliable information on how much alcohol you really need to consume to fettle a cold!

Local History Special Offers

Merchants and Gentry in North-East England 1650-1830
The Carrs and the Ellisons by A W Purdue
Size: 246mm x 173mm   Pages: 304   ~~RRP: £16.95~~ **Now £12.95**

This book follows the progress of the Ellisons of Hebburn Hall and the Carrs of Dunston Hill from their mercantile success in the seventeenth century to their solid gentry and land-owning status in the nineteenth century.

The main source of research is drawn from the wealth of papers collected by both families providing considerable information about social and family lives of the North East elite during the period 1650-1830.

The Official History of Sunderland AFC 1879-2000
Edited by John Hudson and Paul Callaghan
(Hardback) ~~RRP: £24.99~~ **Now £9.99** (Boxed) ~~RRP: £39.99~~ **Now £15.00**
Size: 275mm x 220mm   Pages: 336   **Full Colour**

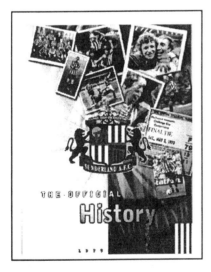

Every season since the club's formation in 1879 is examined in detail - a saga that covers six League Championship, two FA Cup wins and seven promotions, with equal attention to the disappointing near misses, and the crushing blows of relegation.

This book with over 400 illustrations is the most comprehensive account of the club's 120 year history, recording the high and low points, the deadly serious and the lighter moments, all in great detail.

Please Note: there will be a charge for postage and packing on all publications.
To order any of the above publications contact:
Business Education Publishers Limited, The Teleport, Doxford International, Sunderland, SR3 3XD
Tel: +44(0)191 5252410 Fax: +44(0)191 5201815 email: sales@bepl.com